The Soul of the City:
LE PETIT THÉÂTRE DU VIEUX CARRÉ
OF NEW ORLEANS

by
Dr. Rebecca Fichter Hale

The Soul of the City:
LE PETIT THÉÂTRE DU VIEUX CARRÉ OF NEW ORLEANS
By Dr. Rebecca Fichter Hale
Book Copyright © 2007 Dr. Rebecca Fichter Hale
Library of Congress Control Number: 2006938586

ISBN 97809676748-5-8
Printed in the United States of America
Second Edition

Published by Rock Press, Inc.
4611 South University Drive #450
Davie, FL 33328 USA
www.Rock-Press.com

Direct inquiries and/or orders to the above address.

All rights reserved. Except for use in a review, no portion of this book may be reproduced in any form or by any means, electronic or mechanical, including photocopying, recording, or by any information storage and retrieval system, without the express written permission of the publisher.

Designed by Melissa Macy
Cover photographs by Laura Silverberg and Richard Hale

The Soul of the City:
LE PETIT THÉÂTRE DU VIEUX CARRÉ
OF NEW ORLEANS

by
Dr. Rebecca Fichter Hale

Acknowledgements

This book is dedicated to Emile Fichter, the author's father, whose love, encouragement, and respect for education inspired the researcher to complete her dissertation and this book.

The author wishes to express sincere appreciation to the late Professor Lowell Swortzell, Chairperson of her dissertation committee, and to Professor Alistair Martin-Smith and Professor Cheryl (space dot space dot) Frederic, for their invaluable guidance and assistance in the preparation and development of this research.

The writer wishes to thank her talented publisher and close friend Tracey Broussard, whose expertise guided the author in completing this project. During the many years that the author has known Tracey, she has been an inspiration and has helped make her a better teacher.

The researcher is grateful to all people who agreed to share their memories of Le Petit Theatre through interviews, especially Leon Contavesprie, Vatican Lokey, Stocker Fontelieu, and the late Arthur Tong.

The author is very thankful for the help of her long-time friend, Kathleen Higginbotham, without whose support and computer expertise her dissertation would not have been possible. The researcher also wishes to thank her stepmother Patricia Fichter and friends Katherine Marie Harding, Peggy Laurel, Rene J.F. Piazza, and Tom Higginbotham, as well as her many friends, family members, and students for their encouragement.

The writer wishes to acknowledge her husband, Richard C. Hale, for his love and support. She especially thanks him for not complaining that his wife spent so much time in New York while attending New York University and completing her doctorate in 2002.

Table of Contents

ACKNOWLEDGMENTS   v

PREFACE   xi

CHAPTERS

    I   LE PETIT THEATRE:
    ITS ORIGINS, ITS PHILOSOPHY,
    AND AN OVERVIEW OF THE THEATRE   1

    II   TEDDY'S PLAYHOUSE FOR CHILDREN:
    CHILDREN'S THEATRE AT LE PETIT   57

    III   MAIN-STAGE PRODUCTIONS   89

    IV   LE PETIT THEATRE:
    THE CONTRIBUTIONS OF THE PAST,
    THE REALITY OF THE PRESENT,
    THE PROMISE OF THE FUTURE   121

BIBLIOGRAPHY   143

APPENDICES

A	THE INTERVIEWS	171

C. Stocker Fontelieu	173
Lyla Hay Owen	192
Don Marshall	206
Arthur Tong	209
Lois Crandell	221
Bryan Batt	223
Janell Wattigny	225
Julie Winn	229
Vatican Lokey	231
Maurice "Moon" Landrieu	256
Keith Briggs	257
Leon Contavesprie	261
Ricky Graham	276
Michael Arata	279
Terri Gervais	284
Edward R. Cox	294
Vatican Lokey	296
Lucy Daigle	299
Rosa Deutsch	301
Leon Contavesprie	312
August Staub	314
Sonny Borey	315
Jim Word	321
Luis Barroso	333
Lucy Daigle	356
Veleka Gray	358
Leon Contavesprie	359
Leon Contavesprie	362
Sarah Kary	363
Leon Contavesprie	367
Vatican Lokey	369
Leon Contavesprie	374
Luis Barroso	377

	LEON CONTAVESPRIE	380
	DAVID CUTHBERT	386
	GARY RUCKER	387
	DOUGLAS LEAL	388
	ERROL LABORDE	393
	STEPHEN THURBER	395
B	CHILDREN'S THEATRE PRODUCTIONS AT LE PETIT	397
C	MAIN-STAGE PLAYS AT LE PETIT	407
D	LE PETIT CHILDREN'S THEATRE PRODUCTIONS PERFORMED AT OTHER LOCATIONS	447

ABOUT THE AUTHOR   449

Preface

This book is based on the dissertation <u>Le Petit Théâtre du Vieux Carré of New Orleans, Louisiana: 1968-2001</u>. This dissertation was written by Dr. Rebecca Hale as part of the necessary requirements in completing her Ph.D. in Educational Theatre from New York University in the Fall of 2002.

Le Petit Théâtre du Vieux Carré is an outgrowth of a group organized in 1916 as the New Orleans Chapter of the Drama League of America. In 1917, this organization became the Drawing Room Players, so named because one-act dramas and comedies were performed in the drawing room of one of its members. When the members of the association expanded, they leased space in the Pontalba Apartments, an historic apartment building in the French Quarter. The new theatrical space was christened "Le Petit Théâtre du Vieux Carré."

Le Petit Theatre continues to contribute to the New Orleans theatrical community. This theatre, located in the historic French Quarter, remains a vital part of the New Orleans community and the New Orleans theatrical scene.

1

LE PETIT THEATRE:
ITS ORIGINS, ITS PHILOSOPHY,
AND AN OVERVIEW OF THE THEATRE

The Drama League of America was established in 1910 with hundreds of chapters throughout the country for the purpose of encouraging the production of good drama and providing an organization for communication between theatrical groups (Hughes 367). Le Petit Théâtre du Vieux Carré of New Orleans, Louisiana, is an outgrowth of an organization formed in 1916 as the New Orleans Chapter of the Drama League of America. In 1917, this association, led by Louise Nixon, Rhea Goldberg, Helen Schertz, and Martha Robinson, became the Drawing Room Players, so named because one-act dramas and comedies, in both English and French, were performed in the drawing room of one of its members. They also performed plays for members of the military who were stationed throughout the city during World War I. A local newspaper account of the early efforts of the Drawing Room Players mentioned the group:

> The Players are building an enviable reputation for artistic interpretation of unusual plays and the delightful manner in which they are staged. In all the little theater movement of the country there is no single group who are giving more thoughtful attention to detail than those purely amateur artists of New Orleans. (Wallfisch, "Big Dreams" 4:1)

The Drawing Room Players became the nucleus of Le Petit Theatre.

Many small social groups, devoted to the arts, existed in New Orleans at this time. The Literary and Musical Club, the Causerie du Lundi (devoted to the production of plays in French), and the Shakespeare Society primarily were social organizations, most of whose members formed the Drawing Room Players (Chapman 15).

A major influenza epidemic curtailed theatrical activity in New Orleans in the winter of 1918-1919, when it affected eleven per cent of the population and killed two thousand people. The malady subsided by May of 1919, and theatrical activity resumed. The Drawing Room Players assembled in increased numbers, anxious to recommence acting (Chapman 17-18).

The Drawing Room Players aspired to express themselves through the medium of amateur theatricals. Because of the interest these theatricals generated, the group needed a facility larger than members' homes. When the organization expanded, they leased space for seventeen dollars and fifty cents per month in the Pontalba Apartments, a national historic landmark in the French Quarter built in 1850 for Baroness Almonaster de Pontalba. A large room with an adjoining porch in the apartment building was transformed into a small stage and an auditorium, seating 184 people. The members, none of whom were paid, were responsible for every aspect of the theatre, from directing to set construction to box office. The initial membership consisted of 500 subscriptions. The new theatrical space was christened "Le Petit Théâtre du Vieux Carré." The Irish playwright and nobleman Lord Dunsany, a strong supporter of the Little Theatre Movement, visited the city on November 9, 1919, and formally launched the new playhouse with his commendations and good wishes (Dodds, "Big Birthday" C10). One-act plays, such as The Romancers by Edmond Rostand and Suppressed Desires by Susan Glaspell and George Cram Cook, were performed the first two seasons.

Lord Dunsany, born Edward John Moreton Drax Plunkett, an Irish novelist, poet, and playwright, was known for writing fantasy. Not only did he write over seventy books, but also, at the invitation of author William Butler Yeats, Lord Dunsany composed plays for the Abbey Theatre, including The Glittering Gate (1909) and The Laughter of the Gods (1919). His short plays, such as A Night at an Inn performed at Le Petit in 1921, were popular with the Little Theatre movement in the United States (Drabble 303).

Later in 1919, fire destroyed New Orleans' French

4

Opera House, and, as a reporter for the local newspaper wrote, "The heart of the old French Quarter has stopped beating" (Dabney 402). There was a clamor from the public to rebuild immediately, which fiscal problems prevented. Another cultural venue was needed to fill the void. According to one historian, Le Petit provided an outlet for people to view live theatre:

> Le Petit Théâtre du Vieux Carré was the reorganization of the Drawing Room Players, created in 1916 [sic], and the answer to the clamor that more be admitted to amateur dramatic work than was possible when the efforts were confined to private homes. It improvised a playhouse in the lower Pontalba building, later built its own theater on St. Peter Street. (Dabney 402)

Success and a growing audience (membership in 1922 had grown to 1,000, with a waiting list of 300) warranted the move to a permanent, more spacious facility. This same year under the guidance of Harold W. Newman, chairman of the theatre's Board of Governors, the present site at the corner of St. Peter Street and Chartres Street was purchased for $25,000, with another $25,000 needed to convert the property into a theatre. The premises measured 90'10" on Chartres Street by 132'8" on St. Peter Street (Chapman 70).

The original building, erected in 1789 by Hilario Boutte and later known as the Orue-Pontalba Building, was owned by

Joseph de Orue. The architect was Gilberto Guillemard. De Orue received permission to build a balcony over the sidewalk, but before it could be finished, the building was damaged by fire in 1794. In 1795, de Orue entered into a contract with Boutte to repair the damage. However, before Boutte and his crew could refurbish the building, de Orue sold it to Don Almonester y Roxas, who later sold it to his friend, Joseph Xavier de Pontalba. Boutte completed the project according to the original contract (Vieux Carre Survey).

    The corner portion of the property originally was the residential palace in 1797 of the seventh governor of Louisiana, Don Manuel Gayoso de Lemos. After the governor's death in 1799 from yellow fever, the property was transferred from one owner to the next. In the mid-1800s it became a restaurant and saloon, known as "The Suckling Calf." The property had fallen into decay by the time it was purchased by Le Petit Theatre in 1922. The stage and auditorium were built in 1922 but did not join the corner property (which the organization rented) on the St. Peter Street frontage. Three small, shed-like buildings facing St. Peter Street had to be removed in order to erect the auditorium. Architect Richard Koch designed the theatre building in Spanish Colonial style in conformance with the surrounding buildings. This was one of the first serious attempts to construct a modern building in the traditional style of the Vieux Carre (Chapman 70-71). Noteworthy in Koch's design for this theatre is what now is considered the typical French Quarter courtyard, with a paved ornamental space containing flower beds and a fountain. Fountains were rare in the French

Quarter before this time. Koch's inspiration came from the Spanish gardens he had seen and studied, especially the Alcazar Gardens of Seville. Such gardens had no historical precedent in New Orleans, but have since become the norm ("Architectural Gems" F:9). Ethel Crumb Brett, an actress, long-time Le Petit volunteer, and the first female technical director in the South, contributed to the courtyard design (Anniversary Program). The theatre's location, which remains the same today, is 616 St. Peter Street, across the street from Jackson Square and St. Louis Cathedral.

    The audience in 1922 entered the theatre through three doors into a foyer, or lobby, which was nine feet by twenty-nine feet. During intermission, complimentary coffee and cigarettes were served from tables in one corner of the lobby. In a telephone interview, board member Leon Contavesprie commented that the tradition of serving complimentary coffee (but not cigarettes) at intermission continued until 1999 when board members decided to eliminate this small expense (approximately $250 per month) (11 Nov. 2000). Two small stairways with iron railings led to the auditorium. A balcony, seating thirty-two, was adorned with a wrought-iron railing. The stage was twenty-three feet in depth and fifty-nine feet, six inches, in width. The proscenium was seventeen feet high and twenty-nine feet wide (Chapman 71-78). Louise Nixon, one of the founding members of the Drawing Room Players and whose portrait hangs today in the lobby of Le Petit, commented:

> Into the spacious room once graced
> by the beauty and culture of France

> and of Spain we are led, and we sit
> among the remnant of our people
> who still cherish the charm and
> romance of New Orleans as you and
> I know it, and in a restful glow of
> softened light we enjoy our evening
> of culture and of art, amid
> surroundings and an approach no
> other American city can afford.
> (Dodds, "Big Birthday" C10)

The organization financed the building from a bond issue bearing seven per cent interest for six years. Opening night audience subscriptions totalled more than $20,000, allowing Le Petit Theatre to become one of only a few little theatres in the United States to develop financially without outside assistance (Baldwin 2). The dedication of the new playhouse read: "to every man, woman, and child who loves New Orleans" (Wallfisch, "Big Dreams" 4:1).

It was during this period when the founders of Le Petit moved into the permanent facility on St. Peter Street that the French Quarter was transformed from a long-neglected section into an area of charm and beauty. Le Petit Theatre helped revitalize the French Quarter (Dabney 403). The founders of Le Petit, who included civic leaders, writers, educators, and businessmen, brought about a major reawakening of interest in the city's historic area—"a section which had deteriorated into a dilapidated tenement, filled with immigrants and shunned by Orleanians" (Pitts, "Budding Theatre" 2:9). Both the remodeling of the Pontalba Apartments into a temporary facility for the original Drawing Room Players and the renovation of the property on St. Peter Street into a permanent theatre prompted similar activities among neighbors. Ultimately, there was interest in making the French Quarter an art center. Citizens in the community talked of restoring the old French Quarter with the hope of making it "the Greenwich Village of New Orleans" (Wallfisch, "Big Dreams" 4:1). The New Orleans theatre community viewed Greenwich Village as a mecca of creativity because of the Provincetown Players, playwrights such as Eugene O'Neill, Susan Glaspell, and George Cram Cook, and actors and artists who lived and worked there.

> Every large city is symbolized by some particular thing: New Orleans' symbol will be the Petit Theatre, for that in turn is symbolical of the artistic endeavor of New Orleans, and of the distinguishing charm that lies below Canal Street—the soul of the city. (Barbee 11)

The aim of the Little Theatre Movement in the United States was to combat a dearth of theatre outside of New York City for many areas of the country. The geographical distances between cities made it rare for many sections of the country, such as New Orleans, to see professional productions. The original goal of Le Petit Theatre was as follows:

> to present plays of a type that

> otherwise would never be seen in New Orleans with the purpose of keeping drama as an art and as an educational and spiritual influence alive. (Deutsch and Higgins 23)

Le Petit Theatre was established as a community-wide venture that relied on amateur actors. In the early days, the only requirements for membership were the desire to join and the annual fee of ten dollars before the fixed limit of subscriptions was reached. With this policy, which attracted the culturally elite regardless of their social or financial status, membership rose rapidly and enabled the theatre to be economically sound (Deutsch and Higgins 5). However, the perception by the general public of the exclusivity of Le Petit created problems in later years when membership declined. As Broadway critic, producer, and specialist on little theatre work Kenneth MacGowan stated:

> The theater finds that the fact that it does not appear to be open to the public has spread abroad among the lower middle classes of the city the notion that this theater is really an exclusive social club where only the members appear on the stage. To break down this social prejudice is a real problem for Le Petit Théâtre du Vieux Carré. (MacGowan 225)

10

The public's perception of Le Petit's exclusivity was not an unusual notion since a closed social structure existed in New Orleans. Evidence of this appeared in the festivities surrounding Mardi Gras during this time period. Mardi Gras organizations, called "krewes," limited membership by social class. Members of krewes staged balls and parades. Advertised as the "greatest free show on earth," the Mardi Gras parades could be attended by anyone. However, the average New Orleanian in the 1920s could not be a member of a krewe or participate in any of the select festivities of the krewe, such as the Mardi Gras balls. It would not be surprising to find that many of the founding members of Le Petit were members of the krewes as well; however, since the names of krewe members seldom were revealed publicly, this could not be proven.

At its inception, the membership of the theatre was divided into two types: active members and sustaining members. All those who purchased season memberships were considered sustaining members. The active members, who consisted of board members and anyone the Board selected to serve as an active member, were those who were responsible for producing the plays. The original active members conducted workshop productions and membership drives, provided business help, and voted on theatre issues. Additional members could be added to the active membership at any time. According to Lucy Daigle, current board member, as of 1998, the classification of sustaining member has been eliminated; all people who purchase season memberships today are considered to be active members and are allowed to vote (14 July 1998).

In the early years of Le Petit, members directed themselves in productions. Acting coaches were employed during the second season until the members realized the necessity of engaging a full-time person to direct and manage the theatre. Oliver Hinsdell became the first director in 1921 and directed until 1923 (Chapman 57).

Hinsdell planned for the inaugural season in the new location to consist of a group of short plays one month and a long drama the next. Seven programs were scheduled for the season. Since the leaders of Le Petit wanted to encourage original works, <u>The Falcon and the Lady</u> by Los Angeles playwright Margaret Penney, was selected as the first play in the new theatre (Chapman 81-82). Hinsdell resigned from his position after two years, rather than endure the intervention of the Board. Although he was qualified as a director, Hinsdell was not allowed to do his job, a trend which has continued throughout much of Le Petit's history. The Dramatic Committee chose the plays, and a committee of three, of which Hinsdell was often the minority member, selected the casts (Chapman 94-95).

At least one play per season was performed in French in the early years of the theatre, beginning in 1920. <u>Le Passant</u>, written by Francois Coppee and directed by M. Ravaux of the New Orleans French Opera, was the first production at Le Petit performed in French. Causerie du Lundi was a small social group devoted to the production of plays in the French language. Among the group's members were some of the founding members of the Drawing Room Players (Chapman

15). French Consul-General Barret commented in 1922 on the deep relations between France and New Orleans, as well as the artistic triumphs of Le Petit Theatre. He conferred upon the membership the palm of the French Academy as a recognition by the French government of the work done by Le Petit Theatre in spreading interest in the French language (Chapman 80-81).

The incorporation of Le Petit Théâtre du Vieux Carré occurred on May 20, 1922. According to Article III of the Act of Incorporation, this corporation was established for the following purposes:

    (1)   The encouragement and cultivation of a taste for drama, literature, and fine arts.

    (2)   The presentation of dramas, comedies, and other types of plays.

    (3)   The acquisition of a theatre building.

The Board of Directors considers Le Petit Theatre to be one of the oldest continuously-running community theatres in the United States. As earlier-established theatres halted productions during World War I and World War II, plays continued to be performed at Le Petit:

> Chicago is credited with the first little theatres—three opened in 1907—but Le Petit is considered the first major little theatre established in the South and Southwest. And more importantly, it is widely recognized as the oldest continuously-operating community

theatre in the United States.
(Dodds, "Big Birthday" C10)

    The researcher has discovered that the Footlight Club was established in 1877 in the Jamaica Plain area of metropolitan Boston, Massachusetts. Since 1878, regular season performances have been presented each year at Eliot Hall, owned by the Footlight Club. The American Association of Community Theatres considers the Footlight Club to be the oldest continuously-running amateur community theatre in the United States.

    In 1923, the Workshop Theatre was formed at Le Petit to allow novices to gain experience before appearing in main-stage productions. The purpose of the Workshop was to act as an adjunct theatre and to perform original and experimental plays that the Board would not allow to be a part of the major season. Operating without a budget for costumes or scenery and with only a small amount of money for publicity, originally board members exclusively previewed the Workshop plays during the summer before the regular membership was allowed to see them. Eventually, productions were performed for all members during the year at times when there were no main-stage plays. Between 1926 and 1929, audiences attended thirty-six Workshop plays. A committee decided when an actor in the Workshop had sufficient ability to perform in a main-stage production (Chapman 195).

    On Sunday, November 2, 1924, six hundred students from three New Orleans high schools were invited to a free performance of the main-stage production, <u>The White-Headed</u>

Boy. This was an attempt to extend Le Petit outside its closed membership circle (Chapman 107). After being urged by many members who wanted their children to receive the cultural benefits of the theatre, Harold Newman, chairman of the Board of Directors, announced that junior memberships would be extended to those under eighteen years of age. These junior memberships were restricted to 500 who could attend special matinees on Sundays, rather than at night, so it would not interfere with their study or sleep hours (Chapman 108).

In 1925, the Little Theatre Orchestra, consisting of seventeen musicians, was established. A sum, not to exceed $100 for the purchase of music scores, was allocated. Musicians did not receive a salary but were given free tickets to each play for that season (Chapman 148).

Growth in adult membership increased at such a rate that the corner building was purchased by the organization in 1925 and joined the theatre as part of the full plant that Le Petit claims today (Chapman 117). The corner building and the theatre auditorium were connected by the present loggia, which opened into the courtyard.

In 1928, the Board of Governors voted to spend $15,000 on improvements to the theatre, which included the extension of the entire backstage area to allow for the production of plays of greater scenic magnitude. Also, an entirely new lighting system was installed at the cost of $12,000 (Chapman 169).

In 1929, Kenneth MacGowan visited New Orleans as part of a tour of the principal little theatres in the United States.

15

He regarded Le Petit as one of the five outstanding Little Theatres in the country (Chapman 181). After attending a performance of <u>Saint Joan</u>, MacGowan commended the theatre:

> First an exceptionally fine pace in the direction, such pace as I rarely have seen among amateurs and not too often among professionals. And, second, the single fact that the performance which will be given tonight and all this week is backed by a larger body of interested and organized playgoers than any little theatre rejoices in—if we reckon the 3500 members in proportion to the size of this city. That is what makes Le Petit Théâtre du Vieux Carré one of the soundest, healthiest and most progressive producing theatres in the United States. He [the director, Walter Sinclair] has given Shaw's play as handsome and illusive a production as it is likely to have anywhere on this continent.
> (qtd. in Chapman 181)

Also, during the run of <u>Saint Joan</u>, the Board deviated from its "members only" policy by opening the last two performances to the public, at a cost of one dollar per ticket. The members of the Board felt that the educational value of this production would be beneficial to the public ("<u>Saint Joan</u> Opens" 11).

A number of momentous events occurred in 1935. The Board of Directors decided to create a school of theatre, in which acting classes were taught by actors who performed in the main-stage productions. Both the acting school and the Workshop Theatre fed talent into the major season (Chapman 538). During this seventeenth season of the theatre (1935-36), severe internal battles of the Board, concerning the selection of directors, resulted in the Board's interviewing many different directors for the season. Actor/writer/ director Bernard Szold, who eventually was employed for the season, believed that a community theatre represented the entire community. He was a proponent of open casting, which resulted in a change in production policy. Szold selected actors for their dramatic ability, rather than typecasting them, as had occurred previously (Chapman 242-243).

The Children's Theatre, sponsored jointly by the New Orleans Junior League and Le Petit Theatre, was inaugurated in 1937, performing productions on the main stage (Deutsch and Higgins 23). Chapter Two will explain more about children's theatre activities at Le Petit.

The major innovation in 1938 was the installation of air conditioning, of which specific requirements were silent operation and minimal machine space. In the winter of this year, film and theatre actress Margaret Tallichet portrayed the female lead in the production of <u>The Play's the Thing</u>. Before her performance at Le Petit, Tallichet had appeared in <u>The Virginian</u> with Henry Fonda and had screen tested for the roles of Scarlett

O'Hara and Carreen O'Hara for the film Gone With The Wind, roles that eventually went to Vivien Leigh and Ann Rutherford, respectively. Because the film's producer, David Selznick, believed Tallichet would benefit from the direction of Bernard Szold, she became the first professional artist to appear at the theatre (Chapman 266). One reviewer praised Tallichet's performance in The Play's the Thing, while criticizing the playwright for writing only one female role. He described Tallichet as lovely and graceful and excused her tendency to emote too much "because she, like the audience, feels that what little feminine touch there is must be accented" (Jones 18).

    The theatre thrived economically until the beginning of World War II, when a significant decrease in membership occurred. To increase revenue, in 1941, the Board decided to sell two city lots which lay directly behind the theatre, fronting on Chartres Street and running parallel to St. Peter Street. The property was sold for $11,000 (Chapman 294). This proved to be an unwise decision, since the value of the lots today is hundreds of thousands of dollars. An additional effort to increase revenue occurred in 1946, when Le Petit Théâtre du Vieux Carré became the playhouse of New Orleans Little Theatre Productions, Incorporated, the producing organization. This was a legal arrangement that allowed a substantial tax advantage (Chapman 342).

    Since the newly-appointed director, Monroe Lippman, taught at Tulane University, Le Petit and Tulane established an affiliation in 1947. This appealed to both students and professors because Tulane lacked a satisfactory theatre or performing space. Tulane professors who directed chose classics that had not been performed previously at Le Petit, thus exposing the membership to new plays. University officials employed Le Petit staff members, such as the publicity director and the technical director, to teach at Tulane. The expanded university departmental staff produced an expanded curriculum (Chapman 346-347). The affiliation received nationwide attention, and Lippman was invited to participate in a discussion concerning the merger at the American Educational Theatre Association Convention in 1948 (Chapman 363). The local affiliation continued until 1953 when the Department of Theatre and Speech at Tulane received its own theatre on campus.

    In 1951, with the consent and encouragement of the directors of Le Petit Theatre and New Orleans Little Theatre Productions, Incorporated, the Guild of Le Petit Théâtre du Vieux Carré was formed. Membership was open only to female members of New Orleans Little Theatre Productions, Incorporated, in good standing and was limited to 500. The Guild, primarily a social organization, promoted the welfare and best interests of the Theatre by inviting prominent people of the entertainment world to visit the Theatre (Constitution I:2).

    The internal revenue code of the United States Government concerning theatre admissions was amended in 1956. As a result, attorneys advised the Board to discontinue its dual corporate structure. Therefore, the New Orleans Little Theatre Productions, Incorporated, the producing company of the theatre, was dissolved, and the consolidated organization became known as Le Petit Théâtre du Vieux Carré. To insure the benefits of the new exemption, attorneys further advised that the charter of the new organization should provide for the disposition of its assets, in the event of the dissolution, for some civic and educational purpose. The new charter provided in the event of the organization's dissolution that an even division of its surplus would be divided among Louisiana's top three universities, Tulane University, Louisiana State University, and Loyola University of the South, to be used to further the dramatic arts at each university (Chapman 424-425). Louisiana State University in New Orleans (LSUNO), which later had a one-year affiliation with Le Petit, did not exist at the time of this charter.

The Board of Governors, who managed the Theatre, mandated in 1956 that the Board would consist of nine to fifteen members, which included the following: Chairman of the Board; President; Vice-President; Secretary; Treasurer; and Heads of the Play-Reading Committee, Membership Committee, House Committee, Building Committee, and Publicity Committee. As it was established then and continues today, the Chairman of the Board is the chief executive officer who presides at all meetings of the Board of Governors. The president presides at all meetings of the members and is the social head of the organization (Articles of Incorporation 5:2). Attempts have been made to eliminate the Play-Reading Committee, but it still exists today. As former Chairman of the Board Michael Arata stated:

> I'm trying to get rid of the Play-
> Reading Committee. You barter now

> over plays; the best plays are not always chosen. Some plays are outdated. We need someone with a strong vision to select the plays.
> (Personal interview, 11 Nov. 2000)

Upon hearing from the researcher about Arata's comment, actor/board member Contavesprie responded by telephone, "As long as I'm on the Board, there will be a Play-Reading Committee" (11 Nov. 2000).

The 1957-58 season set a record for memberships with 5,450. During this season, the balcony in the theatre was extended by two rows (Genre, <u>Anniversary Program, 1966-67</u>). Also, the Board eliminated student memberships; however, theatre students at Tulane and Loyola could attend the dress rehearsal of each show.

A major renovation of Le Petit began in March of 1961 and was completed in October 1963 at a cost of over $300,000. A fund had been started out of theatre income to make a rebuilding project possible. All of the theatre's surplus income since 1952 had been deposited into a special building fund, and no other revenue from any source was solicited or accepted. The auditorium, which held 460 people (and continues to do so today), and the main stage were unchanged, but the remaining structures were demolished and rebuilt. A second, smaller stage was built in a section of the building that originally was erected in 1789. This building was damaged by fire in 1794 and rebuilt in 1795; however, the damage had not been repaired adequately. The wall, known as a party wall because it was shared with the owner of an adjacent building, was unsafe; this portion of the building was condemned. It was necessary to restore the wall, or the building would have become a ruin ("Chartres Side To Be Reconstructed" 1).

As workmen began demolishing the wall, Fred Wohlford, director of the Vieux Carre Commission, literally ran from his office across the street from the theatre and ordered the workers to cease. Lionel Favret, head of the contracting firm rebuilding the property, told Wohlford that the Commission had approved the demolition of the wall. An argument ensued, and Wohlford called the police to settle the dispute. The building inspector arrived and issued a stop-work order. Thirty minutes later, the head of the department of regulatory inspections arrived and revealed that the co-owner of the party wall had agreed to the demolition. The stop-work order was rescinded, and the workers proceeded with the demolition (Madden 7).

The new, smaller stage, which was to be used as an experimental-rehearsal theatre and was known initially as the Players Theatre, was actually an extension of the stage in the main theatre. During productions on the main stage, this extension facilitated the movement of props and scenery and relieved cramped conditions backstage. Over the stage extension were a storage area and dressing rooms for the actors. Other changes included a new coffee room and box office. The patio, which included a fish pond, was restored to its former beauty. The Newman Memorial Library, named in honor of former Chairman of the Board Harold Newman, was built above the entrance foyer overlooking the patio (Chapman 490).

The significant event of 1961 was the appointment of C. Stocker Fontelieu as Managing Director/Executive Director, a post he held from 1961 until 1985. Fontelieu was the first native New Orleanian to direct at Le Petit. Until 1961, Le Petit Theatre was managed by a Board of Governors with a paid professional staff and a Managing Director. The Managing Director was in charge of play selection (with the Play-Reading Committee), casting, rehearsal, and technical aspects of all stage productions. He or she was responsible to the Board of Directors for the safekeeping of all physical property placed at his or her disposal (By-laws II). With the appointment of Fontelieu, the position of Managing Director became that of Managing Director/Executive Director, a position Fontelieu held for twenty-four years, during which time he directed over one hundred plays. According to Fontelieu, the Managing Director/Executive Director is responsible for hiring all the different directors each season and is in charge of public relations. He or she must answer to the Board of Governors. Once Fontelieu retired, the one position became two separate jobs (Personal interview).

Fontelieu instituted the Teen Club in 1962, which was not restricted to members. Many of these youths had worked with Fontelieu when he directed at Gallery Circle, another New Orleans community theatre. The Teen Club, which welcomed all people aged thirteen to twenty, met on alternating Saturdays for the purpose of indoctrinating young people in all phases of theatre. Guest speakers gave presentations on various aspects of theatre (Fontelieu 13).

23

Tulane University drama professor/director Richard Schechner in 1967 directed the Eugene Ionesco play <u>Victims of Duty</u> at Le Petit. Ellen Stewart, founder of La Mama Experimental Theatre Club in New York, saw the play and wanted the Le Petit actors to perform the play at La Mama. Unfortunately for the actors, the Board of Governors at Le Petit proclaimed that they did not sell subscriptions in New York City and refused to grant the necessary six hundred dollars needed for plane fare. The production, therefore, did not go to La Mama (Owen). The Board had no interest in venturing into uncharted territory, even though it was an honor for Ellen Stewart to invite the actors. An association began in September of 1969 between Le Petit Theatre and the Department of Drama and Fine Arts at the University of New Orleans (called Louisiana State University in New Orleans—LSUNO—at that time). This was a new educational venture for advanced and highly experienced graduate students in drama, using the facilities and staff of Le Petit Theatre and the graduate faculty at LSUNO. Students' participation was by invitation only and involved three years of graduate study leading towards a Master of Fine Arts in drama. August W. Staub, Chairman of LSUNO's Department of Drama and Fine Arts, observed:

> The cooperation and enthusiastic support for the project on the part of the Board of Directors of Le Petit Theatre is an indication of the willingness of the community to support major innovations in

> dramatic production and education. LSUNO is indeed grateful for Le Petit Theatre's generous support of this aesthetic and educational program. This support is indicative of the true cultural strength of New Orleans. The program will certainly attract much national attention and comment. It will add just a bit more shine to our cultural luster.
> (qtd. in "Theatre, School Plan Program," 2:12)

What seemed to be an excellent idea lasted only one year. Louisiana State University in New Orleans had a relatively new theatre department, which began operation in 1966. Influential board members at Le Petit believed it was more prestigious for the theatre to be associated with a more established university, such as Tulane University, rather than the fledgling LSUNO (Staub).

The experimental Players Theatre, accommodating 150, became a children's theatre in 1970. Children and adults performed in plays for children on this stage, instead of using the main stage. Initially, the children's theatre was named Children's Corner. Luis Barroso, an actor, director, and teacher, was appointed as the first full-time children's theatre director at Le Petit in 1970. According to C. Stocker Fontelieu, there were five or six children's plays a year, which justified employing a full-time director (Personal interview). Later, Children's Corner became known as Teddy's Playhouse for Children, in honor of Theodora "Teddy" Sciacca, who was a playwright, lyricist, composer, and president of the Board of Governors. Chapter Two will examine key children's theatre productions and will explain more about the history of the children's theatre at Le Petit.

Le Petit prospered as adults, accompanying children to Children's Corner plays, began to populate main-stage productions in the early 1970s (Tong). Membership for the main-stage productions was 8,000 with a waiting list of a few hundred:

> We couldn't fit them all in. And this was not with an open box office. You couldn't just buy a ticket like you can today.
> (Fontelieu, Personal interview)

Most seasons in the 1970s opened with a musical, such as Oklahoma! (1970), Fiddler on the Roof (1971), Hello, Dolly! (1972), My Fair Lady (1973), 1776 (1974), Funny Girl (1975), and Shenandoah (1976). Musicals at Le Petit have been both popular and profitable.

After achieving its highest season subscription rate in 1970, memberships lagged in 1974, and the Board authorized the allocation of money for television commercials, advertising upcoming productions. Also, at this time, area high school and college students had the opportunity to purchase season subscriptions at reduced prices to dress rehearsal performances only. The season consisted of seven plays with each play having twelve performances and at least one dress rehearsal.

After a revival of interest in the late 1970s, memberships again decreased considerably in the 1980s:

> Probably, the biggest turnaround occurred in the five years over the '80s that I was there, from '80 to '85, that the membership started to take a tumble. I mean a serious tumble. (Fontelieu, Personal interview)

For years, the board members clung to the belief that the theatre could thrive financially through season memberships and resisted exploring other financial opportunities, such as grants. With the emergence of the Saenger Theatre in 1980 as a facility for touring professional productions, as well as the rise of other community theatres in New Orleans and the suburbs, competition affected the finances of the theatre. The Saenger productions often featured celebrity actors, such as Elizabeth Taylor in <u>The Little Foxes</u> (1981) and Yul Brenner in <u>The King and I</u> (1982), which drew huge audiences:

> One problem is not one for which the theater [Le Petit] is to blame but, nonetheless, one which it has to face, and that is the changing market—a market in which the potential audience now has more experimental and university

alternatives from which to choose as well as professional road shows at the Saenger. (Laborde 17)

C. Stocker Fontelieu cited additional reasons for the decline in attendance at Le Petit:

> This is when certain Board Members felt possibly Stocker had burnout, and Stocker had done as much as he could do with all of this. That may well have been true, I don't know, but the membership did start to go, and, with it, went the resources, and with the resources, then the staff members had to go. It was a domino effect. The physical look of the place took a tumble. The physical look of the plays took a tumble.... But, you know, by then, restaurants had caught on. "Let's really promote dining out." Dining out doesn't mean running to the restaurant at 6:00, and leaving at 7:15 to get to the theatre. Dining, you go at 7:30, and that's the evening's event. National sports have taken hold of things now. The Saints [a professional football team] are entrenched in the city now. You

know the entertainment dollar can only go so far. The community had so many other theatres. The Beverly [a professional dinner theatre] had opened. This whole new dinner theatre thing came along. So, all of a sudden, there were so many people now vying for the entertainment dollar, who had not been, that things just started to tumble. They [Le Petit] haven't rallied to this day. (Personal interview)

After determining that season subscriptions did not produce enough money to maintain the theatre, the Board instituted the open box office policy in 1981. While continuing to promote to the public the benefits of purchasing season memberships and being reluctant to alter this policy, the Board announced in the media that tickets could be obtained for individual productions. Fears that an open box office would result in a loss of season subscriptions did not materialize. Season memberships decreased by only seven per cent, whereas individual ticket sales compensated for the decrease. However, because of rising costs in operating the theatre, the money from season memberships and the open box office was not sufficient to balance the budget. In another attempt to increase revenue, the Board authorized individuals to rent the theatre and/or the courtyard for parties, weddings, luncheons, and style shows. Production companies were allowed to rent the facilities to film commercials; a commercial for Guess Jeans was filmed at the theatre. The Board also sought corporate sponsorship for the first time during the 1980s at the suggestion of director C. Stocker Fontelieu and others:

> I instituted something when I was there, called "co-produced by." In other words, let's say Whitney Bank wants to put up $5,000.00. Le Petit and Whitney Bank of New Orleans presents <u>The Time of Your Life</u>. It's a co-production. Contributions, donations to the theatre to help them get through the rough times.
> (Personal interview)

Banks, hotels, furniture stores, and bakeries were willing to do this. Shell Offshore, Incorporated, agreed to contribute corporate support. Organizations were encouraged to purchase tickets for employees. DePaul Hospital bought all tickets for one performance of <u>The Philadelphia Story</u> as an activity for its employees, and R and L Financial Services used its performance of <u>Auntie Mame</u> as a birthday party for the president's wife (Dodds, "Le Petit Succeeded in Going Public" 2:17-18). Businesses or individuals who chose to co-produce received a full-page advertisement in the playbill and one free performance of that play to use however they wished. Offering discounts on season memberships to high school and college students as well as teachers was another method used to generate income during the 1980s; these discounts continued to be offered until the 2000-2001 season. The Board finally realized that it was necessary to pursue financial avenues other than relying solely on season subscriptions. Director Fontelieu commented:

> It's virtually impossible anymore for a community theatre to survive on box office alone, especially with an operation like ours. We have a big overhead just keeping the doors open. Actually, we should have done what we're doing now ten years ago, instead of crying about the lack of money.
> (qtd. in Dodds, "Le Petit Succeeded in Going Public" 2:17-18)

Actress Helen Hayes visited Le Petit in 1983 for a fund-raiser for the theatre and commented as follows:

> Good community theatre is essential to the continuation and growth of culture in our country. It provides accessible entertainment and enlightenment for those who wish to be observers, a wonderful avocation for many talented citizens, and a training ground and showcase for those aspiring to professional theatre careers. Le Petit Theatre is not just

good. It is magnificent community
theatre. The professional approach
of your board and your staff, plus
the excellence of your theatre plant,
attract outstanding talent and
provide unusually high quality
productions. I know that your
theatre is for the first time in its 67-
year history struggling with
financial problems. It is a credit to
your strength that these problems
have not plagued you sooner,
considering that you're the oldest
continuing non-professional theatre
in the nation [sic]. It is also to your
credit that you are proceeding with
strong plans to alter the situation.
You have so much more to offer
than most community theatres that I
cannot but believe that you will be
successful.
(qtd. in Wallfisch, "Big Dreams" 4:2)

After Fontelieu retired, his successor Mary Ellen O'Brien was appointed Managing Director/Artistic Director. O'Brien, a native of St. Louis, had lived in New Orleans less than four years but already had directed six plays at various theatres. She had teaching experience at several universities and had masters' degrees in drama and directing from Yale

University and Tulane University. Armed with a desire to increase interest and attendance at the theatre, O'Brien expressed her desire to recharge marketing and public relations activities. She wanted to see the theatre rented for independent productions and, eventually, to offer lunch-time theatre. She also intended to bring in guest designers for each production (Laborde 18). Her additional plans for the theatre included offering playwriting workshops, acting classes, and experimental productions in Children's Corner, which would continue to house children's productions as well (Dodds, "Turning New Page" Lagniappe 13). In the spring of 1986, the newly-created Louisiana Shakespeare Festival presented <u>Twelfth Night</u>. This production was directed by Tulane University drama professor Buzz Podewell as part of the interaction between Le Petit and local universities that O'Brien had hoped to encourage.

O'Brien's choice of the play <u>Pigeons</u>, written by her husband, a local playwright and university professor, proved to be controversial. Answering questions about this play, O'Brien responded: "Some people ask if that is nepotism, but nepotism is when a job is given to an incompetent; my husband is a professional" (qtd. in Laborde 18). Critics commended the director for taking a risk and producing a new play, which rarely happened at Le Petit; yet, the play itself did not receive favorable reviews.

Finances continued to be problematic. During O'Brien's tenure, the full-time production staff of six was trimmed to two to meet budget cuts.

Despite the charges of nepotism and continuing financial problems, O'Brien was stunned when, after one year in her job, her contract at the theatre was not renewed. Expressing her surprise, she responded:

> The theatre had never had such a big box office; we were able to raise over 90 percent of our operating budget. We [O'Brien and the Board] worked well together. I think they took my requests (for a raise and increased vacation time) as a display of ingratitude. I gave twelve to fourteen hours a day to that theatre; this is no way to end it.
> (qtd. in "Life's Too Short" 51)

One aspect, unaddressed by O'Brien, was noted by long-time board member Rosa Deutsch in speaking about the sole female occupant of the director's chair:

> We had one lady who was a wonderful actress, but she was no manager at all. And she would have checks on her desk to pay musicians or this or that, and she would just forget to pay them. People were very unhappy about that.
> (Personal interview)

Even so, board member Lary Hessdorfer concurred with

O'Brien that her demands could not be met:

> There were big advances last year, but we couldn't meet some of the things she was asking for.
> (qtd. in "Life's Too Short" 51)

When the decision was made to replace O'Brien, both she and the title of Managing Director/Artistic Director were dismissed. The new position was Executive Director: "The Board of Governors wanted someone to run the show, but not necessarily to choose the show, too" (Dodds, "Curious Case" 4:10).

The new Executive Director, Don Marshall, was employed at the theatre from 1986 until 1991. Before accepting the job at Le Petit, Marshall served for nine years as director of the Contemporary Arts Center in New Orleans, a multi-media organization featuring theatre, music, dance, and art. Pat Haun, then Chairwoman of the Board, encouraged the Board to appoint Marshall: "We wanted someone with business talent, artistic talent, and creative talent" (qtd. in Dodds, "Marshall" Lagniappe 1).

Since he was cognizant of Le Petit's shrinking audiences, at the beginning of his tenure, Marshall had several ideas about how the theatre could attract more people:

> One of the first things we have to do is work with the younger people who are involved at the theatre to attract young professionals to our shows. There should also be more

> emphasis on selling the individual shows, and if people like them, then maybe they'll subscribe to a whole season. I also think we should add an extra weekend of performances, because with the current schedule, it doesn't allow for word of mouth to build up the house.
> (qtd. in Dodds, "Marshall" Lagniappe 1)

Marshall also intended to give new directors the opportunity to stage experimental productions, using the Children's Corner. He believed that new directors had very few outlets in New Orleans, and Le Petit should provide them with a place to perform (Dodds, "Marshall" Lagniappe 1). Marshall supported local playwrights: <u>Le Veau Qui Tete</u> (<u>The Suckling Calf</u>) by local playwright Dalt Wonk was performed in 1987. <u>Le Veau Qui Tete</u> was an historical pageant written as a tribute to Le Petit Theatre's seventieth anniversary. The first act related events surrounding the founding of Le Petit, and the second act was a potpourri of numbers from past productions on its stage (Gagnard, "Le Petit Celebrates" E12).

    Marshall encouraged other activities at the theatre, in addition to the regular season of plays. Both the New Orleans Classical Music Festival and a production entitled <u>New Vaudeville</u> were held in 1989. Carl Mack, a native of Rochester, New York, organized his vaudeville show because of a lack of a showcase for variety artists. Additionally, Marshall instituted the Family Fine Arts Series. The Family Fine Arts Series presented scenes from Shakespearean plays that were performed by students and faculty members of the New Orleans Center for Creative Arts, a performing arts high school. Special school performances were given for children who normally would not have access to Shakespearean productions. Adults could attend weekend performances for a nominal fee. Also, full-length main-stage productions of <u>A Streetcar Named Desire</u> and <u>The Glass Menagerie</u> were performed at the theatre during the school day for high school pupils, giving them an opportunity to be exposed to plays by Tennessee Williams. It was noted:

> Under the prodding and encouragement of Executive Director Don Marshall, who had plenty of experience working with both artists and governing boards during his years as director of the Contemporary Arts Center, the theatre's French doors have been thrown open, and this prime piece of property—underutilized for so long—can today be legitimately called a performing arts center. (Dodds, "Le Petit's New Image" C8)

Several of Marshall's innovations helped restore Le Petit to some financial stability. These included the new projects previously mentioned, a revitalized stage program, increased audiences, especially in the Children's Corner which routinely sold out for performances, and a higher community profile. Marshall resigned his position in the fall of 1991: "Marshall's decision to leave after five years followed conflicts among the Board of Directors over their role in running the theatre" (Dodds, "First Nighter" E:1). Seven board members resigned at this time also because of an ongoing battle over the direction that the theatre should take. A major issue was whether the theatre's Board should be policy-making only, deferring management to a hired staff, or also take charge of management. It was decided that the Board would continue to have a strong presence.

    The seven members of the Board had requested the resignation of board member Emmett J. Johnson. Upon the resignations of the seven members, Emmett J. Johnson was named Chairman of the Board. Johnson also served as Executive Director until the employment of Lawrence J. Knowles in June of 1992. During this interim period, various local directors were given the opportunity to direct productions, such as <u>Fiddler on the Roof</u>, <u>Fences</u>, <u>Applause</u>, and <u>Sweet Bird of Youth</u>.

    Knowles, the new Executive Director, recognized the fact that Le Petit had a very strong Board, "and that can be both positive and negative. But we have developed a working relationship, and I do run the theatre on a day-to-day basis" (qtd. in Dodds, "First Nighter" E:1). During 1992, Knowles directed one play, <u>Summer and Smoke</u>, and the other five plays in the season were directed by various local directors. He envisioned using the Children's Corner as a "black-box space for a more select target audience. The board is very open to that idea" (qtd. in Dodds, "First Nighter" E:1). It was at this time that Le Petit installed new theatre seats that were wider and had cushioning on the backs and bottoms. New patio furniture and plants, new paint for the interior of the theatre, and dark red carpeting inside the auditorium were welcome additions (Dodds, "First Nighter" E:1).

Knowles' cited complaints about his relationship with the Board, and his incumbency lasted only one year. Knowles said that he resented the lack of communication between himself and the Board, particularly in having to learn about the Theatre's activities from the newspaper. He also would have preferred to deal more in artistic expression and less in management (Dodds, "Time to Change Course" Lagniappe 18). David Cockerell, whose title was changed from Executive Director to Managing Director, succeeded Knowles. The plays that were performed during the 1993-94 season, once again by guest directors, included West Side Story, The Baby Dance, The Pirates of Penzance, and The Taming of the Shrew.

Board member Emmett Johnson assumed the day-to-day operations of the theatre in the 1994-95 season when David Cockerell resigned. Cockerell departed after serving one year because of his "too-good-to-miss opportunity to continue his education at Oklahoma City University" (Dodds, "Time to Change Course" Lagniappe 19). Le Petit's top salaried post was not an easy one to keep filled. Serving in an interim capacity, Johnson dictated the tone, direction, and philosophy of the theatre to board members who often were overwhelmed by his intense and analytical approach. Although Johnson helped restore financial discipline to the theatre, some board members considered his control to be a stranglehold (Dodds, "Time to Change Course" Lagniappe 18). Trophies, A Life in the Theatre, La Cage aux Folles, and The Sisters Rosenweig were some of the plays performed during this season by various directors. As the exodus of directors (executive director, managing director, interim director) continued yearly, audience attendance at Le Petit plummeted.

Local actors who performed frequently at the theatre asked to meet with the Board to address certain issues. Their main request was to be paid for performing at the theatre and to be reimbursed for parking during rehearsals and performances. The Board agreed to consider reimbursing the actors for parking, but denied their requests to be paid for performing. The Board intended to continue operating Le Petit as a community theatre with amateur actors. As a group the actors decided not to perform again at Le Petit until Michael Arata, at that time Chairman of the Board, invited them to return. However, the by-laws remain the same, and actors are not supposed to be paid for performing at Le Petit. The researcher has discovered that a local Equity actor was paid to perform in the 1999 production of City of Angels. When the researcher telephoned board member Contavesprie to confirm this, he responded:

> Our policy is not to pay performers. However, actor Bert Pigg, who is in Equity, was paid Equity scale to

perform in City of Angels. I
understand he is no longer in Equity,
and he wasn't paid to perform in
Barnum, our first show this season
[2000-2001]. If an Equity member
wants to be on stage, he or she can
perform but won't be paid by us.
(11 Nov. 2000)

Also, director Sonny Borey paid for New Orleanian Patrick Mendelson to return home in 1999 to perform in Grand Hotel (Contavesprie, 11 Nov. 2000).

Joel Rainey, who previously had worked at a professional children's theatre in Baton Rouge, Louisiana, was appointed Executive Manager in 1995. During his employment at Le Petit, Rainey directed a production of The Secret Garden. Other productions by guest directors included Carmen Jones, The Heiress, They're Playing our Song, and Steel Magnolias. Stocker Fontelieu, who had not directed at Le Petit since 1985, directed a production of The Woman in Black. Robert Landry, Chairman of the Board at this time, appointed Fontelieu Director Emeritus, hoping that the honorary position could be expanded to a point where Fontelieu would serve as a liaison between Le Petit and the theatre community. The full-time position that Fontelieu once held had changed substantially through the years. While Fontelieu had directed almost all of the theatre's main-stage productions during his twenty-four-year tenure, the position held by Rainey had become a low-profile desk job (Dodds, "Eighty Years at Le Petit" Lagniappe 20).

Rainey followed his predecessors and exited his position after one year. "The Board and I do not see eye to eye on a number of items. As a result, the work atmosphere is no longer bearable," Rainey wrote in a letter to the Board (qtd. in "Rainey Is Leaving" E10).

Because of declining attendance, in 1996 Le Petit instituted its Sunday Salon on the first Sunday of each month. In the courtyard at the theatre, local actors performed scenes from plays, and poets recited their original poetry as the audience sipped tea. Occasionally, local artists displayed their art work. The goal was to get people acquainted with Le Petit to see what was offered. The Board of Governors hoped to attract new people to the theatre and to welcome back old members (Tong). After three years, waning attendance resulted in the discontinuation of this event, according to board member Daigle (14 July 1998).

The 1996-97 season began with the musical <u>Sophisticated Ladies</u>, directed by Sonny Borey, who later would become the theatre's artistic director. After the premiere performance, Le Petit Theatre celebrated its eightieth birthday with a black-tie party. This celebration, at which actress Delta Burke was the guest of honor, served as a fund-raiser for the theatre (Dodds, "Fancy Ladies" E:9). The second production of the season was <u>Laughter On the 23rd Floor</u>, directed by the late Keith Briggs, who became the new Managing Director in 1997. Briggs had directed a critically acclaimed production of <u>The Heiress</u> during a previous season. He first performed at Le Petit at the age of seven in a production of <u>Peter Pan</u>. New Orleanian

Briggs, a former educator in the local school system for many years, stated his objectives:

> My primary objectives will be to increase corporate funding and to open up the theatre to tourists who don't know that there is this wonderful theatre here. We've got to get a new audience base.
> (qtd. in Dodds, "Local Director to Head Le Petit" Lagniappe 24)

Membership in 1997 fell from 7,000 to 2,000. The theatre was $350,000 in debt, so Briggs decided to close Children's Corner. His idea was to have performances of children's productions on the main stage for elementary and high school students during the school day (Briggs). A production of <u>The Passion of Dracula</u> in the fall of 1997 proved to be successful financially, making a profit of $15,000. According to board member Leon Contavesprie:

> Keith shifted the children's theatre productions to the main stage, and when he did, we made a profit of $15,000 on one show, as opposed to losing $800 per show on a lavish children's production.
> (29 July 1998)

In April of 1998, audiences of over 1,000 elementary school children viewed a two-character version of <u>The Lion, the Witch,</u>

and the Wardrobe that made a $7,000 profit (Contavesprie 29 July 1998). However, Le Petit continued to operate in debt.

In September of 1997, Le Petit served as the facility for the world premiere of the musical Pretty Baby, based on Louis Malle's 1978 film. The Board of Le Petit was contacted by the producers of Pretty Baby, who were interested in an out-of-town opening for the play with Broadway aspirations. Since the play is set in Storyville, an area that once existed in New Orleans, Le Petit seemed a logical theatre to host the production. The producers of Pretty Baby paid Le Petit $15,000 to rent the theatre. Both New York actors and New Orleans actors, Equity and non-Equity, were cast in the production. The Equity actors performed under Equity guest artist contracts (Briggs).

In January of 1998, citing health reasons, Briggs resigned. The popular musical Gypsy replaced Briggs' scheduled production of A Few Good Men since the Board felt a musical would generate more income. Gypsy would not have been performed were it not for the generous donation from Mr. and Mrs. Brunswick G. Deutsch, long-time supporters of Le Petit (Papatola, "Stripped-down Gypsy" Lagniappe 23).

On April 5, 1998, after a very heated, vocal Board meeting, Michael Arata, a local actor and lawyer, was named Chairman of the Board of Le Petit Theatre. Arata is the first actor ever to serve in this capacity. Among his many plans for the theatre, the reopening of Children's Corner became a reality:

> I hope to restart the children's
> theatre. We have some

reconstruction plans for the space itself. I would like to use it during the day for children's plays and at night as an experimental theatre, especially for works by new local playwrights. (Arata)

Since this interview with Arata, not only has the children's theatre flourished, but also the space has been utilized for adult, theatrical productions. There is a scarcity of performing spaces in New Orleans, so other theatre groups welcome the opportunity to rent a place to perform. The Director's Studio, as this smaller theatre is known when not in use as a children's theatre, provides this opportunity. Le Petit has benefitted from the success of the play, <u>Late Night Catechism</u>, which had been running indefinitely since July of 1999 in the Director's Studio until the arrival of Hurricane Katrina. The show generates $50,000 per month in revenue, with a net profit of $35,000 to $40,000. Capacity crowds have flocked to see this production (Contavesprie, 26 Jan. 2000).

The Tennessee Williams/New Orleans Literary Festival, held every year since 1987, provides additional revenue to the theatre. A group of New Orleans citizens committed to promoting the cultural heritage of the city and fostering the development of cultural literacy founded the festival in the city that Tennessee Williams considered his spiritual home. The founders' goal is to serve the community through educational, theatrical, and literary programs. The festival's organizers rent space each year at Le Petit to host this event, which includes a book fair, lectures, panel discussions, and workshops. The festival's Board and Le Petit's Board have co-produced a Tennessee Williams play each year during the festival. Both organizations co-produced <u>Cat on a Hot Tin Roof</u> in March 2000. However, in the future because some of the Le Petit board members have expressed the desire not to be bound to performing a Tennessee Williams play as part of its season, the festival may produce a play on its own.

    For years the Board, clinging to the idea that season subscriptions provided sufficient revenue, resisted applying for grants. The late Arthur Tong, theatre photographer and long-time volunteer (over thirty years) at Le Petit, encouraged the Board for years to seek grants. Finally, in the 1990s, the Board received its first grant from the National Endowment for the Arts. The Theatre was also the recipient of a City of New Orleans Municipal Endowment Grant for the Arts of $3,500 from annual payments stipulated in the franchise of Cox Cable and administered by the Arts Council. State Representative Mitch Landrieu, a former actor at Le Petit, was instrumental in having the Louisiana legislature appropriate $300,000 in 1998 for capital improvements to the theatre. These monies provided for bathroom accommodations for the physically challenged, the repair of a stairwell, and the renovation of the outside balcony of the theatre. The Board spent $100,000 of the grant on the installation of a new lighting system, which the technical crew used for the opening production of the 2000-2001 season. After viewing the 1998 production of <u>Hay Fever</u>, Cheryl Sims, a representative from the Gertrude Ford Foundation, granted

$50,000 to be spent in any way that the Board chose (Contavesprie, 26 Jan. 2000). This grant has been renewed every year since 1998. In an effort to finance programs that catered to the ethnically diverse, Harrah's Casino in New Orleans contributed $5,000 to the 2000-2001 production of <u>Little Shop of Horrors</u>, which boasted a multi-cultural cast (Contavesprie, 11 Nov. 2000).

    In addition to the appointment of Arata, other significant personnel changes occurred in 1998. The positions of president and vice-president were eliminated; this required amending the by-laws. At the same time, the Board was increased from fifteen to thirty-six members. Also, the Board paid an application fee to the New Orleans Arts Council for two interns to help with fundraising. An organization within Le Petit, called Friends of Le Petit, was established to aid in fundraising.

    The dissolution of Le Petit was mandated to create a more favorable tax status to allow its continuation. Three local universities stood to benefit from the demise of the theatre. Board member Contavesprie noted:

> Numerous rumors existed two years ago about the closing of Le Petit. Officials from Loyola, Tulane, and L.S.U. got word about this, and their fangs were out. We can't turn it over to universities. They would sell it, close it, and use the money for their own programs.
> (7 Nov. 1999)

Therefore, provision was made in the by-laws to reflect this concern. According to the new by-laws, in the event of the dissolution of Le Petit Theatre, the ownership of the organization would transfer to another New Orleans arts organization, not specified. The building must be maintained as a theatre, and there would be no monetary transactions (Daigle, 26 Oct. 1999).

In June of 1998, Le Petit Theatre announced the employment of Roland Henry "Sonny" Borey, III, a long-time local director, teacher, and costume shop owner, as Artistic/Executive Director. Arata referred to Borey as "a progressive, ambitious artistic director who will set a style for our theatre that we think audiences will respond to" (qtd. in Papatola, "Le Petit Theatre Staging Revival" B4). Local professional actress Terri Gervais responded:

> He knows how to get things done. Sonny has a following of people who know he does good work. I absolutely think he will turn Le Petit around. Given the first show he's directing [42nd Street], it will have good people in it, a lot of publicity, a real positive edge to it; and he will get a lot of people back. The theatre has lost a lot of money with many people not renewing. I bet people have gotten subscriptions when they found out he was taking over. I can

> even see a documentary being done on him in a year or two on one of the cable stations.
> (Personal interview)

Borey, who prefers directing musicals, directed two productions his first year, beginning with 42nd Street and closing with the first local production of City of Angels. Borey's duties include overseeing all productions, as well as being responsible for the day-to-day operations of the theatre. His plans for invigorating the former children's theatre space with a mix of children's theatre and small-scale shows co-produced by Le Petit have come to fruition.

Although the expenses of running Le Petit total close to $25,000 per month and the theatre is in debt, the appointments of Arata and Borey have given both the Board and the community reason to be optimistic about the future of this historic theatre:

> Le Petit has run down for the last ten years; its glory is fading. I'm trying to get new people— local people, business people— interested. It's a valuable landmark for the community and theatre as a whole. Le Petit has a central location in the city. Le Petit has a prime location. I want to restore the creative bravura that this theatre needs—like the excitement and

creativity that the original people in 1916 had. Coming to the theatre is something you can't get on television. I want to restore the creative vitality of this theatre. (Arata)

In the late 1980s and continuing into the 1990s, membership sharply declined. Increased crime in New Orleans (New Orleans was rated as America's most dangerous city in the years 1994-95) and the perception by local citizens that the French Quarter had a higher crime rate than other parts of the city no doubt contributed to this decline. Theatre patrons, particularly the elderly, complained about the lack of available parking in the French Quarter, which necessitated walking a few blocks from the theatre to a parking lot. Fearful patrons expressed concern about having to pass large groups of "grunge people," who inhabited the French Quarter in the mid-1990s, on the way to the theatre. The Board did not address their fears, and many patrons did not renew their memberships. However, according to statistics compiled by the New Orleans Police Department in December 1999, crime in the French Quarter decreased by forty per cent from 1996 to 1999 (New Orleans Police Department). Reports such as this should encourage patrons to return to Le Petit. Also, with Borey at the helm, the Board was optimistic about the future.

For the 1999-2000 season, the Play-Reading Committee allowed Borey, the Executive/Artistic Director, to choose the plays for the season. This was a major concession instituted by the Board to lure Borey. In an attempt to adhere to the original philosophy of Le Petit by presenting plays that audiences might not see anywhere else in New Orleans, Borey chose <u>Grand Hotel</u>, <u>Lettice and Lovage</u>, <u>Falsettos</u>, and <u>Kiss of the Spider Woman</u>, as well as the well-known <u>Cat on a Hot Tin Roof</u>. Although subscriptions increased in 1998, only a slight increase occurred in 1999. Board member Daigle attributed this to the selection of plays. The majority of the season subscribers wanted to see traditional plays. <u>The Sound of Music</u> was voted the number one choice in a survey. Age may be a contributing factor, as the majority of season members are older. The Executive/Artistic Director chose to expose the audience to a wider variety of plays than many members desired. This was evidenced by the many negative telephone calls received by board members (Daigle, 26 Oct. 1999).

As of July of 2001, long-time board member Errol Laborde replaced Michael Arata as Chairman of the Board. Arata cited his hectic schedule as the reason for his resignation, although he will continue to serve as a board member. Also, the word <u>amateur</u> was deleted from the charter; however, according to Laborde, Le Petit will maintain its non-professional status. Beginning with the production of <u>George M!</u> for the 2001-02 season, any Equity actors who perform at Le Petit will be paid Equity scale. Borey will negotiate with non-Equity actors in key roles for salaries (Laborde, Personal interview).

Le Petit Theatre has been described by performers, visitors, and New Orleanians as one of the most picturesque little theatres in the United States. Its architecture, which blends with the French Quarter, enhances its attractiveness and appeal. The entrance to the auditorium is modeled after the Old Absinthe House, a landmark of strong Spanish and French influence. To the rear of the building and upstairs are the greenroom, dressing rooms, a library, a property room, and a scenery shop. The patio is considered one of the most beautiful in New Orleans (Wallfisch, "Big Dreams" 4:1).

Directors, actors, designers, and board members who were interviewed by the researcher mentioned frequently that the strength of Le Petit is the theatre's facility. Their sentiments paralleled this enthusiastic description of the theatre:

> ...a fine old building, housing a reception area, space for experimental and children's theatre, a lush courtyard and a 460-seat main stage area with a sophisticated lighting system comprising what is generally considered to be among the finest community theatre facilities in the country.
> (Laborde, "Biggest Challenge" 17)

Le Petit has been "the prestige theatre, the place for aspiring performers to take their first step on their way to their Broadway dream" (Laborde, "Biggest Challenge" 17). Bryan Batt, a 1999 Drama Desk nominee for Forbidden Broadway Cleans Up Its Act and who has appeared on Broadway in Sunset Boulevard, Cats, The Scarlet Pimpernel, Saturday Night Fever, La Cage aux Folles, and Seussical, received his theatrical indoctrination at Le Petit, which he felt proved to be an excellent training ground (Personal interview). Batt also produced the play <u>Forever Plaid</u> at Le Petit as a summer production. Jazz musician Wynton Marsalis' initial theatrical experience was performing in the role of Gabriel in <u>Shenandoah</u> at Le Petit at the age of fourteen (Fosberg, "<u>Shenandoah</u>" 12). Actress B.J. Crosby (known in New Orleans as "Lady B.J."), nominated for a Tony Award in 1995 for her performance in <u>Smokey Joe's Cafe</u>, made her stage debut in 1978 at Le Petit (Dodds, "Rapunzel" Lagniappe 6).

Veteran New Orleans actress the late Lois Crandell, who had performed in over twenty-five plays at Le Petit and whose brother Val Winter was one of the original Drawing Room Players, describes Le Petit:

> Le Petit is for me the epitome of local theatre. If I had a choice between a part of a few lines at Le Petit and a big part at another theatre, I'd take the small part at Le Petit.
> (Personal interview)

Julie Winn, formerly a costumer with the Ice Capades and with the New Orleans Opera Association and currently a costume teacher/designer, was a costumer for seven productions at Le Petit and an assistant to the costume designer for twelve productions. Asked if her early experiences at Le Petit prepared her for a career, Winn responded: "When I first worked at Le Petit, I learned so much. I loved it there. I wanted to live there.

It was a great learning experience for me" (Personal interview).

In addition to local actors and designers whose training at Le Petit enabled them to achieve professionally, the theatre hosted celebrities. Nobel Prize novelist Sinclair Lewis acted in Shadow and Substance in 1940. Although Lewis was known primarily as a novelist, he was also an actor and a playwright. He wrote the play Angela Is Twenty-Two, a drama about an older widower who falls in love with a much younger woman. Lewis portrayed the widower role in a tour of the play. For Lewis, life imitated art. At the age of fifty-four, Lewis met and fell in love with eighteen-year-old Provincetown Players apprentice actress Rosemary Marcella Powers, whom he introduced to friends as his niece. Powers and Lewis traveled throughout the South; soon after arriving in New Orleans, Lewis introduced himself to Le Petit director Bernard Szold. Szold knew that Lewis had acting experience and invited him to act at Le Petit. Lewis expressed interest in performing in Shadow and Substance in the role of Canon Skerritt. When Shadow and Substance finished its Broadway run, actor/producer Eddie Dowling who owned the rights gave the first amateur rights to his friend Father Edward Murphy, a priest at Xavier University in New Orleans. Szold asked Father Murphy if he would give the production rights to Le Petit and serve as technical advisor. Murphy agreed and both Lewis, as Canon Skerritt, and Powers, as Brigid, performed in the production (Schorer 654-656).

Other fledging artists honed their craft at Le Petit. The first "Laura," Julie Haydon, in The Glass Menagerie on

Broadway (1945) performed at Le Petit in 1943. Haydon was friends with Eddie Dowling, who had directed her on Broadway in <u>The Time of Your Life</u>. Dowling, who was indirectly responsible for Sinclair Lewis' performance at Le Petit, encouraged Haydon to act at the New Orleans theatre. Coincidentally, Haydon had portrayed the character Brigid in <u>Shadow and Substance</u> in a New York City production in 1938 (Lazarus 24). Billed as "our first guest star from Broadway" (Le Petit program, July 19, 1943), Haydon portrayed the leading role in <u>Major Barbara</u>. "All I remember is she wanted to play that part," responded long-time board member Rosa Deutsch when asked why Haydon chose this role (Personal interview). Actor Ed Nelson, best known as "Dr. Rossi" on the television series <u>Peyton Place</u>, performed at Le Petit in <u>Make Mine Bourbon</u>, a summer production in 1985. Emmy winner (in 1997 for "Guest Actor on a Drama Series"—<u>Murder One</u>) Pruitt Taylor Vince acted in <u>Pigeons</u> in 1986. Actor and make-up artist Edouard Henriques received his initial theatre experiences at Le Petit, which enabled him to design and apply the actors' make-up in the films <u>The Cell</u> (for which he was a 2001 Academy Award nominee) and <u>Armageddon</u>, among others. Film, television, and stage actress Veleka Gray, who starred in six soap operas as nine different characters, performed in <u>The Seven-Year Itch</u> (1967) and <u>Enter Laughing</u> (1968). When asked to comment on her experiences at Le Petit, Gray responded:

> In my case, Stocker Fontelieu and
> Le Petit took me to the next ring in

my career. Since I was five years old, I had done extensive modeling, print work, and enough local commercials at WWL and WDSU [television stations] to be well-known in the city. But even when the regional and national commercials I was cast in enabled me to join the actors' unions so that I was recognized as a professional actress, it was my training at Le Petit that I credit with having transformed me from a mere artisan into an artist. The people with whom I worked at the theatre instilled a respect in my soul for the art of acting and induced me to find the best in myself in performance. This was enormously valuable tutelage for the work I would soon be doing on national TV.
(E-mail interview)

Although the quantity of amateurs who have progressed to professional careers after working at Le Petit is not numerous, many of those who have been successful in the entertainment field cite their experiences at Le Petit as being beneficial to their careers.

Despite financial problems and the frequent exit of

artistic directors, when viewed from an historical perspective these trials will be classified as either the impetus of endurance or the refinement of direction. Optimism was generated by the positive feedback from the community concerning the accomplishments thus far of former of Chairman of the Board Michael Arata and artistic director Sonny Borey. Eva Le Gallienne once said: "The true theater of America must be created by the people themselves. Their demand will create the supply. The theater must be an integral part of the life of the community" (MacGowan 81). Le Petit Theatre is an important part of theatre history in New Orleans and continues to be a vital part of the community.

In 2005, the theatre was in the process of undergoing major changes to the more than 80 year old main stage and auditorium. Planned changes included the digging of an orchestra pit for musicals, installation of a new stage floor, and soundproofing of the area between the theatre's two stages. The new orchestra pit will accommodate 33 musicians and instruments. For some past musicals, the orchestra was seated in the upstairs library with a television monitor facing the stage so performers could see the conductor. Some of the costs of the renovations were raised by the theatre, and the state also contributed money. Until renovations could be completed, shows for the 2004-2005 season were staged in the Children's Corner.

Chapter Two will explore the history of children's theatre at Le Petit and will examine key productions.

2

TEDDY'S PLAYHOUSE FOR CHILDREN: CHILDREN'S THEATRE AT LE PETIT

Children's Theatre, sponsored jointly by the New Orleans Junior League and Le Petit Theatre, began in 1937 with occasional performances on the main stage of plays, such as The Wizard of Oz and Treasure Island. The actors presented a special performance of each play for the orphans of the city. While orphanages are institutions of the past, the tradition of giving free tickets to underprivileged youths continues today. In 1970, the Board decided to have a permanent children's theatre season with at least three productions a year. The smaller stage at Le Petit, originally an experimental theatre known as the Players Theatre, became a children's theatre seating 150. Teenagers and adults performed in plays for children in this theatre, initially known as Children's Corner.

The Board appointed Luis Barroso, an actor, director, and teacher, as the first full-time children's theatre director. Prior to his employment at Le Petit, Barroso had directed the children's theatre at Gallery Circle Theatre in New Orleans. Gallery Circle Theatre had only one performance space used by both its children's theatre and adult productions. Barroso welcomed the opportunity to have a permanent facility for children's productions (Personal interview, 23 Oct. 1999). According to Jim Word, actor, former theatre historian, and current Le Petit business manager:

> The Theatre [Le Petit] hired him [Luis] in 1970 to come here and that was the beginning of what was called the "Plan des Enfants," which means the Children's Forum. That period from 1970 up to, I would say, 1978, was known in New Orleans as the golden age of children's theatre. We were— Luis, myself, a lot of people that you know around town today—Becky Allen, Peggy Scott LaBorde, Pam Vergas, John Garret, Kenny Wesson— all of those performers . . . Ricky Graham . . . all of them came out of that children's theatre program. So it was not only great entertainment for kids, it was a terrific audience development tool for all of the theatres in town— not just this one—but it also produced some of

> the first line talent that you see in
> the city today.
> (Personal interview)

The late Arthur Tong, who eventually became Le Petit's photographer, unofficial historian, and long-time volunteer, accompanied Barroso from Gallery Circle. Arthur Tong's interviews with his candid comments proved invaluable to this writer. No one loved Le Petit, especially the children's theatre, more than Arthur Tong. He graciously spoke to this writer about Le Petit and lovingly shared scrapbooks that he treasured of productions at the theatre. According to many actors and directors who worked with him, Tong taught them more about stagecraft than they learned in college.

In addition to photographing Le Petit's productions and actors, Tong took other photographs that he cherished. One of his prized photographs, that he shared with this writer, was of Pope John Paul II, when the Pope visited New Orleans. The photograph shows the Pope standing in his Popemobile waving to the crowds in Jackson Square, with the sign <u>St. Peter's Street</u> (the street sign on the corner where Le Petit is located), in full view in the picture. Arthur Tong died in 2004 at the age of 81, and he will be missed. A portrait of Arthur William Tong now hangs in the lobby of Le Petit.

Luis Barroso was the only permanent staff member for the children's theatre at that time. Other staff members either were volunteers or were employed on a "per show" basis (Tong). According to Barroso, the Board admitted they were completely unschooled in children's theatre, so they trusted his expertise (Personal interview, 23 Oct. 1999). This trust proved beneficial; by the third show, the children's theatre supported itself.

Although tickets for Children's Corner could be purchased as season memberships, individual play tickets were sold (and still are today). Parents who accompanied their children to the children's plays often decided to acquire subscriptions to the main-stage productions, thus making the 1970s one of the most prosperous periods for Le Petit (Tong). The run of each play included sixteen performances over four weekends with the curtain at 1:00 p.m. and 3:00 p.m. on Saturdays and 2:00 p.m. and 4:00 p.m. on Sundays.

One local critic remarked that the Children's Corner flourished in its first year of operation. After viewing a production of The Wonderful World of the Brothers Grimm, he commented:

> If the current production is indicative of the work he [Luis Barroso] has been doing, something very special is going on over there. Everything is bright and vivid in Barroso's production, from the handsome set to the glittery, showy costumes. It's a polished little jewel of a show, and the audience I saw Saturday loved it, strained their necks and stood up to catch a better glimpse of the action.

> (Cuthbert, "Children's Theater Blossoming" 1:21)

In 1971, Le Petit became a member of the Southwest Theatre Conference, the American Educational Theatre Association, and the American Community Theatre Association. According to Barroso:

> We performed a children's show for the Southwest Theatre Conference, and it was suggested that we apply for the Winifred Ward Award. We submitted samples of our work. (23 Oct. 1999)

In its third year of operation (1973), the Children's Corner won the Winifred Ward Award for excellence in theatre for children. This prize honors a theatre company, performing for young audiences, which has been in operation at least two full years and not more than five years. To win this award, a theatre company must have attained a high level of artistic production, sound management practices, and have stimulated community interest in its endeavors.

The Board initially had two goals for the children's theatre: to provide a service to the community and to cultivate an audience for the future (Barroso, 23 Oct. 1999). The creation of Children's Corner filled a void in New Orleans cultural activities by presenting live entertainment for the whole family to enjoy:

> This has been accomplished by

> presenting the classic stories for children in the form of mini-musicals. All productions are original works, or original stage adaptations by local playwrights and composers. Favorable reviews plus exhilarated approval from parents gave Children's Corner its success. Some shows were repeated and reworked every four years. Each time we repeated them, we refined them. The audience changes. The kids grow up.
> (Barroso, 23 Oct. 1999)

Critic Al Shea felt that the Children's Corner addressed a two-fold need in the community: to provide children with the experience of attending a live show and to enable children to share in the wonderment of a simple story unfolding before their eyes (Shea, "Soapbox" 33). Tong mentioned how engrossed one child became when he viewed <u>The Brave Little Tailor</u>:

> One day we were doing a production called <u>The Brave Little Tailor</u>. A gnome kidnaps the little tailor and puts him in a sack. Well, a little boy got so involved in the play that he jumped on stage and started beating up the gnome. We thought it

> was so funny that at curtain call, we brought him up on stage to take the curtain call. That was the funniest thing to happen on that stage.
> (Personal interview)

Other benefits included learning discipline and developing a taste for the theatre (Shea,"Soapbox" 33).

A patron related his experiences attending a Children's Corner production with his sons:

> I must admit that taking the children to see <u>Raggedy Ann and Andy</u> was not my idea of a perfect Saturday afternoon, but the experience has made me a lifetime fan of theatre for children. The boys behaved exceptionally well throughout the performance, and we had some great communication as we drove home talking about the production.
> (Danflous 43)

Since most children's television shows are action-oriented, Barroso believed that children's plays should move constantly. He interspersed long scenes with music, "But I require that the songs be intelligent ones. The five or six songs I use in each show must develop plot and characters" (qtd. in Danflous 42). Barroso sought to provide the audiences with an experience equal to that of productions on the main stage. He utilized music, dance, lights, set, and costumes: "I always wanted them to have a magical hour in the theatre" (Barroso, 23 Oct. 1999). A local critic described one of Barroso's productions:

> Sleeping Beauty is a gem of many facets, all of which your children—and you—are bound to find delightful. The actors are bright and full of bounce; the costumes, lighting, and technical effects all first rate and then some. And since Barroso's musicals have original scores by Fred Palmisano, your kids get a tuneful and excellent introduction to the world of musical comedy. (Cuthbert, "Le Petit Sleeping Beauty" 2:6)

Beginning in 1971 and lasting for three years, the Calliope Players, a touring children's theatre associated with Le Petit, performed in area shopping malls. Besides entertaining at the malls, the Board hoped this group would serve as advertisement and enticement for future audiences to the Vieux Carre theatre. To attract families for Labor Day in 1971, the manager of a local Travelodge Motel engaged the Calliope Players to perform (Tong).

Barroso served as Children's Corner director from 1970 until 1978. His collaborators included the late composer/pianist Fred Palmisano, librettists Sharon O'Brien and Ricky Graham, designers Larry Kelley and Jim Word, actress/playwright/director Lyla Hay Owen, the late choreographer Judy Latour, the late Arthur Tong (a long-time volunteer at Le Petit), and costumers Ann Casey and Cecile Casey. Two adult musicals that Graham and Palmisano produced, <u>Tunes</u> and <u>A Night on the Town</u>, were an outgrowth of their work with Barroso. As Barroso commented:

> Another function that we served is that we trained people. We took the time to show them how to work, impressed upon them the importance of coming to rehearsals on time. I was at the theatre full-time, and there was a continuity to the work. And I don't think you see any of that now.
> (qtd. in Cuthbert, "Phantom Barroso" E:3)

"Working in the Children's Corner with Luis Barroso in the late '70s provided some of the most exciting theatre experiences in my life," commented Ricky Graham, one of only a few local performers who for years has been able to support himself by acting exclusively in New Orleans (Personal interview).

In 1978, Barroso resigned because of disagreements with the Board.

> It was the first time there was Board interference, something very petty. In order to expand my audiences, I

> had bought a set of little chairs
> because I had a little bit of money
> left over from one of my budgets.
> And a board member said that that
> was a capital investment. These
> little plastic chairs. They are still
> using them. And I guess that I was
> just at a point where I was just
> indignant that I was being given
> grief over something.
> (Barroso, 23 Oct. 1999)

Barroso rented the children's theatre at night for the musical revue <u>Tunes</u>, on which he collaborated with Palmisano. The success of <u>Tunes</u> caused the Board to ask Barroso to produce it for the main stage, where it became known as <u>Tunes II</u>. The Board refused Barroso's subsequent request to perform the play <u>Night Time Naughties</u> at night in the children's theatre, citing the inappropriate title. The incident of the chairs, along with the denial of theatre rental, caused Barroso to vacate his position at Le Petit (Barroso, 23 Oct. 1999). Board of Directors Chairman, Adrian Benjamin, Jr., expressed surprise that Barroso felt disagreements with certain board members necessitated his resignation. "We've all had words, but never words we had to part over. Everyone on the Board admires his ability and gives Luis full credit for the creation of Children's Corner" (qtd. in Dodds, "Barroso Resigns" 6:3). Barroso responded: "I don't know how much longer I would have stayed; an artist needs to move on" (23 Oct. 1999).

Barroso toiled at various theatres in the New Orleans area for two years; then the Center for Puppetry Arts in Atlanta offered him employment as producing director. He returned to New Orleans briefly in 1984 to direct a twenty-five-minute version of Pinocchio at the Italian Village of the New Orleans World's Fair. Barroso directed at the Center for Puppetry Arts as well as the Alliance Theatre for eight years. Both Robin Hood and The Adventures of Raggedy Ann and Andy, originally staged at Le Petit, were presented at the Alliance during Barroso's tenure (Barroso, 23 Oct. 1999). Since becoming a New Orleanian again in 1986, Barroso's involvement with Le Petit has been limited mainly to acting, although Sonny Borey coaxed him into directing Puss in Boots in 1998.

When Barroso departed and his collaborators worked on projects at other theatres, attendance at Children's Corner declined. The name Children's Corner suggests that children have a special place in the theatre, yet the history of children's theatre at Le Petit indicates that children have not been treated specially. The Board often has treated the children's theatre as an after-thought, a step-child to the main-stage productions. By the time Don Marshall became Executive Director in 1985, the Children's Corner season had dwindled to one play. Marshall directed his attention toward solving woes on the main stage and did not place a priority on the children's plays. He soon discovered that "there were all these talented people who wanted to see it [Children's Corner] happen again" (qtd. in Dodds, "Revival of Children's Corner" E5). The first production during Marshall's tenure was a revival of Rapunzel, one of the original golden age musicals. The following year, Children's Corner instituted a four-show subscription series that by 1990 had grown to 1,400 members. To celebrate the twentieth anniversary of Children's Corner, Marshall revived The Emperor's New Clothes, the first production at the theatre. Robert G. Lee directed the play, and Barroso, the original director in 1970, starred as the Prime Minister (Dodds, "Revival of Children's Corner" E5).

In 1992, Children's Corner was renamed Teddy's Corner after the death of Theodora "Teddy" Sciacca, a playwright, lyricist, composer, and former President of the Board of Governors. Sciacca wrote the book, music, and lyrics for How to Stay Young Forever and Make Mine Bourbon, produced on Le Petit's main stage, and the children's production of The Golden Touch. Gayle Batt, a board member and past president, commented:

> Her contributions to Le Petit were immeasurable. She was a theater member for many years, publicist for the women's guild, and an extremely active board member, a harmonizing spirit on the Board. In addition, she made a creative contribution to the theater as a playwright.
> ("Deaths" 14)

Le Petit employed Edward R. Cox as artistic director of Teddy's Corner in the spring of 1997. Later that same year, the late executive director Keith Briggs, faced with declining attendance in Teddy's Corner, decided not to use the facility for children's plays. Instead, he opted for weekday productions for children on the main stage:

> It's partly a question of finances, naturally, but it's also a question of service. The Children's Corner audience has been dwindling. By coordinating with the schools, and by finding out what kind of plays the teachers would like to see presented, we will be able to offer worthwhile theatrical experiences for much larger groups of kids.
> (qtd. in Wonk, "Curtain Call" 9)

However, at a meeting at which teachers were invited to suggest titles of plays their students would like to see, Briggs did not take any of the recommendations.

Briggs intended to use the smaller theatre for rehearsals or as a second adult theatre, where shows that were worthwhile but not appropriate for the main stage could be performed (Personal interview). This idea did not materialize, and the children's theatre became a storage facility during Briggs' tenure. Once again, the authority figures at Le Petit gave little consideration to providing children with a performance space of their own. Actor Vatican Lokey, who attempted to reinvigorate the children's theatre and served as its last Publicity Director, commented:

This is the end of Children's Corner as we know it. They may continue doing some kind of shows for kids, but not these lavish musicals we have come to expect.
(qtd. in Wonk, "Curtain Call" 9)

Teddy's Corner remained closed for only one year until the departure of Briggs. The theatre reopened with a production of <u>Puss in Boots</u> in 1998, which starred original cast members Edward R. Cox and John Grimsley from the 1977 production. Former New Orleans theatre critic Richard Dodds described the music in <u>Puss in Boots</u> composed by the late Fred Palmisano as "specifically and decidedly show music, and his knowledge and mastery of the form were unsurpassed in New Orleans" (qtd. in Papatolo, "Pair of Palmisano Shows Return" E7).

Teddy's Corner, since 1998 referred to as Teddy's Playhouse for Children to attract more children to the theatre, experienced a modest increase in attendance. However, the production costs of <u>Sammy the Sorcerer's Unsightly Halloween</u> totaled $6,000 and generated only $2,500 in revenue. This type of deficit prompted board member/actor Leon Contavesprie to respond that he would prefer to have the children's theatre perform a less elaborate play. Contavesprie cited as an example a two-character version of <u>The Lion, the Witch, and the Wardrobe</u> that had proved to be profitable for the theatre a few years ago (29 July 1998).

Business manager Word acknowledged that it is more difficult to produce children's theatre today, citing rising costs and a lack of commitment from the actors, at least at Le Petit where the actors are not paid. However, Word stressed the importance of children's theatre:

> But it is important that we continue doing it. Children's theatre brings kids to the arts, which helps develop audiences for the future. Attending the arts—theater, symphony, ballet, opera—is instructive in all kinds of ways for young people. It teaches them something about how to express themselves and how to behave in those situations; how to be a receptive, responsive audience. (qtd. in Cuthbert, "Kidstage Vet Back" Lagniappe 18)

However, reducing the number of performances of each children's show from sixteen over four weekends to eight (or fewer) suggests a lack of commitment by the Board. A 1996 production of Wily and the Hairy Man had only two performances, disallowing word-of-mouth publicity to generate larger audiences.

Le Petit announced that Teddy's Playhouse for Children would present three plays for the 2000-2001 season: The Bepuzzled Pilgrim, Lafitte the Pirate, and An Afternoon with Aesop. The choice of a play by Wayne Daigrepont, an experienced children's theatre performer and director, provided a glimmer of hope. Daigrepont, who originally wrote The

Bepuzzled Pilgrim for his Porta-Puppet acting troupe, expanded the show by writing new songs for its Le Petit premiere. Performed by Daigrepont and Vatican Lokey, the interactive puppet musical pleased both children and adults (Cuthbert, "This Thanksgiving Act" Lagniappe 16). Lafitte the Pirate was replaced with an interactive celebration of poetry for children, Limerick Junction, staged by Gary Rucker and Dane Rhodes in April of 2001 for eight performances over three weekends. According to Rucker, the already-established Limerick Junction proved to be an attractive alternative "because the Board felt there was not enough time to mount a production of Lafitte the Pirate" (Personal interview). Reviewer David Cuthbert remarked that the children in the audience seemed to enjoy the production; however, he emphasized the sparce attendance ("Playing With Poetry" Lagniappe 15). An Afternoon with Aesop was performed in June of 2001.

Debate among board members continues concerning the types of plays to be performed in the children's theatre: either the lavish musicals staged in the 1970s during what members refer to as "the golden age of children's theatre," or the smaller-scaled (small cast, minimal costumes and sets) productions that board members such as Contavesprie favor. The important issue is providing children the opportunity to view theatre, whether the play has a large or minuscule budget.

As a means of tracing the history of children's theatre at Le Petit, the researcher chose to examine the following children's theatre productions:

The Little Mermaid (1971)
The Emperor's New Clothes (1974)
Lafitte (1975)
Raggedy Ann and Andy's Musicland Capers (1978)
Rapunzel (1978)
Cinderella Battistella (1989)
Pinocchio Commedia (1997)
Puss in Boots (1998)
Rumplestiltskin (2000).

    Children's theatre flourished locally, as evidenced by the opening on the same weekend in May 1971 of four plays besides Le Petit's production of The Little Mermaid (Cuthbert, "Youth Theaters Boom" 2:16). Lyla Hay Owen wrote the book, music, and lyrics for this local production with musical arrangements and piano accompaniment by the late Palmisano. Director Barroso also performed as the narrator and singer of the show's theme song. When Barroso had asked Owen to name her favorite fairy tale, she responded with The Little Mermaid; therefore, he commissioned her to write her version of the Hans Christian Anderson tale for Children's Corner (Owen).
Reviewer Neil Curran critiqued the performances by the cast, particularly Dianne Aime as Merganser the witch, as excellent. He commented on Barroso's superb direction and described the set and colorful costumes as being better than most of the other productions in the city (Curran).

    Critic Cuthbert described the production as both fun and delicately touching. He praised Fanny Casey's elaborate costumes, Tong's lighting, and Palmisano's songs, especially the simple melodies of "Together You and Me" and "She Smiled at Me, She Likes Me." Cuthbert commented on the handsome set with designer Word's witch's niche and the "glitteringly, gloriously green underworld of the sea." He commended the cast, most notably the Mermaid and the Prince, as portrayed by husband and wife Sharon and Phillip Beard. While Cuthbert lauded most of Janice Roger McCarthy's choreography, his only negative comments concerned the "much too involved and bizarre final dance sequence" ("Petit <u>Mermaid</u>" 1:17).

In addition to the three plays that were performed during the 1973-74 season—<u>Rumplestiltskin</u>, <u>Aladdin and the Magic Lamp</u>, and <u>Rapunzel</u>—the Children's Corner presented three plays as part of a summer repertory: <u>The Emperor's New Clothes</u>, <u>Rapunzel</u> (a second time), and <u>Take Me to the Treasure</u>. Barroso had participated in an acting session conducted by Claire Jones at the Southwest Theatre Conference. Jones, director of the Oklahoma City University Children's Theater, wrote <u>Take Me to the Treasure</u> and, at Barroso's invitation, directed the play at Children's Corner, the only occasion that another person directed during Barroso's tenure (Cuthbert, "Too Darn Hot for Theater?" 2:12).

The researcher experienced heightened enjoyment of a personal favorite, <u>The Emperor's New Clothes</u>, watching Nancy Fichter, the researcher's sister, perform the role of Lady-in-Waiting. Fond recollections of the production include the lavish costumes and the expert singing, especially of the Lady-in-Waiting. This is another instance in which Le Petit has served as a training ground for a young performer, as Fichter eventually became a professional singer.

Critic Cuthbert referred to writer O'Brien's adaptation, set in an 18th Century kingdom ruled by a vain emperor with a penchant for finery, as funny and inventive. He praised Barroso's direction as brisk and farcical and commended composer/pianist Palmisano's work. However, he described the production as physically undistinguished and "without that showy sparkle we expect from the Children's Corner" ("Emperor's New Clothes" 2:5).

Reviewer Suzanne Joslyn Fosberg criticized Barroso's production as being too formulaic, lacking any surprise element. In a later critique of a 1978 production, Fosberg commented similiarly about Barroso's direction. Upon discovering this, the researcher interviewed Barroso a second time to ask for his response to the reviews. Barroso commented that Fosberg's criticisms did not affect his directing in any way, nor did he change his directing style after her reviews. He agreed that the plays were formulaic:

> I always asked my writers to stick to the original story as much as possible. That's what they were—formulaic.
> (14 Jan. 2001)

Fosberg believed that children's theatre should be educational. Barroso, while acknowledging educational content in theatrical presentation, advocated children's theatre as entertainment:

> To me, theatre first and foremost

should be entertainment. People
don't want to be hit over the head. I
think the kids were educated; they
saw lights, scenery, costumes. Once
those children walked into the
theatre, they saw magic. In The
Emperor's New Clothes, they saw
farthingales and high wigs. In
Raggedy Ann and Andy, I set it in
the 1930s, so they saw costumes
from that time period.
(14 Jan. 2001)

The logistics involved in transporting children to Le Petit, such as the narrow, winding streets of the French Quarter and the lack of safe parking, can be daunting for some parents; therefore, parents may be joyful simply to have their little ones entertained at the theatre.

Fosberg questioned why Le Petit could not perform plays dealing with children's problems ("The Emperor's New Clothes" 14). Outside the microcosm of the Vieux Carre, libraries and individual schools in the metropolitan New Orleans area did present educational plays during the time of Fosberg's reviews. From an educator's viewpoint, plays dealing with children's or adolescents' problems are better performed in school settings where students have access to teachers and counselors who can respond appropriately and initiate intervention if necessary.

As a preamble to the bicentennial celebration, Lafitte

premiered in 1975. Critic Bill Rushton commented that director Barroso departed from "the sort of campy extravaganza one is accustomed to expect" and praised Barroso for producing an original, revisionist history of the Battle of New Orleans, "couched in a language and a style that even a child can understand" ("Lafitte's Surprise" 2:1). Barroso collaborated with playwright O'Brien, choreographer Latour, composer/lyricist Palmisano, and set designer Larry Kelley for a play originally envisioned for a cast of thirty and later trimmed to eleven. O'Brien's play suggested a number of parallels between the Battle of New Orleans and the Vietnam War. Rushton described Lafitte as both a play and a method—behind the stage in its collaborative effort by five of the city's best theatrical specialists and in its on-stage content and message, concluding:

> Lafitte pointedly suggests that we can learn from our history and not merely be victimized by it. Lafitte is a minor masterpiece of entertainment.
> ("Lafitte's Surprise" 2:1)

Reviewer Cuthbert praised the production of Lafitte for its blending "of history and fancy with spirited song and lively dance for an enjoyable family entertainment." The rousing, hearty spirit of Palmisano and O'Brien's songs, "Barataria," "Coming Together," and "All the Way Back," received commendations in the critique. Cuthbert cited Kelley's outstanding design of the raked stage and atmospheric rough-hewn set, as well as Fanny Casey's appropriate period costumes

("Spirited Song" 2:13).

In his review of the 1978 production <u>Raggedy Ann and Andy's Musicland Capers</u>, James Perry praised director Barroso for his inventiveness and commended Children's Corner for becoming "a weekend wonder for many a local youngster in search of enrichment." Lyla Hay Owen wrote the book, music, and lyrics for this play, as well as its predecessors, <u>The Adventures of Raggedy Ann and Andy</u> and <u>The Further Adventures of Raggedy Ann and Andy</u>. Jim O'Quinn provided the musical arrangements, while David Potter, the technical director, also designed the sets. Perry lauded the cast for having fun in presenting the play. He cited Cynthia Owen as Sugar Flower for her excellent singing and leads Jan Perron as Raggedy Ann and Edward R. Cox as Andy for establishing a lively tempo throughout the play. Perry concluded his critique with these words:

> Invention and creative magic are what Barroso is known for. And he's built a large following of youngsters and their parents (who insist they are taking their youngsters to see the children's plays). But nobody's being fooled. Barroso and his colleagues stage their productions for discerning adults as well as young fans. And it pays off. ("More Creative Magic" C8)

Critic Martin Covert referred to <u>Raggedy Ann and</u>

Andy's Musicland Caper as a "sometimes snappy, sometimes sentimental, always satirical musical adventure," and praised Barroso for not sparing "his usual bite in putting on a children's show with an hysterical adult sensibility." He commended all performers, particularly Cece Casey for her tap-dancing ability and her commanding presence as Lulu Lullaby Lu and Cynthia Owen as a "Southern belle with the voice of an angel" (Covert, Ann and Andy 12).

The 1978 production of Rapunzel featured as the Fairy Godmother, Lady B.J. (B.J. Crosby), one of the first African-American performers to appear at Le Petit in a role other than a maid or butler. While she criticized Barroso's formulaic production, reviewer Fosberg called Lady B.J.'s performance "the one saving grace to Rapunzel." Lady B.J. later became a Broadway actress nominated for a Tony Award. Fosberg cited the success of Children's Corner but felt the 1978 Rapunzel "sacrificed charm for slickness" in comparison to the 1974 production. As Fosberg concluded her tenure as theatre critic at the New Orleans Courier in 1978, she acknowledged the vast increase in opportunities to view children's theatre in the New Orleans area, unlike five years earlier ("Farewell" 11).

Reviewer Lynn Cunningham cautioned future audiences of Le Petit's Rapunzel to "dismiss any preconceived notions of wicked witches, damsels in distress, diminutive fairy godmothers, and dashing princes." For example, Tinsel Holiday, a tinkerbell turned disco queen, replaced the luminous Fairy Godmother. Rapunzel, although imprisoned in a fortress, had a sense of humor, especially when entertained by her warden, Tacky, a hateful hag with a big nose. Cunningham praised all performers, especially Judy Langford as Tacky and Lady B.J. as Tinsel Holiday. She cited O'Brien's adaptation as far-fetched but effective and Palmisano's music and lyrics as varied and witty, with the adults in the audience appreciating the jokes more than the children. Cunningham expressed amazement to discover that the small Children's Corner stage could handle a tower and a forest, as well as musical numbers and choreography ("Rapunzel Pleases" D4).

Critic Richard Dodds viewed Rapunzel as a vehicle for the talents of Langford, costumed in "a gaudy 1940s dress, out-of-date hairdo, and a false nose." Dodds noticed the enjoyment of the children in the audience, but he felt the adults responded more to the witty dialogue. He commended all actors and noted that Palmisano wrote a new song (in addition to the original songs in the 1974 production) for the vocal talents of Lady B.J. ("Review: Rapunzel" 1:24).

A new collaboration created the 1989 production of Cinderella Battistella. Composer Palmisano combined with writer/lyricist/costumer Bob Bruce, writer/lyricist David Cuthbert (the critic), and long-time New Orleans Recreation Department theatre director the late Ty Tracy to present a 1950s New Orleans variation on the Cinderella story, which included numerous local idiosyncrasies. Palmisano chose the name Battistella in the title because he liked the rhyming aspect of it and the familiarity of the name for New Orleanians (Cuthbert, E-mail interview). Battistella Seafood is a famous seafood market in New Orleans. Muppet-like puppets, designed by Jeff

Kent, included Cinderella's chauffeur Berl Crawfish (read "boiled crawfish") and Cinderella's hairdresser Buster of Boutte (Buster crabs are harvested in Boutte, a city near New Orleans). Such idioms delighted New Orleans children and adults. Cinderella's godmother sent Cinderella to the Twelfth Night Ball; at this Ball, Cinderella met her future husband, Prince of King Cake Bakeries. Twelfth Night (January 6) is the beginning of the Mardi Gras social season in New Orleans. According to Arthur Hardy, Mardi Gras historian, in 1870 the Twelfth Night Revelers debuted:

> This unique group made Carnival history at its 1871 ball when a young woman was presented with a golden bean hidden inside a giant cake, signifying her selection as Mardi Gras' first queen and starting the "king cake" tradition. (20)

Enough of the original Cinderella story remained to help children relate.

Reviewer Dodds commended Palmisano's simple, hummable melodies and more sophisticated tunes, as well as Tracy's skillful direction. He praised the vivid performances of Eva Earls as Cinderella, Shirl Cieutat as the evil stepmother, Becky Allen and Ginger Guma as Cinderella's stepsisters, and Katherine C. Arthurs as the fairy godmother. The stepsisters, Tangipahoa and Feliciana, were named after two Louisiana parishes. Based on his fifteen years of periodic visits to the Children's Corner, Dodds noted the signs of an entertained contingent:

> no running to mama, no scraping of chairs and no palavering with neighbors. From a back-of-the house vantage point, all those little heads remained fixed firmly on the stage. ("N'Awlins-Set" E:10)

Dodds also commented on the laughter of the adults in the audience. The Board acknowledged the appeal of <u>Cinderella Battistella</u> to adults by having two performances at night, a departure from the previously day-time-only shows ("N'Awlins-Set" E:10).

In his praise for the quartet and the production, critic Shea mentioned in his review that the collaborators of <u>Cinderella Battistella</u> recently had triumphed with their production of <u>Silver Scream,</u> a spoof of Hollywood, performed in the Blue Room of the Fairmont Hotel. Shea lauded Bruce's humorous costumes, the entire cast, especially Eva Earls, "the city's answer to Marilyn Monroe," and commended every facet of the production: "The show succeeds on every count" ("Review Round-Up" 33).

Edward R. Cox staged <u>Pinocchio Commedia</u> in April of 1997 at the children's theatre, known now as Teddy's Corner Theatre for Children. Critic Dodds mentioned that Le Petit was attempting to reinvent itself since the once-thriving enterprise had faltered during the late 1980s and early 1990s. The energetic and elaborate staging by Cox of the familiar Pinocchio tale, told in this version by a bumbling troupe of players acting in a show, impressed Dodds. Cox incorporated masks and clown make-up worn by the actors as part of the story. Dodds remarked that Cox directed the sixty-minute production with a clarity not always present in children's theatre. The cast, particularly Damien Midkiff as Pinocchio, Adriano Mulino as Gepetto, and Vatican Lokey as the Cricket, received commendations from the critic. Dodds complained about the pre-recorded accompaniment to most of the late Palmisano's songs, his only criticism of the production ("Teddy's Corner Looks Back," Lagniappe 17).

Reviewer Dalt Wonk initially presented a brief history of the character Pinocchio in his critique: "The real Pinocchio, written by an Italian journalist under the pen name of Collodi, first appeared as a serial in a children's magazine in 1881." Wonk acknowledged the problems an American theatre could face in staging Pinocchio since audiences expect Walt Disney's version of the tale. The critic expressed his pleasure at viewing Le Petit's version of Pinocchio, written by John Simons, calling attention to the following:

> little moments of magic scattered throughout the show, such as the charming dance of the marionettes (choreography by Amy Embry) and the dogfish scene with its underwater bubbles. ("Good Wood," 45)

He commended Cox for the white-faced commedia players who donned masks when they became characters in the story. The cast, particularly Lokey, received praise from the reviewer. As the narrator, Lokey exhibited a natural grace and restraint to the stylized movement of the commedia ("Good Wood," 45).

When historian/business manager/actor Word returned to New Orleans in 1997 after a career as a professional theatre artist in New York and Atlanta, he found children's theatre struggling (Cuthbert, "Kidstage Vet Back" Lagniappe 18). In response to that situation, Word, Barroso, and other children's theatre veterans reunited for <u>Puss in Boots</u>, staged in 1998. Children's productions returned to Teddy's Corner after a one year's hiatus from the children's theatre stage during Briggs' tenure. Director Barroso returned to Le Petit to helm this staging and brought some of the performers from the old days with him. Although reluctant initially, Barroso agreed to help revitalize children's theatre at Le Petit at the request of Executive/Artistic Director Borey:

> When Luis was here, our children's theater was at its zenith. Everyone remembers those shows, and they remember how good they were. (qtd. in Cuthbert, "Once Upon a Time" E2)

Only a few actors attended the audition, so Barroso called upon veteran children's theatre performers and artists for help. According to critic Dominic P. Papatola:

> The effort pays off in a production

that's glorious to look at, from Cecile Casey Covert's firecracker-bright costumes to Jim Word's whimsically silly set design to the swirling cape of a not-very-scary bad guy named The Evil Okra. ("Puss in Boots" Lagniappe 25)

The Le Petit staging, with book and lyrics by O'Brien and music by Palmisano, had a distinct Louisiana flavor. The setting occurred in Dry Prong, Louisiana, and the music, provided by a four-piece on-stage band, was a blend of light rock, Broadway-style showtunes, and country-western songs. Papatola commended John Grimsley, known in New Orleans more for directing than acting, for his engaging performance in the title role: "[Grimsley] creates a stage character kids can identify with and he makes acting look like so much fun." Papatola concluded by saying that this production presented an excellent introduction to live theatre for children ("Puss in Boots" Lagniappe 25).

Reviewer Wonk described the musical Puss in Boots as "a smooth and immensely likable production." He commended the cast, especially Shea, Cox, Margie O'Dair, and "an irrepressible John Grimsley as the rascally feline" and concluded his critique with this comment: "This zestful trifle filled the house and gives further hope that Le Petit has truly risen like the phoenix" ("A Different Children's Story" 83).

In his review of the February 2000 production of Rumplestiltskin, Wonk noted the intense involvement of the children in the audience, who often commented aloud to the actors. He commended Walker's set and lighting, as well as Brian Rosenberg as Rumplestiltskin for his engaging manner with the audience. He referred to Rosenberg as "the kind of comic villain kids really warm up to" ("Sublime Rhyme" 48).

Critic Cuthbert found both gold and bits of straw in <u>Rumplestiltskin</u>. He recommended the play as a way to introduce children to the world of musical comedy. He praised Bill Walker's clever set of a large book with painted pages that turned to provide backdrops. Prince Michael (Jeff Poucher) and Princess Millicent (Cari Pope) celebrated their wedding anniversary by reading from the book of their adventures: the fairy tale <u>Rumplestiltskin</u>. Cuthbert lauded Cari Pope as Millie, the miller's daughter; Megan Staab as Queen Brunhilde the Beastly; and Scott Sauber as the stuttering servant Gottlieb for their comic timing. He commended director Daigrepont for not allowing excessive mugging by the cast. His major criticism concerned the lack of clarity by the singers in both individual songs and chorus numbers. Cuthbert concluded his comments by saying that children's theatre had the potential to entertain as well as to engender audiences in the future ("<u>Rumplestiltskin</u>" Lagniappe 20).

In July of 2001, the Board employed Brandt Blocker as permanent director of Teddy's Playhouse for Children. Blocker had directed, acted, and served as a music and vocal director at area theatres and high schools. All performers in the children's theatre were to be between the ages of thirteen and twenty-one, a departure from the past.

Blocker's productions were consistent money-makers. During his tenure, audiences were treated to delightful productions on the small stage of You're a Good Man, Charlie Brown, Honk!, and Cinderella. Blocker also directed Leader of the Pack, Five Guys Named Moe, and Grease to both critical and financial success on the main stage.

In 2004, Blocker resigned to pursue other interests. The plays of the 2004-2005 season were directed by two very prominent New Orleans actors/directors, Gary Rucker and Sean Patterson.

The children's theatre at Le Petit has been known by various names, such as the Player's Theatre, the Children's Corner, Teddy's Playhouse, Teddy's Playhouse for Children, and the Director's Studio. As of July of 2005, the new name is Muriel's Cabaret at Le Petit Theatre. An agreement was made with Muriel's Restaurant for the naming rights. Muriel's Restaurant is one block from Le Petit across from Jackson Square and had been offering pre-show dining packages.

Regardless of its name, the children's theatre at Le Petit entertains as well as fosters audiences for the future. Teddy's Playhouse for Children (under all its monikers) has accomplished the original goals established by the Board: to provide a service to the community and to cultivate a future audience. The researcher hopes that the children's theatre at Le Petit will remain as much of a priority with the Board as the main-stage productions.

No list of plays of the children's theatre exists; therefore, the researcher has included a chronological list of plays in Appendix B. Chapter III explores key main-stage productions at Le Petit.

3

MAIN-STAGE PRODUCTIONS

The researcher developed the following criteria for analyzing main-stage productions at Le Petit Theatre:

(1) The time period covered is divided into five periods (1968-73; 1974-80; 1981-88; 1989-94; and 1995-2001);

(2) The productions selected include one musical, one comedy, and one tragedy to represent each period, plus two additional recent plays;

(3) At least two reviews are available;

(4) At least one person involved in the production (actor, director, costume designer, etc.) was interviewed by the researcher.

Based on these criteria, the researcher chose to examine the following main-stage productions:

Who's Afraid of Virginia Woolf? (1968)

The Importance of Being Earnest (1971)

Hello, Dolly! (1972)
1776 (1974)
A Streetcar Named Desire (1977)
Scapino! (1977)
Evita (1985)
Brighton Beach Memoirs (1987)
Amadeus (1988)
The Women (1990)
My Fair Lady (1991)
M. Butterfly (1992)
Laughter on the 23rd Floor (1996)
42nd Street (1998)
Ma Rainey's Black Bottom (1999)
Kiss of the Spider Woman (2000)
Barnum (2000).

 New Orleanians flocked to the theatre in the early 1970s. The unique concept of fledgling dinner theatres, such as the Beverly Dinner Playhouse, proved popular and successful. At the same time, Le Petit set its own attendance record with an all-time high season subscription base of 8,000.

Local actors enjoyed performing at Le Petit. Auditions were competitive, often with fifty or more actors attending tryouts. Ricky Graham, an actor, director, and playwright, commented about his experiences on the main stage at Le Petit:

> The main stage was as much like a Broadway theatre that one could find for miles around. It was a thrilling privilege to work there back

then [in the 1970s].

(Personal interview)

Since 1946 Stocker Fontelieu has been involved as an actor, director, producer, or in some other capacity in 474 stage productions at theatres in the New Orleans metropolitan area. His resonant voice can be heard in the New Orleans area in numerous commercials. The researcher asked Fontelieu to name his most memorable plays during his long career at Le Petit. He named such productions as Who's Afraid of Virginia Woolf?, The Elephant Man, A Man for All Seasons, and West Side Story. When asked why these selections were special, Fontelieu responded:

> Well, first of all, the scripts are outstanding. You start with a brilliant script, and then, as always, in community theatre, you pre-decide, if you get quality people, and, in the instance of all of those, I was able to get "star" quality people to appear in all roles.
> (Personal interview)

For the time period 1968-73, the researcher chose the tragedy Who's Afraid of Virginia Woolf?, the comedy The Importance of Being Earnest, and the musical Hello, Dolly!. Fontelieu directed one of his favorites, Edward Albee's Who's Afraid of Virginia Woolf?, in 1968. The college president's daughter Martha and her pedantic husband George have invited younger couple Nick and Honey to their home at 2:00 a.m. In addition to the intense verbal sparring between George and Martha, George attempts to entertain his guests with a variety of games of the most vicious and disconcerting nature.

Reviewer Frank Gagnard first expressed his surprise, albeit a pleasant one, that Le Petit attempted such a play, considering the language that could have offended some audiences, and applauded Fontelieu for not sanitizing the script. Gagnard alluded to past productions at Le Petit of other plays in which directors laundered the script's dialogue, so as not to offend any audience members. Fontelieu directed the text verbatim. Secondly, Gagnard assumed that Fontelieu would cast the "predictable powerhouses" for this intense drama. However, he amazed the acting community by casting two new faces as well as two familiar faces in unfamiliar roles. Gagnard described the production as "rewardingly cast by its director," and commended the performances of David Stone, Mary Margaret McCrea, and Jann Bell Simpson, as George, Martha, and Honey, respectively. He found actor Michael Zimmerschied "attentive to the outlines of the part but lightweight for the faculty alley cat Nick is stated to be" ("Le Petit's 'Virginia Woolf'" 2:5). He concluded that the actors succeeded in conveying the maturity and stamina of the text.

Critic Danny Greene expressed astonishment that an amateur theatre could produce such a difficult play as <u>Who's Afraid of Virginia Woolf?</u> so well. In one section of his review, Greene mentioned the ridiculousness of comparing the play to the movie. Nevertheless, in another paragraph he stated this production carried "all the impact and emotional discord of the movie" ("Top Cast Masters 'Virginia Woolf'" 15). He also praised the professionalism of the cast.

Joseph Larose, critic for the conservative Catholic newspaper, <u>Clarion Herald</u>, highly recommended the play to his adult readers. He cautioned potential audiences about the frankness and vulgarity of the language, but noted that this aspect of the play was relevant and should not be overemphasized. He praised director Fontelieu for his natural staging and the four actors, particularly McCrea for her outstanding interpretation. In conclusion, Larose expressed this sentiment: "Adult audiences should find LPT's 'Virginia Woolf' provocative and disturbing but honest and powerful theater" ("LPT's 'Virginia Woolf'" 2:3). Provocative and disturbing, as well as thought-provoking and powerful, describe the researcher's reaction to viewing this production, which she attended as a high school student. With the exception of Gagnard's criticism of the actor in the role of Nick, the three reviewers praised the cast, the director, and the over-all production.

In his review of the 1972 production of Oscar Wilde's <u>The Importance of Being Earnest</u>, James Perry noted that the actors appeared to be a company of professional thespians who impressed him with the perceptiveness of style, era, and customs that each brought to the roles. He commended the actors for making his or her part distinctive. Perry described Roger J. Keller's performance as John Worthing, who discovers at the play's end that his fraternal fabrication is factual, as "sheer pleasure," delivering Wilde's witty dialogue in flawless diction. "This actor's gift for underplaying is ideal for this kind of theater, and his stage presence is unequalled among the local thespians" ("Characters" Lagniappe 17). Reviewer Larose felt that the wheels of artificiality and sophistication, on which <u>The Importance of Being Earnest</u> was mounted, squeaked in Act I. However, he compared Sharon Beard's scintillating portrayal of Cecily Cardew in Act II to a well-oiled machine that glided smoothy. He also commended Francis Fuselier's set and Fontelieu's staging, as well as actors Keller, Blair Ziegler, Olivia Bamforth, Don Campora, and Mattie Brammer in the roles of Worthing, Algernon, Lady Bracknell, Reverand Canon Chasuble, and Miss Prism, respectively ("Truth" 2:4).

    Historically, musicals at Le Petit have attracted the largest audiences. The 1972 production of <u>Hello, Dolly!</u>, one of the researcher's personal favorites at Le Petit, received favorable audience and critical responses. The Board increased the customary run of fourteen performances to fifteen to accommodate additional season ticket requests. "As good-looking a local musical as you're likely to see. Talk about beginning a season on a positive note," commented critic Cuthbert. He praised designer Fuselier's color-coordinated production, as he noted the audience's applause for the multiple sets. The cast received favorable reviews, as Cuthbert specifically mentioned Margie O'Dair's connection with the audience as Dolly Levi and Larry Warner as "the best Cornelius Hackl I've seen." Tony Bevinetto's role as head waiter Rudolf as well as his choreography received commendations from

Cuthbert, as did Peter Dombourian's musical direction. Cuthbert lauded Fontelieu's staging, except for the occasional frozen expressions on the faces of the chorus. He described the production as "the kind of show-stopper community theaters are almost never able to muster" ("'Hello, Dolly!'" 2:4).

Reviewer Joseph Del Papa, critic for <u>Figaro</u> newspaper, described Le Petit's <u>Hello, Dolly!</u> as one of the most lavish local productions ever performed. The sumptuous sets, the beautiful costumes, and most of the cast merited favorable comments. Del Papa commended the performances of Warner, Graham, Ed Hoerner, Marty Prudhomme, and Lisa Bevinetto, as Hackl, Barnaby Tucker, Horace Vandergelder, Irene Molloy, and Minnie Fay, respectively. Drawbacks to the production included O'Dair in the title role and the play itself, which he concluded "seems like a throwback to the bad old days of musical comedies" (Del Papa, "Le Petit's 'Hello, Dolly!'" 4). While he praised O'Dair's stage presence, he criticized her lack of vocal range. The researcher disagrees with Del Papa's evaluation of this play. O'Dair did display a comfortable vocal range. Also, the researcher's sister performed in this production, which heightened her enjoyment. Additionally, the actors, the costumes, the scenery, the musical score, the dancing, the singing—every aspect of this production combined harmoniously to capture the essence of musical theatre and to create a memorable theatrical experience for the researcher.

<u>Hello, Dolly!</u>, the story of inveterate matchmaker Dolly Levi who snares the very frugal Horace Vandergelder, emerged from a number of sources. Playwright Thornton Wilder created

The Merchant of Yonkers from a nineteenth-century Viennese comedy (Einen Jux will er sich machen) (He wants to play a joke) by Johann Nestroy. Nestroy borrowed his plot from the English writer John Oxenford's A Day Well Spent. Wilder reworked The Merchant of Yonkers into The Matchmaker, which premiered in 1954 in London. From these plays, Hello, Dolly!, written by Jerry Herman and Michael Stewart, opened in 1963 (Gagnard, "New Lights" 2:10).

      Parallels exist between Le Petit's productions of The Merchant of Yonkers and Hello, Dolly!. At the initial performance for Le Petit's The Merchant of Yonkers in 1948, the Board welcomed the theatre's new lighting system, which cost $20,000, with this notice in a playbill:

> We are indeed happy to be able to boast, after several years of planning, that we now have one of the finest theatrical lighting control boards in the country. The new board, designed to our specifications...has 80 outlets, each of adequate capacity, and 40 autostat dimmers, which are arranged for grouping under master controls. (qtd. in Gagnard, "New Lights" 2:10)

Coincidentally, twenty-four years later the Board boasted about its new lighting system installed prior to the opening night of Hello, Dolly!. Due to technical advances and the increased cost of materials, the 1972 lighting system cost $63,000 and contained 150 outlets and fifty dimmers. Fontelieu, a Tulane University student in 1948, stage managed The Merchant of Yonkers and directed the 1972 production of Hello, Dolly! (Gagnard, "New Lights" 2:10).

For the time period 1974-80, the researcher selected the musical 1776, the tragedy A Streetcar Named Desire, and the comedy Scapino!. Five different reviewers praised 1776, which opened Le Petit's 1974-75 season. 1776 is the patriotic theatrical ode to the determination, spirit, and historical backbone of the United States. Joseph Del Papa called the production the best musical he had ever seen at Le Petit, and added: "If there is a better community theatre production running anywhere else, I'd like to see it." He commended Fontelieu for assembling the best singing and acting talents in the city. The outstanding individual performances of Reginald Hendry as John Adams, Frank Bennett as Benjamin Franklin, Larry Warner as Thomas Jefferson, Robert Starnes as John Dickinson, Terri Gervais as Martha Jefferson, and Barbara Faulkner-Bernard as Abigail Adams merited praise from the critic. He applauded Chuck Davis as Richard Henry Lee for his rousing rendition of "The Lees of Virginia" ("1776" 14).

Critic Larose called 1776 "a real flag-waving victory for Le Petit Theatre." The cast handled the humor in the script in a likable fashion without resorting to silliness, according to Larose. He commended choreographer Bevinetto for capturing the "gusto and humor of the play nicely." Larose complimented the set designers—Jack Gallier, Larry Kelley, Bill Turnbull, and

Eddy Vedrenne—for taking advantage of the depth of the stage and overcoming the impression of crowding with all the chairs, desks, and tables in the meeting room of the Continental Congress ("LPT Staging Has Joyous Gusto" 2:4). The other three reviews by Janet Giambrone, Shea, and Cuthbert were uniform in their praise, agreeing with the assessments of Larose and Del Papa.

The first of three productions at Le Petit of A Streetcar Named Desire, the best-known New Orleans-set play, appeared in 1977. Tennessee Williams wrote A Streetcar Named Desire when he lived in New Orleans. From the windows of his home, Williams noticed the Desire streetcar, which passed one block from Le Petit Theatre. The Desire streetcar brought fading Southern belle Blanche Dubois to her sister Stella's home. Williams used references in the play to the French Market and Galatoire's Restaurant, both within walking distance to Le Petit Theatre. It seemed appropriate for this play to be performed at Le Petit. Critic Dodds mentioned that despite Williams' New Orleans associations, his plays have not been overproduced here. A friend of Dodds suggested a Tennessee Williams summer repertory theatre; Dodds' article predated the annual Tennessee Williams Festival, which began in 1987. The first performers on Broadway and in the movie of A Streetcar Named Desire have left indelible impressions on audiences; Dodds acknowledged the difficulty performers encounter in portraying these roles and the danger of clichéd characterizations. The reviewer lauded the acting of James Michael Drumm for creating his own Stanley and not relying on

Marlon Brando's vocal and physical mannerisms. However, Dodds criticized Drumm for not allowing Stanley's animal characteristics to surface. He praised the sincerity of Lloyd J. Roux as Mitch and the consistency of Gerrie F. Singer as Stella. Dodds found positive and negative aspects to Gail Smith's depiction of Blanche:

> Gail Smith has the bravura role, and offers a performance commensurate to it. There were times though when it seemed the actress stayed too near the surface, unwilling to let a bit of humanity peek through Blanche's showy exterior.
> ("'Desire' Comes Home" 2:4)

According to Dodds, the three-act play lasted nearly three hours, but it did not drag under Fontelieu's direction ("'Desire' Comes Home" 2:4).

In his review of <u>A Streetcar Named Desire</u>, Perry complimented Smith for the passion and sensitivity that she displayed as Blanche. He praised her commanding stage presence and referred to Smith's performance as "a symphony of desire." The critic expressed his disappointment with Drumm's uninspiring, one-dimensional performance, and referred to Drumm's casting as a major flaw. Singer's scenes with Blanche were convincing, but her scenes with Stanley were not truthful, according to the reviewer. Perry lauded Roux's performance as Mitch, for giving the audience some of its best moments. In conclusion, Perry noted that in spite of the casting error, this dramatization was very powerful ("Major Flaw" B3).

    For a completely different type of play during the same season, Le Petit produced <u>Scapino!</u>, a commedia dell'Arte play about a schemer with a tendency to involve himself in the problems of others. <u>Scapino!</u> was inspired by French playwright Moliere's <u>Les Fourberies de Scapin</u> (<u>The Treachery of Scapin</u>). Moliere borrowed the story outline from the Roman play <u>Phormio</u> by Terence. "For such an illustrious ancestry, the plot doesn't amount to that much," commented reviewer Jack Wardlaw, who cautioned his readers that "<u>Scapino!</u> isn't much like anything you've seen before." Wardlaw mentioned that the unstructured nature of the action placed a heavy burden on the actors, but the actors met the challenge of this play. Mark Campbell in the title role presented a lively and engaging character. John Bishop as Carlo had to set the tone for the entire evening, and Wardlaw felt that the audience responded well to him. Wardlaw praised the rest of the cast for their energy, as they employed the entire theatre as a stage: "The production must stand or fall on the energy and style of the actors. On opening night, it stood tall" ("'Scapino'" B4).

    Although Del Papa admitted in his review his distaste for physical comedy which prevented him from enjoying <u>Scapino!</u>, he noted the audience "was rolling in the aisles while all I could muster was an occasional smile." He acknowledged that the cast had a wonderful time jumping about the stage and pummeling each other with prop sausages. The critic expressed his puzzlement concerning the audience's pleasure for the energy displayed by the cast, particularly Campbell who engaged the audience to participate at the end of the play, much to Del Papa's consternation. He commented about the fun Fontelieu apparently had in putting the cast through its paces. He concluded his critique by complimenting Don Hood for his bright, colorful set, even though it reminded Del Papa more of the Bronx than Naples ("'Scapino!'" 17).

The musical Evita, the comedy Brighton Beach Memoirs, and the tragedy Amadeus represent the 1981-88 time period. Critic Dodds referred to the dramatic spectacle of the finale of Act I of Evita, the story of the influential wife of Argentinian President Juan Peron, as an auspicious beginning, both for the 1985 production and Le Petit Theatre itself. Long-time director Fontelieu had retired, and Mary Ellen O'Brien replaced him. As Managing Director, O'Brien appointed the directors, herself included, for each play. Borey, the current Artistic Director, staged the production of Evita. Dodds mentioned the anticipation and theatrical electricity, to which the researcher can attest, that raced through the theatre both prior to and during the performance. Mitch Landrieu received praise from Dodds for his portrayal of Che Gueverra, who serves as both narrator and antagonist: "His controlled intensity helps spark the entire production." As an aside, Landrieu, currently the Lieutenant Governor of Louisiana, was instrumental in having the state appropriate money for Le Petit in 1998. The researcher viewed this production of Evita, having seen the play twice before, on Broadway and a touring Equity company at the Saenger Theatre in New Orleans; Landrieu far outshone the other two Ches. Dodds also noted the powerful performance of Barbara Bollinger in the title role and Chuck Davis' effective portrayal of Juan Peron. He praised Borey's staging, which preserved much of Hal Prince's inventive direction, David Potter's lighting and set designs, and Elizabeth Parent and Eddy Vedrenne's costumes. Mark Unbehagen received compliments for his spirited and precise orchestra leadership ("Le Petit Opens New Era" D12).

    Critic Amy Worden complimented the management of Le Petit for venturing into unexplored theatrical territory, yet doing so with skilled navigators. Worden praised Landrieu's charisma, natural leadership on stage, and professionalism. She lauded Deleen Davidson as Peron's mistress for her melodic rendition of "Another Suitcase in Another Hall." The attention to detail in the costumes of Parent and Vedrenne impressed Worden. Bollinger received criticism for not having the necessary vocal talents to play Eva Peron. However, Worden felt the show had enough strong points to overcome this ("The Front Row" 43). The researcher disagrees with Worden's assessment of Bollinger's vocal talents, which more than adequately met the challenge of portraying Peron.

    <u>Brighton Beach Memoirs</u>, performed at Le Petit in 1987, is set in the Depression-era 1930s. Louisiana in the 1980s suffered from a high unemployment rate and low economic development due to the oil crisis. Although New Orleanians did not experience as severe a depression as citizens in the 1930s had, audiences could identify with the plight of the Jerome family in the play. Reviewer Shea expressed disappointment

that Le Petit could not hold over <u>Brighton Beach Memoirs</u>, since he felt that more people should have an opportunity to see this production, a sentiment echoed by actor Douglas Leal in an interview with the researcher. Shea described M. Audley Keck's direction as "a brilliant demonstration of directorial dexterity." He commended designer Potter's four-level set and Winn's appropriate costumes. Shea called the ensemble polished professionals and referred to the cast as "perfection" ("Soapbox" 22).

    Gagnard spent half of his review of <u>Brighton Beach Memoirs</u> criticizing playwright Neil Simon for abandoning the humor of his earlier plays and becoming autobiographical. Leal's engaging portrayal of the young narrator Eugene merited praise from Gagnard, as did Miriam Babin as the mother and Vince Caruso as the father. Gagnard commented on Potter's set as comprehensive and vigorously detailed and Winn's costumes as appropriate to the era and neighborhood of the characters ("Simon" E12). When Leal, currently acting in Los Angeles, was asked recently about his experiences at Le Petit, he responded:

> I credit Le Petit Theatre with the foundation for my career. Not having an academic background in theatre, I honed my acting skills in my work at Le Petit Theatre. Opening night of <u>Brighton Beach Memoirs</u>, I got such a rush that I decided to pursue acting as a career right then and there.

(E-mail interview)

The researcher encountered Leal a few years earlier when she directed his sister in a high school production. Leal, more interested at that time in computers, professed little interest in acting. However, in later years he changed his mind and began auditioning. The researcher sat in amazement in the theatre, admiring Leal's excellent performance.

Leal added to his stage credits the following year by performing the leading role in <u>Amadeus</u>. Conflict between Salieri, a minor composer of the Eighteenth Century, and Wolfgang Amadeus Mozart forms the premise of the play. Salieri is jealous of the genius of the vulgar young Mozart. Critic Shea proclaimed that Leal confirmed his growing theatrical reputation with this performance. Director Keck received congratulations from Shea for his astute casting and for rising to the challenge in staging this play. For her chilling, provocative lighting, Amanda Graham received acclaim ("Soapbox" 67).

Reviewer Gagnard described Le Petit's <u>Amadeus</u> as "a game and rather supple production that M. Audley Keck has directed and Cathy Pack has designed." He commended the stalwart cast, particularly Leal, Blair Ziegler as Salieri, and Eva Earls as Mozart's wife. Gagnard cited the need for sharper technical focus, especially from a hissing sound system. His review also mentioned a Mozart music festival held at the theatre in conjunction with this production ("'Amadeus'" E:11).

For the time period 1989-94, the researcher decided to include the comedy <u>The Women</u>, the musical <u>My Fair Lady</u>, and the tragedy M. Butterfly. Clare Boothe Luce's play The Women concluded Le Petit's 1989-90 season. Director Carl Walker set the 1936-era play in the late 1950s. Critic Ed Real expressed dubiousness when he heard about the degree of campiness in this production, and stated his preference for achieving comic effect with dated material by playing it straight. However, Real commended Walker for combining the rapid-fire delivery of 1930s comedy with "a humorously overwrought twist on the play's more melodramatic moment" ("Life" 10). Walker achieved the latter with period musical accompaniment. Although he mentioned the excellent acting of the entire cast, Real especially recognized Terri Gervais Davis as Mary for successfully carrying the melodramatic plot without having many of the funny lines. Jan Jensen, Kathleen Turner, and Heidi Jensen depicted their small roles with finesse, which added to Real's approbation ("Life" 10).

Le Petit's The Women opened with Helen Reddy's song, "I Am Woman." "Yes, I am wise, but it's wisdom born of pain," Reddy sang in the 1972 anthem of women's liberation (qtd. in Dodds, "Winning 'Women'" C5). With the above song lyrics, Dodds began his review and stated that Luce's comedy had pain born of wisdom: "Hers is a wisdom of human nature, and the pain comes from her less-than-sunny interpretation of it" ("Winning 'Women'" C5). Dodds compared this production to a handsome sedan with a well-tuned engine. Costume designer Bernadette Klotz impressed Dodds with her delightful and slightly outrageous wardrobe for the actors. The leading performers, as well as the supporting players, received commendations. Dodds, too, cited Davis for keeping her noble character vital and interesting. Francine Segal as the gossip Sylvia, Helen Blanke as the ever-pregnant Edith, Kim Landon as the icily-clever Nancy, Glenda Byars as the witchy Crystal, and Heidi Jensen as a big-mouthed manicurist gave noteworthy performances as well. The critic concluded by referring to this production as a considerable accomplishment for Le Petit ("Winning 'Women'" C5).

Rosa Deutsch, one of Le Petit's leading ladies both on and off stage and the daughter-in-law of founding member Mrs. Eberhard Deutsch, starred as Mrs. Higgins in the 1991 production of My Fair Lady. Le Petit celebrated its seventy-fifth season with this musical, directed by Max Gorgal, who also designed the sets. Critic Shea called the production "glamorous and graceful," and praised the cast, particularly Chris Carey as elocution expert Professor Henry Higgins, Andrea Alessi as Cockney flower girl Eliza Doolittle, Michael Minetto as Alfred Doolittle, and Deutsch. Carey's singing especially impressed Shea, as did Pamela Legendre's conducting of the fourteen-piece orchestra ("An Auspicious Opening" 36).

In his critique, Dodds noted parallels between My Fair Lady and Le Petit Theatre. George Bernard Shaw's Pygmalion, on which My Fair Lady is based, had its London premiere in 1914, two years before the founders of Le Petit conceived the idea of their theatre. Pygmalion was one of the early attractions (1925) at Le Petit, once the organization moved into its present quarters, and was revived as part of the fiftieth anniversary season. Dodds believed My Fair Lady showcased Le Petit at its most able, lavish, and confident. Despite its length, the musical held the audience's attention throughout its entirety. Gorgal received praise for both his scenery and direction, which maintained a traditional look, with the main novelty being a passionate kiss between Higgins and Eliza at the final curtain. The performances of Carey, Alessi, Deutsch, Minetta, Blair Ziegler as Colonel Pickering, Lary Hesdorffer as Freddie Eynsford-Hill, and Andee Reed as housekeeper Mrs. Pierce received commendations from Dodds. To conclude his review, Dodds praised the actors for not using amplification: "Reaffirming the human voice is a fine way for Le Petit to honor a disappearing theatrical tradition on its 75th birthday" ("'Lady' Showcases Le Petit" Lagniappe 14).

One of the most audacious plays attempted at Le Petit was its 1992 production of M.Butterfly, a bold choice considering the theatre's conservative membership. Playwright David Henry Hwang combined the Madame Butterfly legend with a story inspired by an incredible Cold War saga. Hwang based his play on an actual incident: a French diplomat, stationed in Beijing, had a relationship with the star of the Chinese opera. After living together for years, the diplomat discovered that the dainty companion was really a man and a spy. The challenge of producing this play could be daunting for a community theatre; however, Le Petit succeeded in confronting any obstacles. The brief nudity at the end of the play was a first, to the researcher's recollection, in a Le Petit production. The gasps from the audience during the nudity confirmed the researcher's thoughts that some of the patrons were shocked by this play.

Critics Shea and Dodds offered differing opinions about this production. An inadequate sound system, dull lighting, and both unflattering make-up and an unattractive costume for the character Song Liling caused Shea's negative review. However, Shea noted the spirit and sincerity displayed by Jim Gibbons as diplomat Gallimard and Alphonse Bladergroen, in his stage debut, as Song Liling ("M.Butterfly" 33). The sustained, multi-faceted performance of Gibbons and Bladergroen's unnerving intensity received compliments from Dodds, who expressed his pleasure in viewing this production. He credited director Kenneth Risch with having the actors and designers effectively communicate the play's drama and the playwright's concerns. Set designer Stephen J. Larson, lighting designer Martin Sachs, and costume designer Shawn Stewart-Larson contributed to the impressive look of the production, according to Dodds ("'M. Butterfly' Takes Flight" Lagniappe 18).

The researcher selected the comedy Laughter on the 23rd Floor, the musical 42nd Street, and the tragedy Ma Rainey's Black Botton for the 1995-2001 time period. Although critic Wonk confessed that he usually did not find playwright Neil Simon as funny as most audiences did, he did consider Laughter on the 23rd Floor truly funny and one of Simon's most original plays. Wonk judged Le Petit's 1996 production as excellent. Actors Robert Pavlovich as writer Max Prince and Prince's writers, portrayed by Butch Benit, Roy Dumont, Michael Sullivan, Garth Currie, Marc Belloni, and Jan Chamberlain, received encomiums from Wonk. In addition to these actors, Leon Contavesprie and Laura North as Lucas and Helen, as well as the late director/set designer Keith Briggs, created an accomplished production (Wonk, "Funny Bone" 45).

The manner in which the ensemble brought the characters to life added to reviewer Dodds' enjoyment of Laughter on the 23rd Floor. Briggs' exemplary production allowed the actors to have fun with their roles. Simon created an eclectic collection of characters, and the director's pacing and polish, which avoided slickness by maintaining the human connection, merited praise from the critic. Dodds favorably mentioned the entire cast and acknowledged that Le Petit's resurgence would occur only with continued quality productions ("Cast Gives 'Laughter' Life" Lagniappe 22).

In the midst of a physical and financial revitalization of one of the city's oldest arts organizations, new Artistic/Executive Director Borey opened the 1998-99 season with an ambitious forty-three-person musical, 42nd Street. Borey authorized the purchase of new paint and carpet for the lobby, the boardroom, offices, dressing rooms, and the greenroom, since he believed "if people have a clean place to work, they'll take better care of it, and they'll feel better about it." Amanda Zirkenbach, who portrayed the ingenue role of Peggy Sawyer, noted the changes with appreciation:

> When I did Sophisticated Ladies here (two years ago), it felt a lot different. Things were a lot more on edge. It feels like there's a lot riding on this show, but there's a self-assurance that

the theater's come this far, so it will
be easier to take the next step.
(qtd. in Papatola, "The Little
Theatre That Could" D:2)

Upon entering Le Petit for opening night of 42nd Street, the researcher noticed the freshly-painted lobby and an air of anticipation among the audience. 42nd Street proved to be an appropriate choice with which to usher in Borey's regime. The optimistic tone of the play, with its plot of a chorine who fulfilled her dream of performing on Broadway when the leading lady broke her ankle, paralleled the optimism of director Borey and Le Petit's long-time supporters. Reviewer Papatola proclaimed that any lingering doubts, concerning what Borey could accomplish for Le Petit, were erased at the end of the overture and the beginning of the initial production number. The critic sensed a mixture of exhilaration and relief from the audience. Le Petit's financial plight had become public a few months earlier, and the writer perceived that the audience wanted the production to succeed. Papatola viewed the well-cast, well-chosen, and well-executed production as a triumphant season opener. Actors Zirkenbach, with her kewpie-doll face and angelic voice, Patrick Mendelson, as the young leading man, and Kenneth Risch, as the gruff-but-lovable Julian Marsh, merited favorable comments by Papatola. Borey's well-executed direction, Karen Hebert's inventive choreography, and Derek Franklin's excellent musical direction helped to create an intricate interplay among cast and crew that made the production appear effortless. Although Papatola admitted that the show did have a few technical problems, compared to musicals performed the previous year, "the turnaround is nothing short of astonishing" ("Le Petit Takes Trip" Lagniappe 22).

The Storer Boone Awards, voted on by members of the New Orleans theatrical community, named Le Petit "Theatre of the Year" for 1998 and 42nd Street "Musical of the Year." Other awards included "Best Director" (Borey), "Best Actor in a Musical" (Risch), "Best Actress in a Musical" (Zirkenbach), "Best Musical Direction" (Franklin), "Best Choreography" (Hebert), "Best Costume Designer" (Debby Simeon), "Best Lighting Designer" (Bill Walker), and "Best Sound Designers" (Bret Hanemann and Cliff Stromeyer). The production won more awards than any other nominated play in 1998 ("Awards" Lagniappe 24).

In his review of 42nd Street, Wonk cited the inventiveness and vivacity of the performers in the production numbers "We're in the Money," "Lullaby of Broadway," and "Forty-Second Street." The charm and poise of Zirkenbach and Mendelson and the convincing performance of Risch drew applause from Wonk. Susan Grozier, Marc Belloni, Jimmy Murphy, and Stephen Shapiro received praise for creating an appealing comic world. Wonk's only criticism was for what he perceived as the falseness of the story line of the play ("Style Over Substance" 67).

When the researcher interviewed former Chairman of the Board Arata, he expressed an interest in employing different directors who previously had not directed at Le Petit. African-

American director Tommye Myrick staged the 1999 production of <u>Ma Rainey's Black Bottom</u>. Myrick chose local musicians, rather than actors, Carl LeBlanc, Chile Groove, Eric "Cassius" Clay, and Willie Metcalf, to play the roles of band members. The researcher's husband Richard Hale, a professional musician who is a reluctant occasional theatre-goer, expressed his enjoyment of this production, since he could identify with the musicians. Hale responded favorably to the musicians, whom he found to be convincing, and to the music of the play, as well as the story line, confirming Myrick's decision to cast real musicians. Myrick's bold casting created a few problematic moments of theatre, such as inarticulate delivery and line hesitancy, according to critic Papatola. However, Papatola observed that through the music, the musicians created characters with depth and richness. In the pivotal role of Levee, Clay displayed acting ability, particularly in two galvanizing monologues. Although he cited the imperfectness of the play, both on the stage and on the page, Papatola praised this production as a worthwhile endeavor ("Music Blows Away Flaws" Lagniappe 18).

    For the surprising ease with which they portrayed distinct, droll sidemen, LeBlanc, Groove, and Metcalf impressed critic Wonk. Clay received commendations for his unmistakable conviction in portraying an emotionally complicated role. Wonk complimented John Grimsley's sets and lighting, Helen Ruiz's costumes, and Trish McLain's props for enhancing the sense of reality in the play. He praised the acting of Will Hicks as Ma's harried agent and Joseph Alvarez as Ma's stuttering nephew and cited the repeating of lines and the too-stereotypical white boss as the main flaws of the production ("Bottomed Out" 54).

Le Petit closed its 2000 season with the musical <u>Kiss of the Spider Woman</u>. The opportunity to write a musical with a serious theme—how to stay human in an inhuman situation—appealed to composer John Kander and lyricist Fred Ebb. Karen Hebert received favorable comments from Cuthbert's critique, for both her choreography and her performance as Aurora/Spider Woman, the film femme fatale. In the role of Molina, an effeminate window dresser confined to a brutal Latin American prison, Russell Hodgkinson's funny and touching depiction and his beautiful singing voice impressed the reviewer. In complimenting Jack Jackson for the strength and simplicity that he brought to the role of Valentin, Molina's political prisoner cellmate, Cuthbert also remarked about the rarity locally of finding such a substantial, mature actor who also could sing so well. Other musical highlights included the robust-sounding orchestra, hidden in the theatre's upstairs library and conducted by Jay Haydel, and the singing of Sarah Jane McMahon (Marta) and Joan Slagle (Molina's mother). The reviewer applauded the hardworking male ensemble, led by musical director Franklin and featuring James St. Juniors, Clayton Mazoue, Kevin Champagne, and Sean Richmond. Cuthbert reserved his criticism for technical aspects of the production, such as late or uncertain light cues, microphone feedback, and uncomfortably loud sound levels, problems that he anticipated would be corrected for subsequent performances

("'Spider' Dazzles" Lagniappe 17+).

  Critic Wonk remarked that the standing ovation for the cast of <u>Kiss of the Spider Woman</u> was well deserved. He exalted Hebert for her effortless grace, Jackson for his unforced virility, and Hodgkinson for his tenderness. The brio and conviction with which the actors performed the musical numbers, as well as Borey's staging, and Walker's set and lighting designs contributed to the reviewer's positive comments. Wonk's negative comments concerned inappropriate accents, such as Molina's mother's Irish brogue. He also questioned the reason for having an orchestra, hiding the musicians in a separate room, and wiring the sound through loud speakers. The fact that this somewhat risque production was performed in "the once-stolid halls of Le Petit Theatre" ("Kiss Off" 47) gratified Wonk.

  Unfortunately for Le Petit, not all of the audience shared Wonk's sentiments. Although it was considered an excellent production by critics and the researcher's colleagues, <u>Kiss of the Spider Woman</u> did not set any attendance records. The theatre incurred a loss of $10,000. When the 1999 - 2000 season was announced, subscribers complained about the homosexual content in some of the plays. It should be noted that on July 7, 2000, the Louisiana Supreme Court in State v. Smith upheld the 195-year-old state Sodomy Law that bans private consensual oral and anal sex between partners of the same or different sex. It is not surprising in a state which upholds the sodomy law that these patrons complained about plays with homosexual content. However, this was not the first local production of this play. Students at the University of New

Orleans performed <u>Kiss of the Spider Woman</u> a year earlier without complaints.

In a telephone interview with Contavesprie during his tenure as board member, the researcher questioned him about play selection from the 1999-2000 season, and he responded: "Sonny [Borey] insisted on doing shows of his choice. Next year it's back to basics. Maybe one innovative show, the rest traditional" (7 Nov. 1999). The 2000-2001 season opened with <u>Barnum</u>, which had two additional performances. Artifacts of the showman's life adorned the lobby of Le Petit, where popcorn was sold, and a juggler entertained patrons before the house opened. David Hunt, Amanda Boyden, and Meret Ryhiner, circus professionals with the New Orleans School of Circus Arts, advised set designer Walker about rigging a high wire and taught the cast circus skills for one month. The researcher can attest to the realism with which the cast, most of whom had only limited gymnastics experience, performed circus skills. The precision with which actors juggled, balanced on a medicine ball, and walked on a tightrope added to the enjoyment of the production. A new lighting system, which tripled the theatre's capacity and enabled Walker to isolate areas more effectively, was installed prior to opening night (Cuthbert, "'Barnum' and Borey Circus" Lagniappe 24).

Actor/co-director Derek Franklin referred to co-director Borey as having similar ideas as the title character: "Sonny likes shows with splash, color, and razz-ma-tazz. He's very much like a Barnum in that way" (qtd. in Cuthbert, "'Barnum' and Borey Circus" Lagniappe 22). Although reviewer Wonk referred to the "three-ring razzmatazz" as "an insubstantial treat—theatrical cotton candy," he acknowledged that <u>Barnum</u> would be a crowd-pleaser. The energy with which Borey and Franklin staged the play, as well as Walker's extravagant set, Fried's costumes, and Hebert's choreography, merited compliments from Wonk. He cited the performance of Jimmy Murphy as Barnum, for accomplishing effectively a Herculean set of tasks. Amy Alvarez as Chairy Barnum, Sarah Jane McMahon as Jenny Lind, Fahnlohnee Harris as Joice Heath, Brian Rosenberg as Colonel Tom Thumb, and the ensemble of plate twirlers, stilt walkers, tumblers, and trapeze artists received commendations (Wonk, "In Full View" 65).

In his critique, Cuthbert complimented the competency of the cast in executing the somewhat-risky circus tricks. "The combination of jaunty musical theater, a smidgen of drama and danger and frequent flamboyant flourishes is irresistible," commented the reviewer. Murphy's energetic, engaging portrayal, particularly in singing "There's a Sucker Born Every Minute" and "Join the Circus," received acclaim. Most impressive to Cuthbert was Murphy's tightrope walk, which had the audience holding its breath and then exploding into cheers. Cuthbert exalted Clayton Mazoue's striking Ringmaster and performers Alvarez, McMahon, and Harris, as well as the ensemble of Hebert, Franklin, Andrew Brader, Jesse Quigley, Matthew Mickal, Jeremy M. Horowitz, Maria Karras, Nori Pritchard, and Susan Heflin. Additional praise went to Rosenberg for "bringing down the house singing 'Bigger Isn't Better'" and for embodying the show's eager-to-please spirit.

The beautiful set of the Victorian theatre circus, with its paneled, curtained boxes on either side of the proscenium, and the band, led by Jay Haydel and stationed behind a scrim, contributed to the beauty of the show, according to the critic. In conclusion, Cuthbert referred to Borey as "the mad magician in charge of this illusion, achieved with the hocus-pocus tunnel vision focus of a Houdini" ("Non-Stop Big Top" Lagniappe 13).

    Noises Off followed Barnum and offered excellent performances and received critical acclaim, although attendance did not reach full capacity, and Le Petit lost over $4,000 on the production (Contavesprie, 16 Jan. 2001). In December of 2000, New Cass Productions rented the main stage for its production of A Christmas Carol, praiseworthy for its fresh look at Dickens and its direction and adaptation by Buzz Podewell (Cuthbert, "Here We Go A 'Carol'ing" Lagniappe 13). The success of the February production of Little Shop of Horrors, with overwhelmingly-favorable reviews and audience response, warranted two additional performances. Critic Cuthbert remarked that Little Shop of Horrors could be both a commercial and artistic hit for Le Petit, since it had a much smaller budget than Barnum (Cuthbert, "Le Petit Has a Hit in 'Little Shop'" E:6). Business manager Word confirmed that Le Petit profited financially from Little Shop of Horrors.

    As a co-production with the Tennessee Williams/New Orleans Literary Festival in March of 2001, Le Petit staged Tiger Tail. Tennessee Williams originally wrote a short story entitled, "27 Wagons Full of Cotton," which later became a one-act play. At the urging of director Elia Kazan, Williams transformed his one-act into the screenplay, Baby Doll. Williams used the Baby Doll script with elements and dialogue from the short story to create Tiger Tail. Critics responded to Le Petit's dramatization of Tiger Tail with mixed reviews; however, as part of the festival, the play drew large crowds.

The June production of The Mystery of Edwin Drood and a benefit concert by Betty Buckley closed the 2000-2001 season on the main stage. Both audiences and critics reacted favorably to the plays this season. The 2000-01 season had 900 subscriptions. Word-of-mouth resulted in increased attendance with additional performances of plays, such as Barnum and Little Shop of Horrors.

In the earlier years of the theatre, plays had longer runs. Plays now open on Fridays, instead of Thursdays, and run for three weekends rather than four. In recent years to reduce its deficit, the season has been reduced to five plays from seven in the past. Reviews appear in the Friday Lagniappe section of The Times-Picayune during the second week of productions. Therefore, today word-of-mouth is responsibile for non-season subscribers' attendance more than critics' reviews.

In following the criteria established in the beginning of this chapter, the researcher selected plays for which at least two reviews were available. She consulted a total of thirty-eight reviews by fourteen different critics. One musical, one comedy, and one tragedy represented each of the five time periods from 1968 to 2001. The researcher interviewed at least one person involved in each of the productions. Respondents included directors Fontelieu, Borey, and director/set designer Briggs, costume designer Winn, and actors Gervais, Leal, Contavesprie, Graham, Deutsch, and Lokey.

Chapter Four will explore the present status of Le Petit as well as its plans for the future. The contributions of Le Petit Theatre to the cultural life and theatrical scene in New Orleans also will be discussed. The researcher will conclude with her suggestions for improving the theatre.

4

LE PETIT THEATRE:
THE CONTRIBUTIONS OF THE PAST, THE REALITY OF THE PRESENT, THE PROMISE OF THE FUTURE

Le Petit has grown from a casual gathering of friends who intermittently performed small-scale theatricals in their drawing rooms in 1916 to a theatre with a $500,000 annual budget and a facility valued at five million dollars. Although the Drawing Room Players initially amused themselves by acting in plays, New Orleanians soon realized the cultural opportunities afforded them through these theatrical presentations.

Through key productions on the main stage, children's theatre productions, acting classes (though not taught on a consistent basis), and benefit performances, Le Petit Theatre has contributed to the cultural life in New Orleans. These benefit performances have showcased professional actors, such as Helen Hayes, and, in 2001, Betty Buckley. In recent years, special day-time performances of The Glass Menagerie, A Streetcar Named Desire, and The Importance of Being Earnest for high school students and The Lion, the Witch, and the

Wardrobe for elementary students presented cultural opportunities for children who would not be exposed to the theatre. Additionally, high school students from the New Orleans Center for Creative Arts have performed matinees of Shakespearean plays, such as King Lear, specifically for high school students, as well as one evening performance for the public. Former Managing Director Joel Rainey stated that an asset of the theatre is its education of young people, many of whom experienced theatre for the first time at Le Petit.

Le Petit Theatre has fulfilled one of its original goals: to present plays of a type that otherwise would never be seen in New Orleans. Through its affiliation with Le Petit from 1947-1953, Tulane University professors exposed members to new plays. Current Artistic/Executive Director Sonny Borey continues to fulfill this goal by presenting Grand Hotel, Lettice and Lovage, Falsettos, City of Angels, and The Mystery of Edwin Drood, plays not performed in New Orleans prior to productions at Le Petit. The 1997 world premiere of Pretty Baby afforded New Orleanians an occasion to view an anticipated pre-Broadway production. (Unfortunately, Pretty Baby did not reach Broadway as its producers had hoped.) Local Equity and non-Equity actors benefited from performing with New York actors in Pretty Baby. Co-productions between Le Petit and the Tennessee Williams Festival of plays, such as Tiger Tails and The Seven Descents of Myrtle, have given season subscribers as well as festival-goers the chance to attend lesser-known Tennessee Williams plays.

Other cultural contributions include the children's

theatre, which addressed a need in the community. The children's theatre involved the New Orleans theatrical community by using adaptations of fairytales and original plays by local playwrights, composers, and designers. The children's theatre entertained young theatre-goers, as it developed audiences for the future. Actress/teacher/director Janell Wattigny observed that the children's theatre has provided a service to the New Orleans community:

> One positive aspect of Le Petit's children's theatre is to bring theatre to children and have them exposed to live performances, as opposed to television or video games. It's an opportunity for kids performing and watching, a rare opportunity in this area [New Orleans], as opposed to New York, where I once lived. . . . Le Petit provides a vehicle for kids to view live theatre. Kids from all walks of life are reached. Many kids' families have no means to see theatre. Le Petit has provided a service.
> (Personal interview)

Along with its neighbors, St. Louis Cathedral and Jackson Square, Le Petit has anchored firmly the cultural and social life of the French Quarter. When Borey was asked how he thought

Le Petit had added to the cultural life in New Orleans, he responded:

> Just the building itself, the physical facility itself. Where else can you find something like this? In any city you go to, it's few and far between. Especially the location we're in. Everybody bemoans the fact that we're in the Quarter and all the parking problems. I think it's wonderful we're here. It's absolutely fabulous.
> (Personal interview)

Le Petit has contributed to the theatrical scene in New Orleans by providing beginning actors with training, starting with the 1923 Workshop Theatre, which specifically trained novice actors before they appeared on the main stage. If only professional theatres existed and there were no community theatres, talented beginners would not have an opportunity to perform. Experienced actors have been able to hone their skills at Le Petit by working with highly-qualified directors in a beautiful facility. Le Petit has provided a learning atmosphere for both performers and technical personnel, such as Veleka Gray, Julie Winn, Eduoard Henriques, Bryan Batt, and B.J. Crosby, who all have achieved professional goals.

Today audiences in the New Orleans area have many choices of places to view theatre, with strong theatrical programs at Tulane University and the University of New

Orleans, and an Equity theatre, Southern Repertory, as well as community theatres in the city and suburbs, providing more competition for Le Petit than in its early years. Even though Le Petit in recent years has not surpassed the season subscriptions of the 1970s, theatre patrons continue to support productions at this theatre. For the researcher and loyal patrons, Le Petit still maintains its charm and prestige. Actor/director Lyla Hay Owen commented:

> The plant at Le Petit is so professional. The seating, the acoustics, there is really nothing like it anywhere. And there is nothing like it in New Orleans.
> (Personal interview)

The minor parking inconvenience (mentioned by some of the people interviewed as a major issue) and the perceived danger of the French Quarter (now safer than during the violent years of 1994-95) should be overlooked as reasons not to attend Le Petit.

Actor/board member Leon Contavesprie described his experiences of performing at Le Petit: "This is like being in an off-Broadway house. The history of it, the legend, and lure of the ghosts . . ." (6 Nov. 1997). New Orleans is both a mystical and magical city, beginning with its legends of the supernatural, from voodoo queen Marie Leveau to the ghosts that inhabit certain buildings in the French Quarter, in particular Le Petit Theatre.

One ghostly legend is the tale of married actress

Caroline who fell in love with a fellow married thespian. Caroline's husband confronted her upon discovering her infidelity. She fled her home for the theatre and searched for her lover. Whether or not she found him is not known; however, Caroline plummeted to her death on the gray stones of the theatre's courtyard. Caroline is a benevolent ghost who is thought to be instrumental in aiding backstage personnel (Klein 67). Former assistant technical director Stephen Thurber commented in the documentary <u>Haunted History: New Orleans</u> that Le Petit actors and crew traditionally ask Caroline's help when seeking lost objects. Thurber related his own experience concerning his inability to locate several swords for a future production. He remembered seeing the swords a few days earlier but could not locate them. After asking Caroline's help, Thurber soon found the props (Lindsey). Actor Michael Sullivan conveyed to the researcher a similar Caroline story of his constantly forgetting during rehearsals a hat he needed for a scene. On opening night, Sullivan, totally alone, descended the stairs from the greenroom to the stage, as a voice, presumably Caroline's, warned him not to forget his hat.

    Thurber also commented that he and two colleagues searched the theatre one day for a missing object. This time he was unaided by Caroline. As he approached an upstairs room, he felt foreboding and fear and told the other two not to open the door. They did not listen to him and chided him. As his friends opened the door, a fuzzy human form exploded past Thurber, knocking him to the ground and causing his mouth and nose to bleed. His companions stood totally bewildered.

> It was the most horrific, scary thing.
> His face was so close to mine. My
> friends said I flew back six or seven
> feet. As I flew back, this thing, this
> vision hit me. I needed six stitches
> in my lip...
> (Thurber, Personal interview)

Costume designer Julie Winn recounted an eerie occurrence. She and two others, alone in the theatre working late on a show, were in three different rooms—the greenroom, the costume room, and the library. A piercing scream emanated from the attic. All three, although terrified, ran to the attic and found no one: "We never did find the source of it, and it sure wasn't a voice any of us recognized." Another incident transpired after Winn and other crew members returned to the theatre after dinner. They had locked the theatre and turned off all lights. They returned to discover complete illumination inside the building.

> Nobody else had a key, and even if
> somebody could have gotten into the
> theatre, they couldn't have found all
> the light switches to turn all the
> lights back on that quickly.
> (Longo 182)

When asked if she feared being alone at the theatre, Winn replied:

> When funny things begin

> happening, we just all laugh and say,
> "There goes that ghost again."
> Nothing takes away fear like a good
> laugh with good friends, whether
> they're dead or alive.
> (Longo 183)

The continuation of Le Petit's unique contributions to the city of New Orleans, both to its culture and legends, must be nurtured carefully.

Since the early interviews conducted by the researcher, positive changes have occurred at Le Petit. Much of the increased attendance since 1998 can be attributed to the employment of Borey as Artistic/Executive Director. Former Chairman of the Board Michael Arata described Borey's appeal:

> He has the uncanny ability to get people—whether it's the students here or the people at Orpheus—[Mardi Gras krewe of which Borey is the captain] to work for him. And Sonny works harder than anybody, so when you see what his vision is, you want to get on the bandwagon. He creates things that you want to be associated with.
> (qtd. in Papatola, "New Director, New Directions" Lagniappe 21)

In her interview, Lyla Hay Owen cited the lack of a business manager, the lack of leadership, and the lack of an authority figure as problems at the theatre. Owen mentioned that keys to the costume shop were given freely, often resulting in costumes being borrowed and not returned. The ease with which a stranger could enter the theatre alarmed Owen:

> I've been there during rehearsals; there were people coming through the back door. . . . Once there was a drunk man sleeping in the back between the scenery. I mean, literally! Crawled in among the scenery and just gone to sleep. (Personal interview)

Owen's concerns were addressed when actor/historian Jim Word was appointed business manager in 2001. Also, Borey's leadership and organizational skills have propelled the theatre into the twenty-first century. Stocker Fontelieu commented in his 1997 interview about the lack of organization in which props, costumes, and furniture were strewn about the theatre, especially on the stairs. Costume designer Winn, upon her return to Le Petit after the absence of a few years, complained about the messy costume shop, where it was not unusual for costumes to be thrown on the floor (Personal interview). When Borey took the reins, he insisted that items should be placed in orderly, designated areas (Personal interview). In 2001, scenic artist Michelle Levine lamented the improper storage of costumes on inadequate hangers. Levine agreed to clean the costume shop and appealed to the public for "hard plastic hangers, wooden hangers, or padded hangers," and vowed to replace all wire hangers ("No More Wire Hangers Ever" Lagniappe 12).

  The researcher noted other inefficiencies which Borey and the Board have attempted to correct. Attendance records for some years were missing; employing Word as business manager will rectify this problem. No list of children's theatre productions exists. The researcher has included a list of children's theatre productions in Appendix B with help from Word, who is compiling a list to be kept on file at the theatre. Also, old, unlabeled photographs of productions were discovered thrown in boxes and stacked in the library; one such box was marked "Dishes." As the theatre fell on hard times, documentation was not a priority; keeping the theatre open and paying the light bill was more important. Word was appalled with this situation:

> I have a peculiar affinity for this building and its contents, not just the artistic programming that goes on here. And to come back four years ago on a visit and see what a terrible state of disrepair everything was in then was really awful.
> (qtd. in Cuthbert, "Deja Views" E1)

Word contacted others with ties to Le Petit, such as Fontelieu, Rosa Deutsch, choreographer Linda Fried, and Carolyn Barrois, chairperson of the historic archive committee established in 1999. The group of volunteers labeled and catalogued each photograph:

> One of our goals is to create a data base that will contain a record of every photo, every program, every play and book in the library. Right now there is no place where any of this is written down.
> (qtd. in Cuthbert, "Deja Views" E1)

Donations from local craft stores supplied the workers with frames for different photograph exhibits that now adorn the lobby for each production.

Other changes to maximize efficiency include increasing the staff with a box office manager and a marketing and development director. Four full-time employees have been added to work backstage with technical director Bill Walker. To ensure an influx of new blood and new ideas, the Board expanded from fifteen members to thirty-six in 1998.

In addition to correcting inefficiencies, Le Petit has undergone changes in its philosophy. For years the theatre supported itself exclusively with season memberships. When this was no longer feasible, the Board sought corporate sponsorships, to the chagrin of some of its members, who indicated that it was "beyond the dignity of the theatre to ask for money" (Papatola, "Le Petit Hopes to Stage Major Revival" A:1). Nevertheless, corporate sponsorships, grants, and an open box office policy were necessary changes when memberships declined. For less than the usual ticket price, one Mardi Gras krewe reserves one dress rehearsal performance of each play for its members. Renting the theatre for non-theatrical events, such as private parties, weddings, food tastings, and commercials, also has increased revenue.

    Another change in philosophy involved renting the main stage to other theatre groups, for example, summer productions of <u>Make Mine Bourbon</u> and <u>Forever Plaid</u>. <u>Forever Plaid</u> sold out for seven weeks. Renting the children's theatre, known as the Director's Studio for non-children's productions, has proved to be a wise decision by the Board. <u>Late Nite Catechism</u>, which ran on Thursdays through Sundays in the Director's Studio for many years, gave the theatre a financial boost. Over 20,000 people viewed the play during its first year, many of whom were repeat attendees. The audience-participation play, which features one character, Sister, who regresses her spectators into naughty school children, had been very popular in the predominantly-Catholic city of New Orleans. Regarding <u>Late Nite Catechism</u>'s effect on Le Petit's financial situation, business manager Word stated: "It's gotten us through some pretty awful financial periods and given us a steady operating revenue, which really helps." Arata reiterated Word's comments:

> Without "Late Nite," it could have been "Good Night Irene" for the theater. This show is unlike any other event in the theater's 83-year history, and is unsurpassed in its importance to the theater, both economically and artistically.

(qtd. in Cuthbert, "The PhenomeNun" Lagniappe 22)

Theatre patrons who attended <u>Late Nite Catechism</u> received in their programs a schedule of the plays on the main stage. Arata believed that some audience members were choosing to sample the offerings on the main stage:

> What this show has done for Le Petit, in terms of generating new audiences and in attracting a tourist audience, is mind-boggling. It has also opened up a new arena of thinking for the theater, the results of which I believe will be long-term for Le Petit.
> (qtd. in Cuthbert, "The PhenomeNun" Lagniappe 22)

<u>Late Nite Catechism</u> did not interfere with productions in the children's theatre, even though both shared the same space, since the children's theatre performances were exclusively during the day on Saturdays and Sundays.

The Tennessee Williams/New Orleans Literary Festival, a non-profit organization established in 1987, rents Le Petit Theatre for its yearly festival. In addition to co-productions with Le Petit of Tennessee Williams plays, this four-day festival offers panel discussions, literary readings, walking tours of places frequented by Tennessee Williams, and master classes with established actors, playwrights, and novelists. A book fair is held in the lobby of Le Petit, and most of the festival's activities are held at the theatre, on both the main stage and in the children's theatre. The event culminates with a "Stella and Stanley Shouting Contest," held under the balcony of the Pontalba Building, where the Drawing Room Players originated. Men who attempt to sound like Marlon Brando in <u>A Streetcar Named Desire</u> shout, "Stella!" to judges on the balcony. The contest, which today draws so many participants that elimination rounds are held before the finals, is so popular that in recent years women who yell, "Stanley!" also vie for prizes. Le Petit benefits from the rental fee as well as the exposure from the festival, which now attracts people from all over the country. Former Le Petit Managing Director Don Marshall helped initiate the festival:

> Peggy Scott Laborde [local television personality and documentarian] and I initiated talks about having a Tennessee Williams Festival. Others wanted a literary festival. I wanted to combine a literary festival with Tennessee Williams; this became the beginning of the Tennessee Williams Festival. (Personal interview)

The Tennessee Williams/New Orleans Literary Festival, <u>Late Nite Catechism</u>, and prior productions in the Director's Studio, such as the critically-acclaimed <u>The Compleat Wrks of Wllm Shkspr (Abridged)</u>, represent changes in the original philosophy of the theatre, necessitated by economic considerations. However, in addition to aiding the financial situation of Le Petit, audiences have benefited from these innovations.

To insure the continuation of Le Petit in the community, the researcher would like to offer a few suggestions. First, expand the educational outreach program for underprivileged children. In his interview, Borey mentioned a program called "Educational Arts Project." Children are brought to the theatre three times per year to see plays that are not part of the regular season. This program could include having Le Petit actors go to schools, particularly in underprivileged areas in the New Orleans school system, to present plays. The theatre should apply for educational grant money to cover the expenses of salaries for actors, most of whom would be required to take time off from their regular jobs for these day-time performances.

Second, Le Petit should cultivate younger audiences for the future. Borey indicated that one of the reasons that he chose more current selections during his first year as Executive/Artistic Director was to address this need. The return of the reduced-priced student subscriptions, or allowing students to attend dress rehearsal performances for a nominal fee would help this suggestion. Also, reinstituting acting classes for children and teenagers on a regular basis would be beneficial for aspiring performers and would create future audiences.

Third, involve local universities by encouraging them to allow college credit for internships. Future actors and technical personnel would gain valuable experience from working with theatre professionals. Le Petit would benefit from having extra help and future audience members. Le Petit could offer a "Summerfest," similar to that which occurs at the Omaha Playhouse, which offers four plays in the summer. Two plays are performed at the Omaha Playhouse, and two plays are performed at the University of Nebraska at Omaha. These plays are directed by the staff of the theatre and the university faculty. Since Le Petit's season traditionally ends in the beginning of June, and the new season resumes in September, this event would fill the idle summer months, entertaining audiences and bringing additional revenue to the theatre. As an aside, Bernard Szold directed at both the Omaha Playhouse (1928-35) and Le Petit (1935-40).

      Fourth, encourage people to volunteer at the theatre. Actress Terri Gervais mentioned in her interview that years ago so many people volunteered at Le Petit a special volunteer award was given each season (Personal interview). Costume designer Winn remarked that as a teenage volunteer years earlier she had learned about costuming; upon returning to the theatre to work, she observed that the lack of volunteers prevented the theatre from operating as efficiently as possible (Personal interview). Actor/board member Contavesprie suggested to the Board that each member should spend time volunteering on at least one production each year to become aware of the amount of work involved in mounting a play (Personal interview).

      Fifth, although Le Petit is not considered a theatre for tourists, Contavesprie noted when the theatre displayed a banner advertising a future production, one hundred out-of-towners attended the play. Placing brochures in area hotels was standard procedure at one time; reinstating this option could attract new audiences. French Quarter hotels could offer packages which would include lodging and theatre tickets. One or two restaurants currently offer discounted pre-theatre meals; perhaps other restaurants could avail diners of similar reduced prices. One of the attractions for the researcher, the researcher's friends, and other theatre patrons in attending plays at Le Petit is the experience of an evening in the French Quarter, which involves eating at a downtown restaurant and then attending a play.

Sixth, plays at Le Petit currently open on Friday nights. Reviews of plays appear in the <u>Times-Picayune</u> on Fridays; therefore, one week has elapsed from opening night until the following Friday when the review appears. Le Petit should consider having its first performances on Wednesdays, which was the policy before the run of plays was reduced. Even though audience response in New Orleans is based more on word-of-mouth than reviews, patrons who do read reviews would have more opportunities to view productions if initial performances were on Wednesdays.

Seventh, the Board should not interfere in the artistic process of the theatre. This problem has occurred from the very beginning of the theatre and has caused the theatre to lose very creative, competent directors. The Board should conduct the business affairs of the theatre and allow the Executive/Artistic Director the freedom to implement artistic decisions. Many of the interviewees mentioned the Board's meddling as detrimental to the continuation of Le Petit. A decision should be made concerning the Play-Reading Committee as to how much power it has. Board members on this committee are very serious about choosing appropriate plays for the upcoming seasons, including at one time sending the Artistic Director (Fontelieu) to New York to view the latest theatre offeri ngs. Their interest is commendable; however, the Executive/Artistic Director should have the final decision in choosing the plays each season.

Eighth, for a small fee, Le Petit should offer an indoor ghost tour of the theatre, which would be especially popular during Halloween. Novelist Anne Rice once had an annual Halloween gala at her home, which attracted thousands of people, and daily tours of her mansion were available. Walking ghost tours of the French Quarter pause outside Le Petit to comment on legends; an indoor tour would attract theatre-goers as well as those interested in history and spectral visions.

Ninth, currently five plays are produced each season at Le Petit. The Footlight Club in Jamaica Plain, Massachusetts, offers a season package of four plays with the fifth play as a fundraiser. Similarities exist between Le Petit and the Footlight Club. Both theatres began as social institutions with exclusive memberships. When reduced memberships and economic difficulties arose, both theatres resorted to open box office policies. The fundraiser play has been profitable for the Footlight Club; the Board at Le Petit should consider this option. Although the Footlight Club does not seek professional actors for their fundraiser productions, Le Petit could invite celebrities, such as Delta Burke, John Goodman, and Nicholas Cage who have residences in New Orleans, to perform.

Although Le Petit Theatre had been experiencing a resurgence, challenges exist for its future. On August 29, 2005 Hurricane Katrina wrecked havoc on the New Orleans metropolitan area and its citizens. Every facet of life was affected. The French Quarter, the first part of New Orleans established by early settlers because it was the highest area in a city below sea level, escaped some of the damage that was rampant in most of the other areas of the city. However, Le Petit did suffer major damage, much more than originally discovered. The new orchestra pit, which was in the process of being built, and the new state-of-the-art main stage both filled with water, which has been pumped out. Also, roof damage to the small theatre, recently renamed Murial's Cabaret at Le Petit Theatre, caused water to leak onto the electrical equipment. Fortunately, Le Petit's lobby, theatre offices, costume shop, greenroom, dressing rooms, and upstairs library were unscathed.

Director Sonny Borey had intended to open the 2005-2006 season with the musical Cabaret, to be performed in Murial's Cabaret, a perfect setting. However, most of the actors cast in Cabaret now are scattered all over the country. In an effort to reopen the theatre as soon as possible, the popular And the Ball and All, a funny, very New Orleans play, was performed at Le Petit in January of 2006. Borey hopes to have a full season of plays for 2006-2007, beginning with The Full Monty in September.

In addition to the challenges posed by Hurricane

Katrina, other challenges exist for the future of Le Petit. These include enlarging the subscription base, increasing ticket sales for individual plays, retiring the debt, and increasing the staff. The need for corporate support, grants, and individuals who can contribute money will continue to exist. Chairman of the Board Errol Laborde's comments are positive in his assessment of Le Petit's current situation:

> I think Le Petit's in good shape, perhaps the best shape it's been in financially in some time. And everyone recognizes that we present quality productions in a unique facility that's second to none. (qtd. in Cuthbert, "Le Petit: New Season, New Chairman" E:9)

The membership of Le Petit Theatre has had its share of mistakes throughout its long history, such as the Board's reliance exclusively on season memberships until lack of revenue forced the exploration of alternative sources of income. The theatre has survived decreased attendance, crime in the French Quarter, and a parade of exiting directors in recent years. Doomsayers who predicted the demise of Le Petit Theatre have been proven wrong. Le Petit is alive since its supporters refuse to let it die. Among the strong points of the theatre are its loyal group of members and the beautiful, historical facility. Prior to Hurricane Katrina, in its history, only once has a performance of a play been cancelled when the leading lady's father died. Although it is no longer the only theatre in town as it once was, New Orleanians still hold Le Petit in high regard. Local actors aspire to perform at Le Petit. With the exception of a couple of years when some actors in the community refused to audition in a dispute regarding the policy of not paying performers, auditions draw a large number. The late actress Lois Crandell spoke for many other actors when she remarked that she would accept a small role at Le Petit rather than a larger role at another theatre. Actress/teacher/director Wattigny explained her feelings about performing at Le Petit:

> People can have a completely different feeling, stepping into the theatre from the outside world. It breathes culture. . . . It's a wonderful place, an asset to the city. It combines historic and contemporary; it doesn't lose the historic. . . . Performing there, standing on the balcony at intermission, and watching tourists glance at the building make the experience more formal.
> (Personal interview)

Le Petit is a theatre that has served the community, a theatre that has overcome obstacles and has continued to survive. From the home of founding member Rhea Goldberg Deutsch at 1527 Seventh Street to the Pontalba Building to Le Petit Theatre at 616 St. Peter Street, where Deutsch's daughter-in-law Rosa Deutsch is a benefactor and theatre activist, Le Petit Théâtre du

Vieux Carré remains a fixture in the New Orleans community. Le Petit will continue to serve its community in the capacity to which its founding members dedicated the theatre.

BIBLIOGRAPHY

BOOKS

Baldwin, Edward McCarthy. "A History of Le Petit Théâtre Du Vieux Carré, 1917-1923." Master's Thesis. Tulane U, 1950.

Brian, George C. The Non-Professional Theatre in Louisiana: 1900-1925. Diss. Louisiana State U, 1965. Ann Arbor: UMI, 1965.

Chapman, Frederick L. A History of Le Petit Théâtre Du Vieux Carré. Diss. Tulane U, 1971. Ann Arbor: UMI, 1971.

Dabney, Thomas Ewing. One Hundred Great Years in the Story of the Times-Picayune: From Its Founding to 1940. Baton Rouge: Louisiana State UP, 1944.

Deutsch, Hermann, and Donald Higgins, eds. Le Petit Théâtre du Vieux Carré: An Illustrated Exposition and Narrative Account of the Theatre from Its Inception in March 1916. New Orleans: Sam W. Taylor, 1928.

Drabble, Margaret, ed. Oxford Companion to English Literature. Rev. ed. New York: Oxford UP, 1995.

Gard, Robert E., and Gertrude Burley. Community Theatre. New York: Van Rees, 1959.

Hardy, Arthur. Mardi Gras Guide. New Orleans: Hardy Enter., 2001.

Horn, Barbara Lee. Ellen Stewart and La Mama: A Bibliography. Westport, CT: Greenwood, 1993.

Hughes, Glenn. A History of the American Theatre: 1700-1950. New York: French, 1951.

Klein, Victor C. New Orleans Ghosts, II. Metairie, LA: Lycanthrope, 1999.

Lazarus, A.L., ed. A George Jean Nathan Reader. New Jersey: Associated U, 1990.

LeBlanc, Ray. "Theatre Activity of Le Petit During World War II." Master's Thesis. Louisiana State U, 1965.

Longo, Jim. Ghosts Along the Mississippi. St. Louis: Ste. Anne's, 1993.

MacGowan, Kenneth. Footlights Across America. New York: Harcourt, 1929.

McCaslin, Nellie. Theatre for Children in the United States: A History. Norman: U of Oklahoma P, 1971.

—. Historical Guide to Children's Theatre in America. New

York: Greenwood, 1987.

Maule, Harry, and Melville Cane, eds. The Man from Main Street, A Sinclair Lewis Reader: Selected Essays and Other Writings, 1904-1950. New York: Random, 1953.

O'Connor, Richard. Sinclair Lewis. New York: McGraw, 1971.

Schorer, Mark. Sinclair Lewis: An American Life. New York: McGraw, 1961.

Smither, Nelle. A History of the English Theatre in New Orleans. New York: Blom, 1967.

PERIODICALS

"Architectural Gems." Times-Picayune [New Orleans] 11 June 2000, sec. F: 9.

"Awards Congregate at '42nd Street'." Times-Picayune [New Orleans] 28 May 1999: sec. "Lagniappe": 24.

Barbee, David Rankin. "Le Petit Has Splendid Inaugural." States-Item [New Orleans] 21 Nov. 1922: 11.

"Chartres Street Side of Petit Theatre To Be Reconstructed." Vieux Carre Courier [New Orleans] 31 Mar.-6 Apr. 1962: 1-7.

Covert, Martin. "Ann and Andy—Three's a Charm." Rev. of Raggedy Ann and Andy's Musicland Capers, by Lyla Hay Owen. Vieux Carré Courier [New Orleans] 23 Feb. 1978: 12.

Cunningham, Lynn. "'Rapunzel' Pleases the Kiddies and Adults, Too." Rev. of Rapunzel, by Sharon O'Brien and Fred Palmisano. States-Item [New Orleans] 17 May 1978, sec. D: 4.

Curran, Neil. "Theater/For the Kids . . . Delightful Production at Le Petit and Green Apple Corps." Rev. of The Little Mermaid, by Lyla Hay Owen and Fred Palmisano. Vieux Carré Courier [New Orleans] 14 May 1971: 8.

Cuthbert, David. "New Orleans Children's Theatre Is Blossoming at Le Petit." Times-Picayune [New Orleans] 22 Mar. 1971, sec. 1: 21.

—. "Youth Theatres Boom; Two Shows Open Saturday." Times-Picayune [New Orleans] 2 May 1971, sec. 2: 16.

—. "Petit 'Mermaid' Splash of Fun." Rev. of The Little Mermaid, by Lyla Hay Owen and Fred Palmisano. Times-Picayune [New Orleans] 10 May 1971, sec. 1: 17.

—. "'Hello, Dolly!' Production Is Good-Looking Musical."

Rev. of <u>Hello, Dolly!</u>, by Jerry Herman and Michael Stewart. <u>Times-Picayune</u> [New Orleans] 9 Sept. 1972, sec. 2: 4.

Cuthbert, David. "Le Petit 'Sleeping Beauty' Said Gem of Many Facets." Rev. of <u>Sleeping Beauty</u>, by John Simons and Fred Palmisano. <u>Times-Picayune</u> [New Orleans] 21 May 1973, sec. 2: 6.

—. "Putting It Together for Le Petit's Kids." Rev. of <u>Sleeping Beauty</u>, by John Simons and Fred Palmisano. <u>Times-Picayune</u> [New Orleans] 27 May 1973, sec. 2: 12+.

—. "Too Darn Hot for Theater?" <u>Times-Picayune</u> [New Orleans] 19 May 1974, sec. 2: 12.

—. "'Emperor's New Clothes' Has Brisk, Farcical Style." Rev. of <u>The Emperor's New Clothes</u>, by Sharon O'Brien and Fred Palmisano. <u>Times-Picayune</u> [New Orleans] 24 May 1974, sec. 2: 5.

—. "Le Petit Plans Variety Bill." <u>Times-Picayune</u> [New Orleans] 18 Aug. 1974, sec. 2: 8.

—. "Spirited Song, Dance in Petit 'Lafitte!'." Rev. of <u>Lafitte!</u>, by Sharon O'Brien and Fred Palmisano. <u>Times-Picayune</u> [New Orleans] 25 May 1975, sec. 2: 13.

—. "Comic 'Ann, Andy' Pleases Small-Fry." Rev. of <u>Raggedy Ann and Andy's Musicland Capers</u>, by Lyla Hay Owen. <u>Times-Picayune</u> [New Orleans] 17 Feb. 1978, sec. E: 5.

—. "Phantom Barroso." <u>Times-Picayune</u> [New Orleans] 2 Dec. 1995, sec. E: 3.

—. "Her Not-So-Secret Garden." <u>Times-Picayune</u> [New Orleans] 5 May 1996: D: 2.

—. "Déja Views." <u>Times-Picayune</u> [New Orleans] 23 Aug. 1999, sec. "Lagniappe": 1.

—. "'Rumplestiltskin' Mostly Gold but Bits of Straw Show Through." Rev. of <u>Rumplestiltskin</u>, by Fred Palmisano and Sharon O'Brien. <u>Times-Picayune</u> [New Orleans] 18 Feb. 2000, sec. "Lagniappe": 20.

Cuthbert, David. "Kidstage Vet Back as One of the Boys in the 'Hood'." <u>Times-Picayune</u> [New Orleans] 21 Apr. 2000, sec. "Lagniappe": 18.

—. "Rollicking, Rockin' 'Robin' a Fun Family Show at Le Petit." Rev. of <u>The Merry Adventures of Robin Hood</u>, by Fred Palmisano and Sharon O'Brien. <u>Times-Picayune</u> [New Orleans] 5 May 2000, sec. "Lagniappe": 39.

—. "'Spider' Dazzles, But Its Web Site Under Construction."

Rev. of Kiss of the Spider Woman, by John Kander, Fred Ebb, and Terrence McNally. Times-Picayune [New Orleans] 9 June 2000, sec. "Lagniappe": 17-18.

—. "The PhenomeNUN of 'Late Nite Catechism'." Times-Picayune [New Orleans] 28 July 2000, sec. "Lagniappe": 22.

—. "'Barnum' and Borey Circus." Times-Picayune [New Orleans] 8 Sept. 2000, sec. "Lagniappe": 22+.

—. "Non-Stop Big Top." Rev. of Barnum, by Cy Coleman, Michael Stewart, and Mark Bramble. Times-Picayune [New Orleans] 15 Sept. 2000, sec. "Lagniappe": 13.

—. "This Thanksgiving Act Is No Turkey." Rev. of The Bepuzzled Pilgrim, by Wayne Daigrepont. Times-Picayune [New Orleans] 17 Nov. 2000, sec. "Lagniappe": 16.

—. "HERE WE GO A 'CAROL' ING." Rev. of A Christmas Carol, by Charles Dickens, adapted by Buzz Podewell. Times-Picayune [New Orleans] 22 Dec. 2000, sec. "Lagniappe": 13.

—. "Le Petit Has a Hit in 'Little Shop'." Rev. of Little Shop of Horrors, by Allen Mencken and Howard Ashman. Times-Picayune [New Orleans] 8 Feb. 2001, sec. E: 6.

Cuthbert, David. "Playing with Poetry at Le Petit." Rev. of Limerick Junction, by Dane Rhodes and Gary Rucker. Times-Picayune [New Orleans] 20 Apr. 2001, sec. "Lagniappe": 15.

—. "Le Petit: New Season, New Chairman, New Direction?" Times-Picayune [New Orleans] 14 June 2001, sec. E: 9.

—. "Le Petit Children's Theater Now a Family Affair." Times-Picayune [New Orleans] 26 July 2001: sec: E: 7.

Danflous, Patricia. "The Smell of the Greasepaint . . . The Giggle of a Child." New Orleans Magazine 4 Apr. 1977: 42-43.

Del Papa, Joseph. "Theatre: Le Petit's 'Hello, Dolly!'" Rev. of Hello, Dolly!, by Jerry Herman and Michael Stewart. Figaro [New Orleans] 16 Sept. 1972: 4.

—. "1776." Rev. of 1776 by Sherman Edwards and Peter Stone. Figaro [New Orleans] 18 Sept. 1974: 14.

—. "'Scapino!'—To Each His Own Jollies." Rev. of Scapino!, adapted by Frank Dunlap and Jim Dale. Figaro [New Orleans] 18 May 1977: 17.

Dodds, Richard. "Musicals for 'Kids' Day Off'." Times-Picayune [New Orleans] 3 Oct. 1976, sec. 2: 7.

—. "'Desire' Comes Home." Rev. of <u>A Streetcar Named Desire</u>, by Tennessee Williams. <u>Times-Picayune</u> [New Orleans] 1 Feb. 1977, sec. 2: 4.

—. "Review: 'Rapunzel'." Rev. of <u>Rapunzel</u>, by Sharon O'Brien and Fred Palmisano. <u>Times-Picayune</u> [New Orleans] 10 May 1978, sec. "Lagniappe": 6.

—. "Barroso Resigns Le Petit." <u>Times-Picayune</u> [New Orleans] 14 June 1978, sec. 6: 3.

Dodds, Richard. "Le Petit Theatre Seems to Have Succeeded in Going Public." <u>Times-Picayune/States-Item</u> [New Orleans] 27 Feb. 1983, sec. 2: 17-18.

—. "Le Petit Turning a New Page." <u>Times-Picayune</u> [New Orleans] 24 Mar. 1985, sec. "Lagniappe": 13.

—. "Le Petit Opens New Era with 'Evita'." Rev. of <u>Evita</u>, by Andrew Lloyd Webber and Tim Rice. <u>Times-Picayune</u> [New Orleans] 11 Sept. 1985, sec. D: 12.

—. "Marshall Moves from the CAC to Le Petit." <u>Times-Picayune</u> [New Orleans] 20 July 1986, sec. "Lagniappe": 1.

—. "Curious Case of Le Petit's Newest Change in Direction." <u>Times-Picayune</u> [New Orleans] 24 July 1986, sec. 4: 10.

—. "Le Petit's New Image Augurs Well for the Old Theatre." Times-Picayune [New Orleans] 4 Feb. 1988, sec. C8.

—. "Vaudeville." Times-Picayune [New Orleans] 30 Apr. 1989: F1+.

—. "N'Awlins-set 'Cinderella' Charms Little and Big Folks." Rev. of Cinderella Battistella, by Fred Palmisano, Bob Bruce, and David Cuthbert. Times-Picayune [New Orleans] 30 Nov. 1989, sec. E: 10.

—. "Winning 'Women' Dishes Wicked Comedy at Le Petit." Rev. of The Women, by Clare Boothe Luce. Times-Picayune [New Orleans] 10 June 1990, sec. C: 5.

—. "Revival of Children's Corner." Times-Picayune [New Orleans] 4 Oct. 1990, sec. E: 5.

—. "Mass Resignations Hit Le Petit's Board." Times-Picayune [New Orleans] 18 June 1991, sec. C4.

—. "Big Birthday for Little Theatre." Times-Picayune [New Orleans] 16 Sept. 1991, sec. C10.

Dodds, Richard. "'Lady' Showcases Le Petit at its Best." Rev. of My Fair Lady, by Alan Jay Lerner and Frederick Loewe. Times-Picayune [New Orleans] 20 Sept. 1991, sec.

"Lagniappe": 14.

—. "First Nighter." Times-Picayune [New Orleans] 18 Sept. 1992, sec. E: 1.

—. "'M. Butterfly' Takes Flight at Le Petit." Rev. of M. Butterfly, by David Henry Hwang. Times-Picayune [New Orleans] 13 Nov. 1992, sec. "Lagniappe": 18.

—. "Child's Play: Theater to be Dedicated." Times-Picayune [New Orleans] 21 Oct. 1993, sec. E: 9.

—. "It's Time for Le Petit to Change Course." Times-Picayune [New Orleans] 12 Aug. 1994, sec. "Lagniappe": 18-19.

—. "NOCCA Students and Faculty Team for Shakespeare's 'Lear'." Times-Picayune [New Orleans] 8 Feb. 1996, sec. E: 9.

—. "Counting to Ten: The Tennessee Williams Festival Marks a Milestone." Times-Picayune [New Orleans] 29 Mar. 1996, sec. "Lagniappe": 20+.

—. "Fancy 'Ladies' at Le Petit's Party." Times-Picayune [New Orleans] 15 Aug. 1996, sec. E: 9.

—. "Eighty Years at Le Petit." Times-Picayune [New Orleans] 13 Sept. 1996, sec. "Lagniappe": 20.

—. "Cast Gives 'Laughter' Its Life at Le Petit." Rev. of <u>Laughter on the 23rd Floor</u>, by Neil Simon. <u>Times-Picayune</u> [New Orleans] 8 Nov. 1996, sec. "Lagniappe": 22.

—. "An Explosion of Talent Rocks Le Petit." Rev. of <u>42nd Street</u>, by Mark Bramble, Michael Stewart, Harry Warren, and Al Dubin. <u>Times-Picayune</u> [New Orleans] 20 Sept. 1998, sec. "Lagniappe": 27.

Dodds, Richard. "Local Director to Head Le Petit." <u>Times-Picayune</u> [New Orleans] 24 Jan. 1997, sec. "Lagniappe": 24.

—. "New Directions for Le Petit Theatre." <u>Times-Picayune</u> [New Orleans] 26 Feb. 1997, sec. E: 2.

—. "Teddy's Corner Looks Back for Its New Start." Rev. of <u>Pinocchio Commedia</u>, by Fred Palmisano and John Simons. <u>Times-Picayune</u> [New Orleans] 8 Apr. 1997, sec. "Lagniappe": 17.

—. "Children's Theater Takes the Stage." Rev. of <u>Puss in Boots</u>, by Fred Palmisano and Sharon O'Brien. <u>Times-Picayune</u> [New Orleans] 20 Nov. 1998, sec. "Lagniappe": 3.

Fontelieu, Stocker. "Theater Called Ace of Clubs." <u>Times-Picayune</u> [New Orleans] 9 June 1963, sec. 2: 11+.

Fosberg, S. Joslyn. "'The Emperor's New Clothes': The Usual Fun." Rev. of The Emperor's New Clothes, by Sharon O'Brien and Fred Palmisano. Vieux Carré Courier [New Orleans] 6 June 1974: 14.

—. "'Shenandoah'—A Civil War Pastiche." Rev. of Shenandoah, by Bronson Howard. Vieux Carré Courier [New Orleans] 23 Sept. 1976: 12.

—. "AVE ATQUE VALE—farewell." Rev. of Rapunzel, by Sharon O'Brien and Fred Palmisano. New Orleans Courier [New Orleans] 11-17 May 1978: 11.

Gagnard, Frank. "Le Petit's 'Virginia Woolf' Follows Text Verbatim." Rev. of Who's Afraid of Virginia Woolf?, by Edward Albee. Times-Picayune [New Orleans] 27 Jan. 1968, sec. 2: 5.

—. "New Lights to Be Shed on Familiar Show Plot." Rev. of Hello, Dolly!, by Jerry Herman and Michael Stewart. Times-Picayune [New Orleans] 27 Aug. 1972, sec. 2: 10.

—. "Le Petit Celebrates Its Own History." Times-Picayune [New Orleans] 14 May 1987, sec. E: 12.

Gagnard, Frank. "Simon Was More Fun Before His Destiny Began to Call." Rev. of Brighton Beach Memoirs, by Neil

Simon. Times-Picayune [New Orleans] 25 June 1987, sec. E: 12.

——. "'Amadeus' Lacks Grandeur." Rev. of Amadeus, by Peter Shaffer. Gambit [New Orleans] 21 Jan. 1988, sec. E: 11.

Greene, Danny. "Top Cast at Le Petit Masters 'Virginia Woolf'." Rev. of Who's Afraid of Virginia Woolf?, by Edward Albee. States-Item [New Orleans] 29 Jan. 1968: 15.

Jones, Charles. "Tallichet Helps Brighten Play." Rev. of The Play's the Thing?, by Ferenc Molnar. Times-Picayune [New Orleans] 10 Feb. 1938: 18.

Laborde, Errol. "Little Theatre's Biggest Challenge." Gambit [New Orleans] 13 July 1985: 17-18.

Larose, Joseph. "LPT's 'Virginia Woolf' Is Powerful, Absorbing." Rev. of Who's Afraid of Virginia Woolf?, by Edward Albee. Clarion Herald [New Orleans] 1 Feb. 1968, sec. 2: 3.

——. "Truth Light in Earnest." Rev. of The Importance of Being Earnest, by Oscar Wilde. Clarion Herald [New Orleans] 4 Nov. 1971, sec. 2: 4.

——. "Spirit of '1776'." Rev. of 1776, by Sherman Edwards and Peter Stone. Clarion Herald [New Orleans] 12 Sept. 1974, sec. 2: 4.

LaRue, Michele. "Community Theatre." Theatre Crafts 20:3 (Mar. 1986): 394.

"Lewis to Act Lead Role in Carroll Play." Times-Picayune [New Orleans] 14 Jan. 1940: 11.

"Life's Too Short at Le Petit." Gambit [New Orleans] 28 June 1986: 51.

"Little Theater Renovation Set." Times-Picayune [New Orleans] 27 Mar. 1962, sec. 2: 2.

Madden, William. "Quarter Wall Stirs Up Big Ruckus." States-Item [New Orleans] 31 July 1962: 7.

"No More Wire Hangers Ever." Times-Picayune [New Orleans] 16 Mar. 2001, sec. "Lagniappe": 12.

Papatola, Dominic. "Le Petit Hopes to Stage Major Revival . . . of Itself." Times-Picayune [New Orleans] 4 Apr. 1998, sec. A1.

—. "Changing World Makes Future of Community Theater Cloudy." Times-Picayune [New Orleans] 16 Apr. 1998, sec. E: 7.

—. "Le Petit Theatre Staging Revival." Times-Picayune [New Orleans] 16 May 1998, sec. B: 1+.

—. "New Director, New Directions for Le Petit." Times-Picayune [New Orleans] 22 May 1998, sec. "Lagniappe": 21.

—. "Stripped-Down 'Gypsy' a Disappointment at Le Petit." Rev. of Gypsy by Arthur Laurents, Jule Styne, and Stephen Sondheim. Times-Picayune [New Orleans] 5 June 1998, sec. "Lagniappe": 23.

—. "The Little Theatre That Could." Times-Picayune [New Orleans] 15 Sept. 1998, sec. D: 2.

—. "Le Petit Takes the Trip of Its Life to '42nd Street'." Rev. of 42nd Street, by Mark Bramble, Michael Stewart, Harry Warren, and Al Dubin. Times-Picayune [New Orleans] 25 Sept. 1998, sec. "Lagniappe": 22.

—. "Pair of Palmisano Shows Return." Times-Picayune [New Orleans] 19 Nov. 1998, sec. E.

—. "'Puss In Boots' Will Have Small Fry Purring." Rev. of Puss In Boots by Fred Palmisano and Sharon O'Brien. Times-Picayune [New Orleans] 27 Nov. 1998, sec. "Lagniappe": 25.

—. "Le Petit Tops Big Easy Noms." Times-Picayune [New Orleans] 4 Mar 1999, sec. E: 7.

Papatola, Dominic. "Music Blows Away the Flaws in Le Petit's 'Ma Rainey'." Rev. of Ma Rainey's Black Bottom, by August Wilson. Times-Picayune [New Orleans] 7 May 1999, sec. "Lagniappe": 18.

Perry, James A. "Characters in 'Earnest' Delightful." Rev. of The Importance of Being Earnest, by Oscar Wilde. States-Item [New Orleans] 23 Oct. 1971, sec. "Lagniappe": 17.

—. "More Creative Magic from Children's Corner." Rev. of Raggedy Ann and Andy's Musicland Capers, by Lyla Hay Owen. States-Item [New Orleans] 19 Sept. 1978, sec. C8.

—. "Major Flaws Mars Petit's 'Streetcar'." Rev. of A Streetcar Named Desire, by Tennessee Williams. States-Item [New Orleans] 19 Sept. 1996, sec. E: 10.

"Pillar of Le Petit Theatre Dies at 66." Times-Picayune [New Orleans] 28 June 1992, sec. B4.

Pitts, Stella. "Budding Theater She Guided Helped to Save Vieux Carre." Times-Picayune [New Orleans] 13 June 1976, sec. 2: 9.

"Rainey Is Leaving as Le Petit's Manager." Times-Picayune

[New Orleans] 1 Feb. 1977, sec. E10.

Real, Ed. "LIFE ON THE WICKED STAGE." Rev. of The Women, by Clare Boothe Luce. Impact [New Orleans] 29 June 1990, sec. 10.

Roehl, Marjorie. "'Coach' Fontelieu Leads Le Petit Into Its 60th Season." States-Item [New Orleans] 19 Oct. 1976, sec. B: 4.

Rushton, Bill. "LAFITTE'S SURPRISE." Rev. of Lafitte!, by Sharon O'Brien and Fred Palmisano. New Orleans Courier [New Orleans] 22 May 1975, sec. 2: 1.

Rushton, Bill. "'St. Joan' Opens Monday Evening at Little Theatre." Rev. of Saint Joan, by George Bernard Shaw. Times-Picayune [New Orleans] 21 Apr. 1929: 11.

Shea, Al. "Little Theatre With Big Problems." New Orleans Magazine Sept. 1980: 42.

—. "Soapbox." Rev. of Brighton Beach Memoirs, by Neil Simon. Gambit [New Orleans] 30 June 1987: 22.

—. "Soapbox." Rev. of Amadeus, by Peter Shaffer. Gambit [New Orleans] 26 Jan. 1988: 67.

—. "Soapbox." Rev. of Puss In Boots, by Fred Palmisano and

Sharon O'Brien. Gambit [New Orleans] 26 Jan. 1988: 67.

—. "Soapbox." Rev. of Rumplestiltskin, by Fred Palmisano and Sharon O'Brien. Gambit [New Orleans] 18 Oct. 1988: 33.

—. "Review Round-Up." Rev. of Cinderella Battistella, by Fred Palmisano, Bob Bruce, and David Cuthbert. Gambit [New Orleans] 12 Dec. 1989: 33.

—. "An Auspicious Opening at Le Petit." Rev. of My Fair Lady, by Alan Jay Lerner and Frederick Loewe. Gambit [New Orleans] 24 Sept. 1991: 36.

—. "'M. Butterfly' Disappoints." Rev. of M. Butterfly, by David Henry Hwang. Gambit [New Orleans] 17 Nov. 1992: 33.

Vayda, Priscilla. "Curtain Rises on LP's 80th Season." Times-Picayune [New Orleans] 8 Sept. 1996: "Overture to the Cultural Season": 16.

Wallfisch, Janet. "First and Only Benefit for Le Petit Theatre." Times-Picayune [New Orleans] 25 Mar. 1976, sec. 3: 10.

Wallfisch, Janet. "Big Dreams Fulfilled by Le Petit Theatre." Times-Picayune [New Orleans] 1 Apr. 1984, sec. 4: 1.

Wardlaw, Jack. "'Scapino!' Actors Offer Full Dish of Fun."
    Rev. of Scapino!, adapted by Frank Dunlap and Jim Dale.
    States-Item [New Orleans] 10 May 1977, sec. B: 4.

Wonk, Dalt. "Funny Bone Syndrome." Rev. of Laughter on the
    23rd Floor, by Neil Simon. Gambit [New Orleans] 12 Nov.
    1996: 45.

—. "Good Wood." Rev. of Pinocchio Commedia, by Fred
    Palmisano and John Simons. Gambit [New Orleans] 8 Apr.
    1997: 45.

—. "Curtain Call?" Gambit [New Orleans] 3 June 1997: 9.

—. "Style Over Substance." Rev. of 42nd Street, by Mark
    Bramble, Michael Stewart, Harry Warren, and Al Dubin.
    Gambit [New Orleans] 29 Sept. 1998: 67.

—. "A Different Children's Story." Rev. of Puss In Boots, by
    Fred Palmisano and Sharon O'Brien. Gambit [New
    Orleans] 8 Dec 1998: 83.

—. "Bottomed Out." Rev. of Ma Rainey's Black Bottom, by
    August Wilson. Gambit [New Orleans] 11 May 1999: 54.

—. "Sublime Rhyme." Rev. of Rumplestiltskin, by Fred
    Palmisano and Sharon O'Brien. Gambit [New Orleans] 14
    Mar. 2000: 48.

———. "Kiss Off." Rev. of <u>Kiss of the Spider Woman</u>, by John Kander, Fred Ebb, and Terrence McNally. <u>Gambit</u> [New Orleans] 27 June 2000: 47.

———. "In Full View." Rev. of <u>Barnum</u>, by Cy Coleman, Michael Stewart, and Mark Bramble. <u>Gambit</u> [New Orleans] 19 Sept. 2000: 65.

Worden, Amy. "The Front Row." Rev. of <u>Evita</u>, by Andrew Lloyd Webber and Tim Rice. <u>Gambit</u> [New Orleans] 14 Sept. 1985: 43.

INTERVIEWS

Arata, Michael. Personal Interview. 4 June 1998.

Barroso, Luis. Personal Interview. 23 Oct. 1999.

———. Telephone Interview. 14 Jan. 2001.

Batt, Bryan. Telephone Interview. 9 Sept. 1996.

Borey, Sonny. Personal Interview. 1 Sept. 1999.

Briggs, Keith. Personal Interview. 14 Aug. 1997.

Contavesprie, Leon. Personal Interview. 6 Nov. 1997.

—. Telephone Interview. 29 July 1998.

—. Telephone Interview. 7 Nov. 1999.

—. Telephone Interview. 9 Nov. 1999.

—. Telephone Interview. 26 Jan. 2000.

—. Telephone Interview. 11 Nov. 2000.

—. Telephone Interview. 16 Jan. 2001.

Cox, Edward R. Personal Interview. 6 July 1998.

Crandell, Lois. Personal Interview. 22 July 1996.

Cuthbert, David. E-mail Interview. 27 Feb. 2001.

Daigle, Lucy. Telephone Interview. 14 July 1998.

—. Telephone Interview. 26 Sept. 1999.

Deutsch, Rosemary "Rosa." Personal Interview. 29 July 1998.

Fontelieu, C. Stocker. Personal Interview. 13 Mar. 1996.

Gervais, Terri. Personal Interview. 29 June 1998.

Graham, Ricky. Faxed Interview. 15 Mar. 1998.

Gray, Veleka. E-mail Interview. 4 Nov. 1999.

Kary, Sarah. Telephone Interview. 6 Dec. 1999.

Leal, Douglas. E-mail Interview. 28 May 2001.

Laborde, Errol. Telephone Interview. 9 Oct. 2001.

Landrieu, Maurice "Moon." Mail Interview. 6 Aug. 1997.

Lokey, Vatican. Personal Interview. 29 May 1997.

—. Personal Interview. 6 July 1998.

—. Personal Interview. 29 Sept. 2000.

Marshall, Don. Personal Interview. 7 May 1996.

Owen, Lyla Hay. Personal Interview. 2 Apr. 1996.

Rainey, Joel. Personal Interview. 1 Aug. 1998.

Rucker, Gary. Personal Interview. 20 Apr. 2001.

Staub, August. Telephone Interview. 18 June 1999.

Thurber, Stephen. Telephone Interview. 3 Mar. 2002.

Tong, Arthur. Personal Interview. 24 June 1996.

Wattigny, Janell. Personal Interview. 10 Sept. 1996.

Winn, Julie. Telephone Interview. 11 Sept. 1996.

Word, Jim. Personal Interview. 16 Sept. 1999.

MEDIA

Haunted History: New Orleans. Narr. Michael Dorn. Dir. Jim Lindsey. Greystone Communications, Inc. 1998.

UNPUBLISHED MATERIALS AND MISCELLANEOUS

Genre, Emma. "Anniversary Program of Le Petit Théâtre Du Vieux Carré," 1966-67. Researcher's Private Collection.

"A Joint Statement from Le Petit Théâtre Du Vieux Carré and the Department of Drama and Fine Arts, Louisiana State University in New Orleans: May 6, 1969." Le Petit Théâtre Archives, New Orleans.

Long, Edith. "Vieux Carré Survey of Le Petit Théâtre." The Williams Research Center, New Orleans, Sept. 24, 1964.

New Orleans Police Department, Technical Services Bureau, Information Systems and Services Division. "U.C.R. Reportable Crimes."

APPENDICES

Appendix A

THE INTERVIEWS

INTERVIEWER: REBECCA HALE
INTERVIEWED: March 13, 1996
RESPONDENT: STOCKER FONTELIEU
Executive Director of Le Petit (1961-1985)/Actor

Q. What is your name and title?

A. My name is Stocker Fontelieu. The program listed me as C. Stocker Fontelieu.
I was the Executive Director of Le Petit from 1961 to 1985.

Q. I did go see Woman in Black. So you are directing again. Have you done any productions there since 1985?

A. Later that same year, 1985, I had been asked, prior to departing, would I do A Christmas Carol, not as a subscription play, but just as a play in December—and I did. But this play, <u>Woman in Black</u>, is the only membership subscription play I've done for them since I left in June of 1985. I had been invited back the next year, too.

Q. You were Executive Director, so you were the only one that was directing at that time?

A. That is correct.

Q. I noticed the last few years they even have been soliciting resumes.

A. Over the past 10 to 11 years, they've changed their policy numerous times; and seems like what they have now is what they call a Managing Director who handles the business end of things; and they "job out" each play to a different director; and that's how they do it now. When I was there, I did all the plays.

Q. That's what I thought.

A. There was an occasional guest director, but out of the hundred and some I did there, I did ninety-nine (99%) percent of them.

Q. The children's theatre—have you directed for the children's theatre?

A. Never.

Q. Do you know when that started?

A. Yes. You need a little background on that space where the children's theatre now is. In 1961, 1962, 1963, somewhere in that two-year spread, so much of the building that the Little Theatre housed had been condemned and had to be done something with. So what they did was tore it down to the ground—not the auditorium—the auditorium remained—and we produced during this—but everything else came down. When it was put back up, they added what is now the children's theatre. When that theatre was built, it was called the "experimental theatre." It was not built to be used as the children's theatre. After several years, it functioned as an experimental theatre—the avant-garde, the off-Broadway type of place. I think it was Luis Barroso, if I am not mistaken, possibly in the 1970s, we were interested then in permitting him to do a children's play in there and one thing led to another, and that led to the birth of the children's theatre which was called, at that time, "Children's Corner." In later years, when Teddy Sciacca became very helpful in there, upon her death, they named it "Teddy's Corner." That's the background of the children's theatre. At one time, it was active enough to justify a full-time director. Luis was on our staff as a full-time children's theatre director. They did four or five or six children's plays a year, but only on weekends and only in the daytime—like at 12:00 or 2:00 on Saturday, and 1:00 and 3:00 on Sunday, an hour-long play.

Q. Are they doing a few productions a year now?

A. Yes. About four.

Q. I know they always do one at Christmas.

A. That's right. That could be <u>A Christmas Carol</u>; I've seen the program for next year. Or maybe they are doing it on the main stage and offering it to children, too. I'm not really sure how that is going to be. I'll find out for you, if that's important.

Q. From time to time, I've noticed that acting classes are offered at the theatre. Were you involved in teaching any acting classes there?

A. No. As Executive Director, which could have been called Executive Director/Managing Director, which now is Managing Director, I engineered several of these projects; I envisioned them happening; I saw to their execution, but I didn't have time to do it. If I was going to direct all the plays, which I did, that was pretty much a full-time job. I think in those days we were doing seven plays. They're just doing six now. I think we were doing seven plays a year.

Q. I've had season tickets through the teachers' discount. They offered us reduced prices because of being teachers. A group of us have been going for years.

A. This teachers' discount that you were getting, does that pre-date my departure from there? When did that start? Was it in the mid-eighties? Earlier than that?

Q. I think it was in the early '80s.

A. Because I kind of think I remember introducing that concept to the Board, and I guess they jumped on that and did it. I just couldn't remember.

Q. It was supposed to be for high school students, college students, and teachers.

A. That's it.

Q. We still have our group. Everybody that originally went. . . .

A. That's wonderful.

Q. It was about ten or fifteen ladies.

A. They'll be happy to hear that it paid off. They still have you.

Q. Okay. Do you have an idea of the approximate number of plays that you directed there?

A. Yes. All right. <u>The Elephant Man</u>, which was my second to last play, was the 500th production of the Little Theatre—not my 500th, because I didn't start with it. But let's do it this way. When you figure from that date—those, those, and those [He now points to a copy of the program.]—how many are we talking about? <u>Everybody Loves Opal</u>, is that the first one?

Q. Yes.

A. I think <u>Shenandoah</u> was my 100th, and I did more after that. I really think it is over 150 to be honest with you.

Q. Okay. Which ones would you consider to be your most memorable plays?

A. I'm going to give you the classic example. It's the one I'm working on now. <u>The Elephant Man</u> stands out; our production of <u>Who's Afraid of Virginia Woolf?</u> was a classic. In that category was <u>A Man For All Seasons</u>, <u>West Side Story</u>, and <u>The Elephant Man</u>. I think those four probably. I could almost put all the musicals in there, too.

Q. Why? What was memorable? Was it the actors, or just everything clicked?

A. Well, first of all, the scripts are outstanding. You start with a brilliant script, and then, as always, in community theatre, you pre-decide, if you get quality people, and in the instance of all of those, I was able to get "star" quality people to appear in all roles. Ninety percent of the director's job is casting. You know after that, if they're good, let them go with it. You just stand there, and tell them where to go.

Q. Okay. How were the plays selected when you were director? Did you have absolute authority?

A. No. The Little Theatre, when it began, had a charter and by-laws that spelled out many things as to the operation. One of those spelled out what each Chair of the Board a board member would occupy—and of production and of membership. One was called play reading; that person was the Chair of the Play-Reading Committee. Now, that person could select one, two, three, eight, however many people from the membership of the Little Theatre, to serve on that committee. However, by Charter, the director was a member of that body. Now, they welcomed the director's input, naturally, because they sent me to New York every year to scout plays. However, I had only one vote on that body. I could try and persuade them; I could try and sway them; I could try to encourage them. The one thing they could not do was make me do a play that I did not want to do. Just like I could not make them do one that they didn't want; they did not make me do one that I didn't want. I felt so strongly that there were reasons why that play was not in our best interests. They had to bow to that wisdom, right or wrong. I believe now here ten years after I've gone, eleven years, a play-reading committee still exists. It's still functioning with the same bylaws that were established in the 1920s, or the teens, or whenever it was.

Q. Was there ever a time when there was a play that you felt very strongly about that you wanted to do that they said you couldn't do?

A. Let me say that I'm sure there was, but I can't remember. Nothing comes to my mind.

Q. More or less, the plays that you wanted to do, you got to do?

A. I think so. You know, they respected me and my abilities, and I won't say that I railroaded them. There was no need for that, but there was a mutual respect. They spent a lot of time, those people. They had to read those plays, because we had a rather in-depth discussion of what they were all about—the plots, the themes, all of that.

Q. The people—besides yourself, and besides the director and the committee—these weren't necessarily theatre people? These were just board members.

A. Correct. They did select for their chairman, usually, someone who was knowledgeable, who attended theatre, and who went to New York or London a lot and saw the plays. Yes.

Q. What would you say, as a director there, were some of your most positive experiences?

A. Well, my longevity. No one prior to me had ever done that. To be renewed annually was—made me feel that I was respected and appreciated. I have a cute little aside there. Along with the theatre, it had been going on for about forty years before I arrived, I was the first native New Orleanian to occupy that chair. All directors prior to me had been imported from somewhere else.

Q. What about any negative experiences?

A. Well, like in anything, there are going to be differences of opinion sometimes between someone who sits in the chair like I did; I mean, I'm not going to say that everybody on the Board, year after year after year, fell in love with everything I said and did. I've had the usual snits and personality clashes, but we overcame them all. I think this occurs in any business. It's in the corporate world. The bottom line was that my output grew (a) popular, (b) successful, and (c) membership-getting. You know, and I think for that reason they were careful that I wasn't going to look for another job somewhere else. Probably the biggest turnaround occurred in the five years over the '80s that I was there, from '80 to '85, that the membership started to take a tumble. I mean a serious tumble. When your sister was involved [in the 1970s], we had annual membership of 8,000 people, and we couldn't fit them all in.

Q. I think there was a waiting list.

A. Yes, a waiting list, and this was not with an open box office. You couldn't just buy a ticket like you can today. It started to take a tumble. Now, this is when certain board members felt possibly Stocker had burnout, and Stocker had done as much as he could do with all of this. That may well have been true, I don't know, but the membership did start to go, and, with it, went the resources, and with the resources, then the staff members had to go. It was a domino effect. The physical look of the place took a tumble. The physical look of the plays took a tumble. But, you know, by then, restaurants had caught on. "Let's really promote dining out." Dining out doesn't mean running to the restaurant at 6:00, and leaving at 7:15 to get to the theatre. Dining, you go at 7:30, and that's the evening's event. National sports have taken hold of things now. The Saints [professional football team] are entrenched in the city now. You know the entertainment dollar can only go so far. The community has so many other theatres. The Beverly [a professional dinner theatre] had opened. This whole new dinner theatre thing came along. So, all of a sudden, there were so many people now vying for the entertainment dollar who had not been, that things just started to tumble. They [Le Petit] haven't rallied to this day. They have not.

Q. How unfortunate!

A. I think I heard—don't quote me—but I think that they have 2,200 members.

Somewhere along the line, someone needs to speak to you about Dr. Emmett Johnson. It's more than just finger pointing at him. For the last five or six years, he has done irreparable damage to the theatre as chairman under the guise of doing good. I was not there, so it would just be hearsay, and it wouldn't be right for me to say. He is not there now. You can only serve two three-year terms consecutively; then you must give up your seat. For your paper to be complete, you will need something on Dr. Emmett Johnson.

Q. Now, did he do any directing?

A. There are those who'll say he did. [Laughs.]

Q. But not officially?

A. He tried to run the roost. The tragedy is, from what I understand, it was all under the guise of "I'm doing right for the organization." He believed that; then he did nothing but do damage to it. He meddled in everything.

Q. Are there any actors that you worked with at Le Petit that have gone on to professional acting careers?

A. I almost have to look at the program. None jump out at me except Bryan Batt. I spawned no superstars. I can't think of any. Some have gone on to minor movies, but no one . . .

Bryan is probably as high up as anybody. Maybe I'm forgetting somebody. Pass on that.

Q. When you were directing there, I assume you were given a certain budget to work with?

A. Correct. Let me tell you how that worked. All these people on the Board, each who had a chair, and one of those positions was called Production Chair, and that person controlled the purse strings. In other words, he or she would go to—when a season was selected, that person did a guestimate or an estimate on how much each play would need—the royalties, the costuming, the musical cost, and all that. When she went to the Board and said, "I need $80,000 to produce that season," they would haggle over that, and end up okay. They told her, as the plays went along, "Look, you've got $5,000.00 for this one; you're at $3,200.00, so you know what you've got to do here." So, to answer your question, yes, budgets were determined prior to the start of the season with "X" amount keynoted for each play, and the plays had to be done within the amount. You could borrow from Play Three for Play Two, and then give back, so to speak.

Q. So, for the most part, you were given enough money?

A. I felt so. The Board realized they were in business to produce plays. They were not in business to make money. It's non-profit. All money had to come back into the billing of the organization. There was no one trying to pay big stock dividends to somebody.

Q. When you did a musical, were the musicians union musicians?

A. They were union musicians, but, frequently, they would permit us, for every hired union musician, they would permit us to use a volunteer non-union musician. Now, throw something in, for what it's worth. Theoretically, those guys are meant to be free by union rules, but we'd give them parking money, cab fare, or baby-sitting expenses. We would do that. Usually, in the musicals, the orchestra was our biggest expense.

Q. Did you have a costumer on staff?

A. There was. However, there was a woman named Ethel Crumb Brett. She predates your dates. She, from almost the start of the theatre until about 1970, was on staff. She was the set designer, the costume designer, and makeup designer, and the set decorator. Now, this did not mean that she didn't have a seamstress to sew for her or a carpenter to build for her, and a painter to paint for her, and volunteers to run box office for her. Ninety percent of what I know is from Ethel.

Q. Now, the actors have never been paid, is that right?

A. Right.

Q. I know that there was a meeting a few years ago. . . .

A. Go ahead, you were about to ask about a meeting. The rebel actors wanting to be paid?

Q. Do you know anything about that?

A. Well, just slightly. I know that it happened. Then, of course, the Board dug its heels in, and said it had never been done that way. They did agree to pay parking. Parking in the Quarter is not cheap.

Q. I know that after they had this meeting, that a lot of the actors refused to work there.

A. That is correct. And some, I think, still have stuck to that. I don't know. You know, the ten years I've been gone, I really have been fairly detached from the theatre. I've not attended all the plays; I'll go once or twice a year, and they now have all these guest directors. It wasn't until this current regime came in that they even called me and asked me if I was interested. So, that doesn't mean that my nose was out of joint or anything; but, I would have thought that they might have felt that I have something to offer the theatre other than nothing. So, I've not been that close to what has gone on during Don's [Don Marshall] time. I don't know all the names of the directors.

Q. Well, you went on to direct at other theatres, and to act, and I hear your voice on TV a lot.

A. Yes. The first two years, I did nothing. When my friend, George Kelly, who had the Bayou Dinner Theatre, asked me to guest direct, which I did, then I had so much fun, he said, "Come on, and stay on." He alternated the plays, he and I. I had a good time there. But when we made this final move out to Metairie, we spent too much; and we spent his operating income; and we had to toss in the towel. But in the four years since then, I've done a lot of directing at the Rivertown Rep. I've directed at Southern Rep., appeared in plays; I've acted in plays; I've done movies. However, when this play (<u>Woman in Black</u>) closes Sunday, there is nothing on the books until next December, though. I will say this; they have no retirement plan at the Little Theatre. I was with the theatre for twenty-five years, and walked away with nothing but a handshake. Nothing. No pension, and no retirement. When Ethel [Crumb Brett] finally retired, after forty-five or fifty years, they had to have a special board meeting to come up with a $50.00 a month thing to give her, which they have never met. Having no retirement policy is an interesting point to make, I think, for your paper, for your dissertation. I think, for a prestigious organization that will, next year, celebrate its eightieth anniversary, and consider themselves one of the oldest, if not <u>the</u> oldest, continuously-performing community theatres in the country, to have no policy of retirement for long-time employees, I think, is unbusinesslike, to say the least.

Q. Did you notice anything different about directing the production that you just directed (<u>Woman in Black</u>), as opposed to directing that you did the last time that you were there?

A. Well, they have come upon such hard financial times. They have a much smaller staff now than they were when I was there. Even when I left, our staff had been reduced. There, virtually, is no staff now. There is a technical director whose job it is to design the scenery, light the show. I brought my own stage manager. He did get a lighting operator. I recommended a props and wardrobe person. So, the difference comes under staff that exists now. Now, it is a very different show that you saw. It is highly technical. It took us a week to do a tech rehearsal; it usually takes a night or two. I knew who was going to be there.

Q. Anything else that you noticed different now? How many people showed up to audition?

A. I brought my two men. I knew that I wanted Leon and Walter. So, I didn't have any auditions. I know the acting community pretty well. I don't know the youngsters, I will say that.

Q. How about when you directed there before? Did you have open auditions?

A. Yes. And, I guess when I go back next winter, they are going to want that policy again.

Q. What thoughts do you have about the future of Le Petit?

A. I'll tell you exactly what I told the board members about six months ago. If, by charter, they must stay where they are, must remain there, they can count the years before it's all over. If they have any opportunity—and I'll explain why I'm saying that—to get out, they better take it. The people are getting scared to go in the Quarter; the people are finding it expensive to go in the Quarter; the people don't like that the homeless are all over.

Q. In other words, you think they should leave the building and go elsewhere?

A. I mean they will not last ten more years if they have to stay where they are. That is contributing to their small membership.
Now, there is something in the charter that, if this organization has to go under, has to close, has to do anything, the property is to be equally divided between Tulane, Loyola, and LSU. There was no UNO [University of New Orleans] when the charter was started. So, I don't know if—whether that precludes their being able to make a move. I heard the board chairman once say that that corner was valued at $4,000,000.00, and that's when I said, "Take the money and run!" I do not see—to answer your question—a turnaround, in a positive way, occurring as long as they are where they are. Time has passed that location by. And, it is regrettable. It is a charming place.

Q. I wondered if the building had been declared a historic landmark?

A. I don't think so. Only because the part that would have been declared that was the part they tore down because it was falling apart. It was crumbling. The auditorium was put up in 1921 or 1922. So, I don't think that's old enough to declare it that, and the remainder was done in the early '60s.

Q. Basically, the stage and the auditorium, though, that hasn't changed?

A. Correct.
I know they have newer seats than they had years ago. As far as the physical and the architectural structure, that is what was put up in the 1920s, the early '20s. The backstage area, the dressing rooms. . . that's all upstairs. Nothing is downstairs. That's all above Children's Corner.

Q. You mentioned Tulane—and I know that Tulane was very much involved with the theatre.

A. Dr. Monroe Lippmann, who was head of the Drama Department for a long time, but which had no theatre facility at Tulane, engineered something with Le Petit where they worked together, and students would work there on internships and learn the craft. That's where they worked together. I was part of that program.

Q. It would seem to me that that would be really good to have one of the colleges involved. Do you know why they stopped the program?

A. Because Tulane finally got a theatre. You asked about the backstage. When you are sitting in the auditorium, there's the stage—stage right goes all the way to Chartres Street—you can just stand there and see the traffic go by on Chartres Street if the door was opened. The only thing that is not completely open is the shell that would be Children's Corner across the patio. That stage encloses some portion of that. But, otherwise, all of that is one expansive space, and that's the shop where they build, where the scenery can be wagoned on and off, and all of that. Then, above that, which is the third floor, is warehouses and storage, and there's a lift to let things come down from up there to the stage. As far as the building, you asked about the differences. Everything was so well organized when I was there. Spaces that were meant to be spaces were just that. The greenroom was the greenroom. Now, it's a warehouse, a storage area. The set director's office has now become a clutter. The attic was kept so neatly organized with everything—the wardrobe, the props, the furniture. Now, the stairs are just crawling with stuff that never seems to get back up there.

Q. Was that because of lack of staff?

A. Sure. What's the point of having this marvelous property if you don't have the people to run it? One of their biggest assets right now is a little Oriental man named Arthur Tong. Arthur is a volunteer. And, they work him night and day, seven days a week, and he loves it. He knows he is being used, but he loves being there. That's his life.

Q. I was under the mistaken impression that the Tennessee Williams Festival had something to do with Le Petit. I called someone that I know that was involved in that. She said all they did was rent the space.

A. They are correct.
There have been some other productions there from time to

time. I think <u>Forever Plaid</u> was there.

If the space is available to be rented out, and not interfere with the season, they do it. They have wedding receptions there on Saturday afternoons, parties, all of that. So, the space is available for everything from productions, parties, luncheons, style shows, whatever. And, that's not new. I helped institute that. I also instituted something when I was there called "co-produced by." In other words, let's say Whitney Bank wants to put up $5,000.00. Le Petit and Whitney Bank of New Orleans presents <u>The Time of your Life</u>. It's a co-production. Contributions, donations to the theatre to help them get through the rough times.

Q. Did you find companies that were willing to do that?

A. Yes. Banks, hotels, furniture stores, bakeries. Yes, we did that.

Q. Any additional comments that you want to make?

A. Nothing right now, but, now that you have opened this door, I'll start thinking again.

Q. Thank you for your time.

INTERVIEWER: REBECCA HALE
INTERVIEWED: April 2, 1996
RESPONDENT: LYLA HAY OWEN
Professional Actor/Director/Teacher

Q. You had your own theatre. What was the name of that?

A. People Playhouse. A lot of actors came out of my theatre, too. Playwrights, too. Luis Barroso was the director of the plays, and he commissioned me to write . . . well, he said, "Lyla, what's your favorite fairy tale?" And I said, "<u>The Little Mermaid</u>." So he asked me if I would write it for the Children's Corner. He had that kind of freedom. So I wrote <u>The Little Mermaid,</u> <u>The Red Shoes</u>. . . . I wrote three <u>Raggedy Ann and Raggedy Andys</u>. I wrote the book, music, and lyrics. I wrote the lyrics for some of Freddy Palmisano's work. There was a lot of New Orleans talent creating original works for Le Petit Children's Corner. At that time, I think there was some arrangement with Tulane. We did, for New Orleans, some really avant-things. Le Petit was absolutely the center. It was so exciting; it really was. I think the problems started for the theatre overall in 1970. The Children's Corner was still exciting for the next couple of years until 1975. Then it started to lose its power and its focus—when Stocker left and when Luis Barroso left. They were two very strong, creative people. They evolved interesting work. Everything was fine, and, then suddenly, everything got cut off. Luis came to my theatre, and he did <u>A Doll's House</u>; he worked with me in <u>Uncle Vanya</u> and <u>The Three Sisters</u>. He's a fine actor. He graduated from Tulane. His MFA production was <u>Waiting for Godot</u>. I just worked with Luis this year when I wrote and (Luis) did <u>Phantom of the French Opera</u>. I wrote the play, and he directed it. I didn't go down there and direct. All of my children's things were directed by him.

Q. How long did you have your theatre?

A. About nine years. First, it was on Magazine Street. Then we moved to Apple Street. I wanted just to be an artist again. It is very difficult to be a concierge. One of my favorite stories is—and this tells it all—I was with Phil Yayma in <u>Uncle Vanya</u> and I was getting ready to go on in this pretty little silk dress—literally in the wings, and my little stage manager comes over to me and whispers, "Lyla, Lyla, the toilet's stopped up." Then I had to make my entrance into Chekov's world. It was like . . . I can't be a concierge. But nobody wants to do that part of the work. Everybody wants to be artistic.

Q. In any way was your theatre modeled after a theatre like Le Petit?

A. It was the antithesis of Le Petit. Absolutely, the antithesis. My first plays that my group got together was a group of my "One-Acts," songs. Le Petit didn't do experimental. They never really did experimental.

Q. In the 1930s, they claimed they did experimental, but it

really wasn't because they had to make money.

A. Absolutely. The amount of subscriptions. My God, that theatre was packed. The Children's Corner was packed. The Main Stage was packed. It's pitiful now. One person can't do everything. Joel Rainey tried to do it all, and several other people tried. But poor Joel Rainey.

Q. In the times that you have worked there or performed there, do you know of anyone, other than Richard Schechner, that worked there that could be considered famous? Someone who has gone on to a professional career?

A. Well, I consider myself a professional. Jan Bertram, who was in <u>Everything in the Garden,</u> Stocker directed—it's supposedly written by Albee, but is so unlike an Albee play. Jim O'Quinn—he worked with me for all my music at Le Petit—he is now the editor of <u>American Theatre Magazine</u>. I know that Bryan Batt is in New York. My daughter, Cynthia. I wrote a role for her in one of my <u>Raggedy Ann and Andy</u> shows for the Children's Corner. Luis directed her. I remember Luis in the back yelling, "Cynthia, I can't hear you." Now, today, you can hear her over a thirty-piece orchestra. She's at Le Petit.

I have an interesting story to tell you about something that happened at Le Petit a long time ago. This was in the early 1970s [it was actually 1967], and Richard Schechner, who was then a Tulane University drama professor, directed a play by Eugene Ionesco at Le Petit. It was called <u>Victims of Duty</u>. I was in it. The word had gotten out that this was a really good production. Ellen Stewart, who founded La Mama Theatre [La Mama Experimental Theatre Club] in New York, wanted the actors at Le Petit, myself included, to perform the play at La Mama. We were all excited about going. Unfortunately, when Richard Schechner asked the Board of Governors for $600 that we needed to take the production to New York, the Board refused. One member said, "We don't sell subscriptions to Le Petit in New York." That was that, and we didn't get to go.

The plant at Le Petit is so professional. The seating, the acoustics, there is really nothing like it anywhere. And there is nothing like it in New Orleans. At the time when I was in its glow, and they had all these people designing. . . . There is room, really, at the helm right now leading people. When I come in now (at Le Petit), it used to be that they had someone doing things. Now you have to find your own designer, costumer; you have to do everything.

Q. Approximately how many seats does the Children's Corner have?

A. Arthur Tong could tell you that. Somewhere between 150 to 200. It also depends on what mood that Arthur's in, too. The way he seats.

Q. I would think attendance would be good for those plays?

A. It depends. My plays at the Children's Corner have always been well attended. But then, the next one, everybody starts from scratch, everybody is on their own, and maybe publicity didn't get out in time. People don't know what to do.

Q. Do you have any upcoming plans to direct there?

A. No, I tell you the way they are headed. . . . They talked to me about a couple of plays next year. The only plays that were open, nobody cares about. <u>The Sound of Music</u> and <u>Scrooge</u> at Christmas?
I really don't want to work there at the moment. I have devoted a great deal of my creative energy to this theatre, and I don't need all that aggravation. I really don't think they know what they are doing. The theatre has lost its direction.

Q. What has been your favorite production that you have been associated with at Le Petit?

A. I think my production of <u>The Snow Queen</u>. They were done at other places, my plays. At other universities around the country.

Q. And your <u>Phantom</u> was done recently?

A. It was done last November, December. It was a Christmas production at Le Petit.

Q. Nothing currently going on at the Children's Corner?

A. <u>Li'l Abner</u>.

Q. I was told that a few years ago they had a meeting in New Orleans with all the major actors. The actors thought that Le Petit should be changed. Did you attend that?

A. No. One of my favorite things at Le Petit was when I did
The Rose Tatoo with Ivan Uttal. I would say that was one
of my happiest experiences as an actress anywhere. Ivan
was a great director. But the next year . . . the Board is so
stupid. . . . Ivan wanted to do A Streetcar . . ., and he asked
me if I would do it. And, of course, I would. So he had a
meeting with Don Marshall, and Don said, "Well, you have
to write some proposal." And Ivan wanted to know why,
because they had settled it over a cup of coffee last year.
Don said, "That's the way the Board wants it this year."
And Ivan said, "That doesn't make sense to me. I am not
going to do it."
So, again, the Board decides arbitrarily that this year you
can't do that. So I know Ivan can be pigheaded, but he
decided he wasn't going through all that with the Board. He
said to me, "They just don't know the difference." So he
refused to do it. So it didn't happen. He swears people in
New Orleans don't know good theatre, so why bother.
Ah, Le Petit. They have no direction. One production is
good, the next is wonderful, and the next one is. . . . What?
What is this? Everything is so uneven. It's just like a
restaurant. If one meal is good, but the next is vile, you
can't build a reputation on that.

Q. We notice in our little group, it used to be that all six or
seven plays were very good. There would be some you
liked better than others. Now you are lucky if you get one
that is good.

A. I don't go anymore. I don't support Le Petit anymore.

Q. For us, it is a social occasion.

A. Well, I'm glad for that. But I don't think it's the time. I think it's the leadership. You need an artistic director; you need a good business manager.

Q. How do you see the New Orleans theatre scene at the present time?

A. It's actually. . . . There's nothing I'm interested in . . . really nothing . . . because it's all like community theatre . . . There are real egos getting out there doing . . . la de dah de dah . . . "Do you love me?" There's no . . . you have to have training; you have to have a methodology; you have to have a better vision, I think. For me, it's too exciting to. . . . I've been asked to do an acting workshop—a special acting workshop—for adults. We need people that know how to work, that are not just out there for their egos. Directors. There's some good musical theatre here. But theatre is more than musical comedy. So I feel a great lack—in real directors. And musical comedy is alive and well in New Orleans; there's a lot going on. And the rest of the theatre is pitiful. What about you?

Q. Of course, I find myself spending most of my summers in New York. And even though I feel there's tons of work to do, and, obviously, these classes I'm in, I've been doing a lot of research and even the acting and directing classes, you've got a lot of rehearsing to do. So I go to the theatre. That's why I'm there. I know I'm only there for the summer, so I'll go to Off-Broadway or Broadway; it doesn't matter. I like to see a variety of plays. So, consequently, when I come back—and I want to support the theatre here—but what happens is I'll say, I don't feel like spending $15 to see that. I'd rather spend $30 to see something in New York. I hate to have that attitude, but, yet, you can't help but have it. Even in New York, I don't feel like seeing something that's not going to be good either.

A. I don't want to spend my life watching other people just trotting across a stage, you know, just pomp and circumstance, nonsense—they are boring. They call that acting?

Q. Yes, I know what you mean. I'll go see productions if I know someone in it—like a former student.

A. Yes. I'm going tonight because a darling little actress, Soline McClain, was in my <u>The Snow Queen</u>. She was darling. I've worked with her, so I'm going to be a supportive guidance. The idea of going over there is painful, but I'm going to go. Not because of her, but—because I dread the other work. But, I have been asked to do so many things, and I have not done them. I've refused. I'm sorry, I'm busy. But, look, the bottom line is you can't work on a stage alone. You're working with a director. And if you are working with a director that has no vision, I know why would you turn down a role like that? Because I know theatre is more than one actor. It's the director; it's everybody.

Q. Let me get one more quote from you.

A. Sure.

Q. How do you see the future of Le Petit?

A. Le Petit? Unless they get an artistic director and a good business manager, I think they'll just start renting the place out. Because a business manager is something drastic that they should have. There's no focus. Nobody knows what they're doing there. And they are at odds—everyone's at odds with one another. They keep making one bad decision after another. You know, this man's the third person in four years' time. And I don't think he's the person. But things ebb and flow. Hey, if the right person comes along? Look at Don Marshall. Don Marshall knows the lay of that land better than anybody else. Not that he was a real bitter person. I never thought he was. He's strong in the visual arts, and he's another great mollifier and diplomat—like Stocker [Fontelieu]. He did as well by Le Petit as anybody since Stocker.

But, there was just an artist—Mary Ellen. . . .

Q. I know.

A. Her husband taught at UNO—O'Brien. Wonderful actress! Wonderful lady. . . .

Q. We were in an industrial film together.

A. A lovely lady. But, running a theatre and being an artist are two different things. I don't think the Board understands that. Yet, an artistic director wouldn't give him all this latitude, really—creative. You just got to have a business manager there to make it happen. I don't think one person can do both jobs. It's just not possible. I had a theatre. I know.

Q. I know. For instance, when Stocker directed, he was the only director for the twenty-four years—pretty much. Do you think it's better to have one person directing all the plays like that, or the fact that they get in the so-called "guest artists". . . .

A. I think so. I don't know.

Q. You think it's ideal to have the one?

A. Well, ideal for me would be one director for dramas, one for musicals, and yet another for children's plays.

Q. I agree with you.

A. That's ideal, you know. I think that a straight director, a director of straight plays, could make it happen—with the choreographer and the musical director. But, I think that's the way to do it. Oh, absolutely. Straight through. Because we're not talking, you know, about . . . any great theatre's had a division of one or two people—from the Moscow Art Theatre to a repertory company.
But the design of that plant, the interior design, the backstage, the scenes, dressers, costumers . . . there's something about all of that. It just works.

Q. One thing Stocker told me was that, now, when you go . . . you used to be able to find things in a nice order, and now, when you go into the boxes, you . . . it's really a mess, which he attributed to not enough help.

A. Oh, definitely. They need somebody to volunteer . . . there's nobody organizing. I borrowed some costumes for my old production about a year and a half ago. We did some Shakespearean pieces. And I brought them back after a year. And they had been hanging up, and I put them in a garbage bag to transport them over there. Well, anyway, when I was doing my <u>Phantom</u> this year, I saw them on the floor upstairs with all kinds of stuff piled on top of them. They don't even know what they've got.

Q. From what you could tell, do they have a lot of costumes there?

A. Just between us, they could fill . . . I could have kept those costumes forever. But I wouldn't do that. But there are people who do. Do you know how many people have keys to the costume room that come and go? I've been there during rehearsals, there were people coming through the back door. . . . Once, there was a drunk man sleeping in the back between the scenery. I mean, literally! Crawled in among the scenery and just gone to sleep. Yes! Yes! Yes! It's a shame. Le Petit, literally, is just disintegrating, falling apart. There are wood panels knocked out.

Q. The fact that it's in the French Quarter, was that ever a problem for you . . . directing the acting over there? You know, some people say they don't like to work there because you have to pay to park.

A. You don't have to pay to park! They pay for parking!

Q. Yes, but they didn't always do that.

A. No, they didn't. But they have for years and years, because Stocker always said. . . . They have arranged to do parking, of course, if you are volunteering . . . but the costumers, that was another story. But, at that time, it was a community theatre.

Q. And, of course, originally, in the '20s, when theatre was first starting, that was the place to go.

A. Yes, you could live there. It was real Bohemian. It was okay. I lived in the Quarter, too, and walked to work.

Q. I like going to the Quarter. I don't have a problem with it.

A. Me either.

Q. We're grown women that go in our group. And we go out to eat. So, it's a social thing. But, we don't have a problem with going there. I hear people say, "Oh, I'm not going down there." Well, I'm not living locked in my house either.

A. Anyone who attributes the demise of Le Petit to that—no. I think it has to do with the division of power. It's an interesting era. Nothing's going on. Who cares? Who knows even what's going on? You used to know what was coming up. Maybe they've sent out mailouts. The paper used to do advertising.

Q. Yes, now you don't know until after you've missed a production. There should be a PR person handling it.

A. Exactly. It's the people. Because when I was a teacher, I'd go from school to school. And I could tell you how good that school is when I walk in that office. How they're eating. Shuffling down the hallway with their bedroom slippers on, whatever they're doing. . . . It's the principal. How he or she handles it, runs it. And everybody follows suit, right? It's the leader. It's always leadership. It's leadership. Schools, theatres. In business. Bottom line—that's what it is. There's no leadership.

Q. In any of the productions that you directed, did school children ever go to productions at night or on weekends?

A. No. It wasn't geared for that. Southern Rep is and NOCCA [New Orleans Center for Creative Arts]. They'd do a couple of things on the main stage. But it's strictly for that. That's why they did that. No, there wasn't. No.

Q. I had taken groups of students to see The Glass Menagerie and Streetcar, but that was part of a Tennessee Williams Festival. So I guess they weren't really Le Petit doing that.

A. No.

Q. I often thought that, when plays were really good, it would have been nice, at that time—and I realize the problem, because you're dealing with people that are not being paid, and they work other jobs. You can't just take off at your day jobs. You know, people work various things—lawyers and doctors, and so on—but I've often thought it would have been nice if kids could see some of those plays. And then a lot of them, they're not going to go on their own.

A. Oh, yeah. But, then, the actors, that's another issue. Not being paid. Well, they do, a certain percentage they pay at certain dinner theatres. Look at Kenner Rep. Good leadership. I mean, let's just build another theatre. A better mousetrap. Right? You build a better mousetrap and people will lead a pathway to your door. You can say it's anything. Same thing with my theatre. Looks good.

Q. It must have been fun owning your own theatre. I always say, "If I win the lottery, that's what I want to do." I would love to!

A. UNO. George Wood.

Q. He was a major professor on my thesis.

A. Right before he died, he said, "Oh, Lyla, if I had won the lottery, when my ship comes in, all my money's going to go to theatre."
I disagree with Ivan. People do know good theatre. But if you spend a long time not showing people good theatre, they will kind of get brain dead. But that's what happens. You have one director covering the production values at Children's Corner. You'll look at every play you go to, and there will be something valuable. It was just wonderful.

Q. Thank you very much for your time.

INTERVIEWER: REBECCA HALE
INTERVIEWED: May 7, 1996
RESPONDENT: DON MARSHALL
Former Managing Director at Le Petit (1986-91)

Q. What are the strong points of Le Petit Theatre?

A. The building and the organization.

Q. What are the weak points of Le Petit Theatre?

A. The building and the organization.

Q. Did you also direct at Le Petit?

A. No.

Q. Please elaborate on your first two comments.

A. Mary Ellen O'Brien, who followed Stocker Fontelieu, ran into problems with the Board. They were ready to criticize her. It was a hateful ending to her one-year appointment. I was hired by Pat Haun, who was President of the Board and the first non-traditional member. She was dynamic. The Board should give the actors every possible benefit—the best director, etc.—if not paying them. They should find the best script familiar to audiences, probably through movies. My job at Le Petit was to get money. When you present a good artistic product, people come to the theatre and the theatre makes money.

I wrote grants and expanded the staff. At one point when

the Symphony disbanded, Le Petit was the largest subscription in town. It was left with a $51,000 surplus. They still had the Play-Reading Committee that made decisions about the plays.

By the fourth year, I got bored. I started a series of school groups coming to the theatre during the day; I got grant money to pay actors for taking off of work to perform during the day. Kay Files, the costumer, was paid, but the Board didn't want to pay her. An EXXON member got on the Board, as well as people from the business community. They also got Emmett Johnson, a power-hungry Nazi, a control freak, who hates women. He had his following on the Board. Seven of the sixteen board members got together, met, and wanted to get rid of Emmett Johnson, or they would resign. Emmett Johnson moved to the chairman's spot at the meeting and took control. Seven members resigned. Lary Hesdorfer was one who resigned. Emmett Johnson took over everything. The Board decided they didn't need me, so I resigned.

You became an active member by volunteering. Of 3,600 members, maybe eighty-two were active members. The members sixty years old and over were afraid of change, afraid new people would take over—the first problem I had. I wanted to change active membership. Martha Samuels called Lary Hesdorfer a traitor. The older members would fight change. Lines were drawn between the old and new members.

Peggy Scott Laborde and I initiated talks about having a Tennessee Williams Festival. Others wanted a literary festival. I wanted to combine a literary festival with Tennessee Williams; this became the beginning of the Tennessee Williams Festival.

Q. Getting back to the strong points of Le Petit...

A. The facility and survival. The Board needs to address amateur versus professional theatre. The lack of professional theatre in New Orleans could be traced to the success of Le Petit as an amateur theatre. The building is wonderful; you feel like you're in a European theatre. Emmett Johnson eventually took a leave of absence and went to Paris. Many board members were afraid of him. The <u>Times Picayune</u> made Richard Dodds tone down his original article on the changing of Le Petit.
The charter has prevented the organization from growing. You know, Le Petit bills itself as being the oldest continuously-running community theatre in the country, but it's actually about 26th. You can check with the American Association of Community Theatres about that.
I tried to revive Children's Corner while I was there. I contacted Judy Latour to revive it. I also initiated the subscription series for Children's Corner in 1988. I also introduced the Family Fine Arts Series for school kids. Getting back to the weak points of Le Petit, there is a need to open up; it is too closed; it's not really open at all; it's a community from the 1920s. The theatre also needs to produce quality plays.

Q. Thank you for your comments.

INTERVIEWER: REBECCA HALE
INTERVIEWED: June 24 & 25, 1996
RESPONDENT: ARTHUR TONG
Unofficial Historian/Photographer/Volunteer of over thirty years

Q. There were two theatres?

A. Back in the year 1968, we had two theatres. One was the main theatre; and we had an experimental theatre on the other side of the building, which was in collaboration with LSUNO, and in those days when they did avant-garde plays, etc. That lasted to 1970, and September 1, 1970 . . . we started the Children's Theatre with Luis Barroso and I . . . we started the Le Petit's Children's Theatre. We would have original productions written for us. . . . I'd never buy a published script. The parents would buy the tickets for the kids to see the entertainment. So the parents would be familiar with the fairy tales that were known for a long time.
[At this point, Tong is showing Mrs. Hale a picture of the first show from the scrapbook.]
Our second show was in January of '71, called <u>Aladdin</u>. All our scripts were written by local people; they were made campy; so that way, the adults would be entertained also. Adults will get bored with a production and won't bring the children back anymore, you see? So we had a set psychology about these children's productions. In February and March of '71—the theatre season starts from September

to June. So we did a series of Brothers Grimm stories for our third production. I believe it was three of the <u>Grimm's Fairy Tales</u>. And then when we opened in May of '71, we did the <u>Little Mermaid</u>.

Q. You had someone write that, too?

A. Oh, yes! All our scripts were written for us by one person. Freddy Palmisano wrote all the music for these productions. We have all of the original programs and reviews, too. The next one we did was <u>Mary Poppins</u>. Yes, that's correct.

Q. Is this theatre still a member of the Southwest Theatre Conference? Does it still belong?

A. I think it does, but I don't know.
[Mr. Tong, at this point, has been leafing through a scrapbook of Le Petit Children's Theatre.]
Now, here's a picture of Peggy Ann Scott Laborde, who is at Channel 12 now. She was the "Princess-in-Waiting" of children's theatre here back in 1970. Here is a picture of Peggy at Gallery Circle playing in <u>Rumplestiltskin</u>.

Q. That was a separate theatre? That wasn't here?

A. Yes. We had formed our own group here. What actually happened was . . . Barroso and I had children's theatre over there for two years, but we outgrew the place. They made us an offer over here [Le Petit], so we moved over here.

Q. You were first at Gallery Circle?

A. Yes, for two years with children's theatre. Now, this was an article [referring to the scrapbook] about all the children's theatre in New Orleans at that time. These two paragraphs tell that we started at Gallery Circle, and then we moved over here. The second season of children's theatre would be 1971 and 1972. We opened with <u>Pinocchio</u>. The seats became very dear because of the way we had operated. So we know that we opened the second season with <u>Pinocchio</u>, and then we did <u>Babes in Toyland</u> around Christmastime of '71.

Q. This was adapted by John Simons. Was this somebody from New Orleans?

A. No. He was from Dallas, Texas. We used his script that particular time. That was the first time we used somebody else's script. But it was a tremendous script. Our philosophy was to keep the parents entertained also. They buy the tickets and bring the children. That's why the psychology of children's theatre is altogether different from main theatre. That was from our experience. Then we went into March of 1972. We did <u>Red Shoes</u>.
<u>Cinderella</u> was in May of '72. We had a repertoire of about fifteen plays written for us. And at the end of three years, we had a habit of repeating the plays over. The scrapbook is more accurate and in order than anything else. Then we did <u>Brothers Grimm</u> in July of '72. We did a series of <u>Brothers Grimm</u> tales. We did the <u>Wonderful World of the Brothers Grimm</u> in February of '71. Then we did another <u>Brothers Grimm</u>. . . . I'd have to look that up. Here it is . . . 1977. The third season of Children's Corner, we did <u>Beauty and</u>

the Beast, in November '72. Barroso won the National Award for Children's Theatre from the American Theatre Association. They based the award on the strength of my photos in the newspaper [Dixie Magazine]. I recently had this on display. We won the national honor in our third year. Mr. Barroso had to appear in New York at the annual convention of the American Theatre Association to pick up that award. Then we did The Adventures of Robin Hood in early '73. We only did about four children's shows a season.

Q. You must love the theatre to have done this all these years?

A. Yes. I'll tell you something. I've been going on with this for fifty-two years now. Barroso and I stuck together for nine seasons here. Then he moved on to better things in Atlanta, Georgia, to the Center of Puppetry Arts. It was only recently that he came back to do The Phantom of the French Opera House, written by Lyla Hay Owen.
[At this point, Mr. Tong is showing Mrs. Hale pictures of previous plays.]
Now, we redid Aladdin in the fourth season and that would be in '74.
Then for the close of that season, we did The Emperor's New Clothes. That was the second edition of it.
That year was our 5th season. So children's theatre ground along in existence. When Mr. Barroso left, all the color was gone. We had established such an outstanding reputation in children's theatre in this country. He [Barroso] stayed in Atlanta for nine years as director of the Puppetry Arts

Center.

My career didn't start here, you see. I first started off in 1964 strictly as a photographer for the children's theatre. My heart is in children's theatre because children's theatre is more creative to do because children are fascinated by colors and the theatre stage magic. And that's why I enjoy doing children's theatre better than I enjoy doing adult theatre. The outlook is altogether different . . . a lot of people don't understand that.

I have to refer to the program to see the chronological order of all these plays.

Q. You don't have a list of all this?

A. No. I'm the only one here who keeps records of all this and, frankly, I don't have time to write. I take pictures for a living, you see, and I still do. Right now, I can tell you, as old as I am, I'm just getting to be known all over town. All these years, I kept a low profile because I used to do work of a commercial nature . . . advertising and all that. . . . When the oil rush came along around the 1960s, I concentrated all my time in theatre. . . . Well, that's the story of my life, but it is interwoven with the theatre groups here.

Would you like to continue on the chronological order of the plays?

Q. Yes, please.

A. In 1969, we did <u>Marco Polo</u> at the Trinity Church because we had a touring company also. I was a firm believer in keeping everything in the theatre scrapbook. We had a traveling show in the suburbs that would go touring.

Q. Is that from Gallery Circle or from here [Le Petit]?

A. Yes, it was from here [Le Petit]. It was known as the Calliope Players. We played in shopping centers.

Q. About how many years did that go on?

A. About two or three years, I imagine.

Q. You performed at libraries or shopping centers?

A. Yes, it was mostly Clearview Shopping Center. They would always book us in the month of August for a back-to-school promotion. That is where they tied us in with the children. Somewhere in the scrapbook, it will show that . . . there it is . . . at the Clearview Shopping Center. We presented Rumplestiltskin, Luis Barroso's Calliope Players.
I could give you two histories of the theatre here . . . one about children's theatre, and one about the main stage. Now, we also made an appearance at the Travel Lodge. When there were some merchants that wanted to attract families for holidays, that's how we would get booked. One example would be Labor Day, which is a long weekend—Saturday, Sunday, and Monday. We made an appearance at the Travel Lodge.
This [Mr. Tong is showing Mrs. Hale a particular scrapbook.] is the beginning of my career. I was connected with the New Orleans Recreational Department with their theatre program. These pictures represent a big exposure for

me. As long as I have this material, I am able to prepare for interviews like this one. Now here is a picture of the heyday of our children's theatre. That was the only time the theatre was in the round.

Q. It's different now, right?

A. Yes! Well, it can change. It all depends on the director and how they want to present a play.
Now this was something [showing pictures of <u>Sleeping Beauty</u>] that we recently knocked ourselves out for . . . we got such rave reviews. You see, these Christmas tree lights? They were actors who were roped and could swing down at a moment's notice. <u>Sleeping Beauty</u> had four girls in it. The script was written with one girl for each season, if I can remember correctly. You can see that Barroso and I had a fabulous career here.
Now this picture is the only one of this theatre that I made with a fish-eye lens. I'll have to refer to the scrapbook for the date of that.
Now let me see if I can find . . . here it is . . . this is the play we are going to repeat this winter, <u>A Christmas Carol</u>. Here is a picture from the original <u>Cinderella</u>, and here is one from that Disney film, <u>The Wizard of Oz</u> [Disney did not make <u>The Wizard of Oz</u>]. Now here is a picture of <u>Mary Poppins</u> with Cindy Owens. Here is <u>The Emperor's New Clothes</u>.

Q. That was in '74?

A. Yes, May of '74.

Q. Here is <u>Little Red Riding Hood</u>. Is that '74?

A. No, that's '71. Some of this is out of order. There must be some more pages missing from this one here. . . . This is how children's theatre started at Gallery Circle. This was an interview with the Junior League Women of New Orleans.

Q. This doesn't have anything to do with Le Petit?

A. No. This is just how children's theatre got started.

Q. Do they videotape all the productions now? Or just sometimes?

A. That's been in recent years . . . sometime after Stocker left. When Stocker was here, all they did was still pictures. After Stocker left, we had so many people here. . . . I think Luis stayed nine seasons, and then he left.
[Mrs. Hale and Mr. Tong are going through the scrapbook.]

Q. They did this [<u>The Adventures of Raggedy Ann and Andy</u>] in '76 and they did the <u>Further Adventures</u> in '77. They are both by Lyla [Hay Owen].

A. Yes. Now here is something else when Luis was here, but I can't tell what the date is.

Q. Now the guy, Eddie Enriques, didn't he go on to Hollywood to do make-up?

A. Yes, he was a good make-up man. He's still pretty busy. The last time he came back to New Orleans, about four years ago, he told me that he was working on productions back-to-back. He was very busy because he was a terrific make-up man. He's been out in Hollywood since he left here. Then we had David Potter, who was a technical man for the children's theatre. He also left for Hollywood. He stayed out there. He was strictly involved in the production of film work.

Q. Is he still there?

A. Yes. And the last thing that he did in New Orleans was Ann Rice's <u>Vampire</u>. He was in charge of getting all the locations. Every once in a while he gets to come back to New Orleans with some film company.

Q. Have they ever used this building or the courtyard to do any filming?

A. Well, we have so many stages here along with the courtyard . . . some people used them, but I can't remember what stage or year . . . we get so many commercials and all that, I can't keep track of it.
[At this point, Mr. Tong and Mrs. Hale are browsing through old programs and pictures.]
My negative file is at home, and they are in chronological order. I would tell you all the dates of the productions from that. I cannot tell you the order.
After Barroso left and there were guest directors for every production, it was hard to keep tabs on all the stuff around here.

Q. They've done <u>A Christmas Carol</u> a few times?

A. Yes. It went over well.

Q. What do you like best about working here?

A. The physical plant here is so professional. Good lighting in photography is like good theatre. They work hand in hand, you know. But I enjoy doing children's theatre more than I do adult theatre. Because children respond to stage perception different than adults. They are fascinated by colors and they are fascinated by theatre magic—the special effects and all that goes into a production. The whole psychology is altogether different from adult shows. You can really pull out the stops doing children's theatre. It's so much fun to do a show. They enjoy the shows better than an adult, because it is so sophisticated. What we put on stage, they are fascinated by . . . the lighting, special effects, sound. It puts them in a different world . . . different from TV. I'll give you one example:
One day we were doing a production called <u>The Brave Little Tailor</u>. A gnome kidnaps the little tailor and puts him in a sack. Well, a little boy got so involved in the play that he jumped up on stage and started beating up the gnome. We thought it was so funny that at curtain call, we brought him up on stage to take the curtain call. That was the funniest thing to happen on that stage. Never in my lifetime have I ever seen that.
Ever since Stocker left, things around here are like night and day. Every director does things his way and all that. So it's been pretty hard to keep things up here. When Stocker was here, we got albums for each production.

Q. He left in '84? [It was actually 1985.]

A. Yes, '84. I would have to look that up. I have records at home.

Q. This has been very helpful, and I thank you so much for your time.

A. I wish I could help you more. It's different now with people coming and going. It's been pretty hard keeping things up around here. Nobody wanted to follow the system that we had for years under Stocker. It's a shame because when you fill out applications for grants, you've got to show people what you do with your money so they can give you more. The more you show, the possibilities of you getting money increases. But they don't think that way around here anymore. On the educational side, if you teach grammar school students, you can get grants on that alone; but they don't understand that. It's sad . . . they need the money, and they don't know how to go about it.

Q. Let me ask you this. You know how they advertise that they are the oldest continuously-running theatre? Well, there are some other theatres that dispute that. I have been checking into that. There is one in North Carolina; there is one in Pennsylvania that may have opened earlier. Do you know anything about that?

A. No. I could show you some programs from the very first year on the stage. If there are theatres around the country that have been operating continuously since 1916 . . . I just don't know. But I can say this . . . the very first year they started here, they joined the Theatre Association. I have some documents at home that could help. I know they started in 1916.

Q. Do you think the location here has hurt the theatre at all?

A. Yes and no. Physical locationwise, this is the prime location in the Quarter . . . right next to Jackson Square. But the parking problem here . . . a lot of people resent having to spend $7 to $10 a night to park their cars in order to come see a play. And that could be one of the reasons we are losing ground.

Q. What about the actors? Are they reimbursed for parking?

A. Yes. To a certain point.

[The interview was concluded at this point.]

INTERVIEWER: REBECCA HALE
INTERVIEWED: July 22, 1996
RESPONDENT: LOIS CRANDELL
Actress

Q. In what plays have you acted at Le Petit?

A. <u>Caesar and Cleopatra</u>, <u>Once in a Lifetime</u>, <u>The Cherry Orchard</u>, <u>Hay Fever</u>, <u>Let Us Be Gay</u>, <u>The Women</u>, <u>Affairs of State</u>, <u>Sabrina Fair</u>, <u>The Chalk Garden</u> (1956-57), <u>Once More, with Feeling</u>, <u>Breath of Spring</u>, <u>Five Finger Exercise</u>, <u>The Pleasure of His Company</u>, <u>Not in the Book</u>, <u>Never Too Late</u>, <u>You Can't Take It With You</u>, <u>Any Wednesday</u>, <u>The Lion in Winter</u>, <u>Look Homeward, Angel</u>, <u>My Daughter, Your Son</u>, <u>All the Way Home</u>, <u>Butterflies Are Free</u>, <u>The Chalk Garden</u> (1979-80), <u>The Gin Game</u>, <u>The Dresser</u>, <u>The Last of Mrs. Lincoln</u>. I also performed in plays such as <u>Lost in Yonkers</u>, <u>Driving Miss Daisy</u>, and <u>Steel Magnolias</u> at other theatres in New Orleans.

My brother, Val Winter, was one of the Drawing Room Players, who began Le Petit Theatre. The first play I did at Le Petit was <u>Caesar and Cleopatra</u>, with my brother, Val, as Caesar. I studied at the Conservatory of Music and Drama, later affiliated with Loyola University.

The first time I worked at another theatre, other than Le Petit, was in the 1970s. Le Petit has the best facility in the city. It is the epitome of local theatre. If I had a choice between a part of a few lines at Le Petit and a big part at another theatre, I'd take the small part at Le Petit. At one time, Le Petit was the stepping stone to careers.

Q. What positive and negative experiences have you had performing at Le Petit?

A. Positive: The theatre is magical. There is no comparison between the backstage area at Le Petit and other theatres; Le Petit's is superior. No other theatre in town has a professional stage.
Negative: When I was in <u>The Dresser</u>, the director was poor; I didn't know what to do with myself on stage. But I still enjoyed the experience. June Austen [costumer] once took care of wardrobe. Then, when I performed there more recently, there was no one to organize the costumes. Also, in more recent years, the Board felt it was better to have different directors for each production. I don't like the idea of different directors for every play, maybe two or three at most.

Q. What are your thoughts of the future of Le Petit?

A. I'm definitely in favor of having parking fees paid for actors. In order to pay the actors, the by-laws would have to be changed. As far as location is concerned, Le Petit would lose its charm if it were moved.

Q. Would you like to make any other comments?

A. Well, I performed at Gallery Circle [a former New Orleans theatre] in <u>All My Sons</u>. Stocker Fontelieu was the director. He told me he needed a "quick study" to play the mother. When Le Petit wanted a new director, I recommended Stocker.

INTERVIEWER: REBECCA HALE
TELEPHONE INTERVIEW: Sept. 9, 1996
RESPONDENT: BRYAN BATT
Professional Actor

Note: At the time of this interview, Bryan Batt was performing off-Broadway in the play, Forbidden Broadway. His other New York acting credits include Cats, Jeffrey (the play and the film), Sunset Boulevard, Joseph and the Amazing Technicolor Dreamcoat, The Scarlett Pimpernel, Saturday Night Fever, and Seussical. He was nominated for an off-Broadway award for Forbidden Broadway Strikes Back.

Q. How have your experiences in performing at Le Petit helped you in your professional acting career?

A. I got my early training at Le Petit. It has proven to be an excellent training ground for me.
In the summer of 1995, I produced the play Forever Plaid there. The director said he had to have these five guys from Los Angeles in the production, so I rented the theatre. It was the first production of Forever Plaid in New Orleans.

Q. What are the strong points of Le Petit Theatre?

A. It's a beautiful space. The physical plant is really good. When I brought my friend Donna McKechnie [who acted in the original production of A Chorus Line] to see the theatre, she loved it. She remarked that I must have gotten spoiled performing in such a nice theatre, as compared to so many actors who begin their careers in rather primitive settings or primitive theatres. "What a great training ground!" she said.

Q. What are the weak points of Le Petit Theatre?

A. The theatre needs a new lighting board. I would like to see them update equipment. Historically, New Orleanians don't support the theatre here. People go to the Saenger, but not to other theatres. The foyer of Le Petit could be spruced up.

Q. Would you like to make any other comments about Le Petit?

A. It should remain an amateur theatre; they shouldn't turn it into an Equity theatre. It's a great theatre to have, and some very good productions are performed there. It's the size of an off-Broadway house.

Q. Thank you for your time.

INTERVIEWER: REBECCA HALE
INTERVIEWED: September 10, 1996
RESPONDENT: JANELL WATTIGNY
Actor/Choreographer/Teacher/Director

Q. In what plays did you act at Le Petit?

A. <u>The 1940's Radio Hour</u>, <u>Grease</u>, <u>South Pacific</u>, <u>Gypsy</u>, <u>Sweet Charity</u>, <u>The Trials of the Big Bad Wolf</u>, and <u>Annie Get Your Gun</u>.

Q. Did you work in any other capacity at Le Petit?

A. Yes. I was assistant choreographer for <u>Annie Get Your Gun</u>. I was the choreographer for <u>The 1940's Radio Hour</u>. I directed and choreographed <u>How to Eat Like a Child</u> on both stages. I also taught a summer acting workshop there for children, ages eight to seventeen, for three and one-half hours daily. We performed for day camps at Le Petit.

Q. What positive and negative changes have you noticed through the years?

A. <u>Positives</u>
When I was in charge of the theatre workshop, I got paid. The working space–the theatre itself–has a professional atmosphere. I like the intimacy of the theatre, yet it has a professional atmosphere. Working as an actress, I've worked with a variety of different directors.
In children's theatre, the children gain an extension of the

knowledge they already have of theatre. It gives them an opportunity to experience theatre in a professional setting. Several kids have started at Le Petit children's theatre and have been nominated for "Big Easy Awards" [local theatre awards].

One positive aspect of Le Petit's children's theatre is to bring theatre to children and have them exposed to live performances, as opposed to television or video games. It's an opportunity for kids performing and watching, a rare opportunity in this area [New Orleans], as opposed to New York, where I once lived. Le Petit provides a service to the community.

It's a positive atmosphere for kids acting and kids watching. Kids on stage create positive memories for first-time theatregoers. I've done MTV video and commercials, but no one knew my theatre credits. Le Petit provides a vehicle for kids to view live theatre. Kids from all walks of life are reached. Many kids' families have no means to see theatre. Le Petit has provided a service.

The building itself has historical presence. Some of the building is the original from the 1700s. This building got culturally better as each part was improved. The Children's Corner is where the renovations began. The theatre still maintains the atmosphere of the 1700s with the open-air courtyard.

People can have a completely different feeling, stepping into the theatre from the outside world. It breathes culture. It maintains some historic feeling, yet the updated equipment doesn't interfere with the historic significance. It still has that same old feeling. It has not been so updated as to lose its history.

It helps to educate people with theatre etiquette because of the history of the building, as opposed to the Superdome for ball games. It helps you to grow culturally and helps to experience a part of reliving history in modern times. Because educated people began the theatre, people mistakenly feel organizers are elite. As an educated person, instead of eliteness, more and more people can now experience this theatre, unlike in older days. Most educated people years ago were elite—not so today. The common man can enjoy plays there today. Le Petit introduced culture to the city itself and added richness.

<u>Negatives</u>

When different directors were hired [instead of one long-time director], some actors were less comfortable. Since the actors aren't paid, they must like the people they are working with. Actors should have more knowledge of the tech people, etc., they will be working with. If I'm hired as a choreographer, and they bring in set designers from other cities, this can be a problem.

When there was one artistic director with more control, like in the 1980s, it was better. In the 1990s, there have been too many chiefs and not enough Indians. There is a lot of negative energy; too many people are in charge.

Q. What are your thoughts about the future of Le Petit?

A. It's a wonderful place, an asset to the city. It combines historic and contemporary; it doesn't lose the historic. By keeping its roots in history, it can go on, but it must maintain structure so that the contemporary doesn't shine through it.

The location in the French Quarter is a plus. You wouldn't go in shorts. People make it an evening, an event. Performing there, standing on the balcony at intermission, and watching tourists glance at the building make the experience more formal.

Q. Thank you very much for your time.

INTERVIEWER: REBECCA HALE
TELEPHONE INTERVIEW: September 11, 1996
RESPONDENT: JULIE WINN
Costumer

Q. Tell me about your experiences as a costumer at Le Petit.

A. I was the costumer for six or seven productions and the assistant to the costumer for twelve productions. I had an internship at Juilliard; then I worked at Le Petit periodically at both the Children's Corner and for main-stage productions.
Le Petit was truly a community theatre. No one got paid. There was a great atmosphere then. I learned so much. I loved it there. I wanted to live there. Now the technical crew is paid. When I worked on <u>Secret Garden,</u> I had to work alone; there was no help. There was no major source of volunteers to help me, as there had been in the past. After Stocker Fontelieu, people who came to run the theatre didn't know how to treat volunteers. What was once a wonderful stock of costumes is now a mess. People came in and stole costumes, and the managing director didn't seem to mind. I offered to organize things; they could never get the volunteers. It once was a learning pool. I was a college student when I started at Le Petit.

Q. What do you think the future holds for Le Petit?

A. The problem is that the Board is unwilling to change. There is nothing to attract youth there today. The person who trained me, Eddy Vidrine, is now deceased. I went there because of a crush on a guy. I volunteered. I had never heard of it before. It was an adventure for me. There's no one to help now. My dream would be for me to come there and be hired full-time and cultivate a pool of people—or part-time—to get things in order. They need someone who knows about costumes. Some vintage costumes were on the floor. I hope they get someone who will take charge of things.

Q. Thank you for your comments.

INTERVIEWER: REBECCA HALE
INTERVIEWED: May 29, 1997
RESPONDENT: VATICAN LOKEY
Actor/Playwright

Q. In what productions at Le Petit have you acted?

A. **Main Stage**
>Applause
>Light up the Sky (also wrote the book)
>The Importance of Being Earnest (Jack)
>Sophisticated Ladies
>The Secret Garden (Neville) (also did publicity)
>
>**Children's Corner**
>Beauty & the Beast (Beast)
>Pinocchio Commedia
>Little Mermaid (original)

Q. Have you directed there (Le Petit) or worked there other than as an actor?

A. I did almost all of the publicity in the theatre for, virtually, all of the shows for the '96-'97 season. When I came here five years ago, I knew about Le Petit before I ever stepped foot in the city. When I was studying at the University of Mississippi, Oxford, the head of our theatre department, Dr. James Schoenberger, took about a week to tell us about regional theatres in and around Mississippi, Louisiana, and

Texas. He focused heavily on Le Petit. When I came to Le Petit, I made it a point to learn as much about the place as I possibly could because I knew it would be a great experience.

Q. Do you remember some of the things your teacher told you about us? (Le Petit)

A. Before I came to town, my instructor had given us the information that Le Petit had been the foremost theatre in the country; it was the oldest, continuously-running community theatre in the United States; and we just confirmed that.

Q. There is some dispute about that.

A. Yes, I have heard that. The "continuously-running" part is what's disputed.

Q. I think the dispute is whether you consider that it has been continuously-running since 1916 or 1919.[*]

Q. Where were you originally from?

A. I'm not originally from anywhere. I come from a Navy family, so . . . I was born in Charleston, South Carolina. Most of my time, when I was growing up, was spent in Jacksonville, Florida; Atlanta; or Louisville, Kentucky. I guess I spent the most time in Louisville.

Q. I just went there for the first time a couple of years ago. It's a nice town.

A. Yes, and it's not very dissimilar to New Orleans, I find.

Even the telephone numbers are the same. Both river cities. The difference between working in Louisville and working down here is . . . in Louisville, you can't really work professionally in the city if you're from there. They have a tendency to pull in actors from everywhere else in the country except from Kentucky. Here, you really can't work professionally unless you are from here. And that's the biggest difference, I find, theatrically. Besides the fact that there's a great deal of politics here just in community theatre. There's politics here you wouldn't find in professional theatres, which I think is absurd.

Q. Absolutely. I've told some people that, and they kind of look at me like I'm crazy when I say that; but, I think, in some respects, it would be easier to go to a Broadway audition, because at least I think you would be fairly treated.

A. I find a great deal of problems here are to do with the money. The economics of theatre in the city is just useless . . . It's not like it was here in the '60s and '70s where there was plenty of money for productions, and actors were going from this theatre to this theatre to this theatre to this theatre—and could—for most of the work that they were doing. But, what they were doing was . . . they were coming from an environment that allowed them to do so freely. I really feel like, just from my own personal research, the death knell for theatre in New Orleans came when the Beverly burned to the ground. Nothing, since then, has changed since the Beverly [Dinner Playhouse] burned down.

Q. That's true.

A. All of the other professional theatres in town, with the exception of Southern Rep, closed.

Q. Have you worked in any other capacity, publicity, or . . . ?

A. Yes. I did the costumes for a number of productions. Usually, when I come in to do a show, there's . . . someone needs to come in and do make-up. And I end up doing that. Most of what I do is, I do make-up, costume construction, and prop construction if I'm not doing publicity or if I'm not appearing in the show.

Q. What positive and negative experiences have you had at Le Petit?

A. Positive: Working with Freddy Palmisano. Freddy had a neat attitude to his productions that you can't find in today's shows. His productions, even the simplest stuff, are well thought out, well executed. They are musically sound. Negative: On the negative, it was working with the so-called Board of Directors. When I got here five years ago, I made it a point to find out everything I could about Le Petit. That included going through press releases from twenty years ago. I think that it is safe to say that I know more about Le Petit than the current Board of Directors. The problem is that the people who are on the Board have been there for the last fifteen, twenty years, and these people think that all of New Orleans will turn around for them. I have actually heard a Board member say, 'For every volunteer that walks out the back door, two more come in the front door,' which is totally ridiculous; otherwise, subscriptions would not be down to practically nothing. At one time, you could not get in unless you had a subscription; you could not walk in to the theatre and buy a ticket at the box office. People had season tickets, and people did it because the productions had merit. The Board members, at this time, are concerned more with their own social agenda. They are not concerned with the theatre. They are not concerned with the quality of the productions. What they are concerned with is having a place where they can bring all of their friends; a place where they can have the social pages come and take their photographs at the end of the foyer, and look good. The productions are not even secondary; they're intermediate. The members of the Board, at this point, and for several years, have no theatrical background. None of them have any idea how to run a theatre. Most of them are lawyers or housewives. They have tried, on various occasions, to run Le Petit Theatre like any other business, a practice which has been proven completely irresponsible, theatrically, in so many different theatres across the country in the past several years. Yes, it is show business. But, this business is different from any other business.

Q. What positive and negative changes have you noticed through the years at Le Petit?

A. The only living link to the original family that created Le Petit is Rosa Deutsch and her husband, Brunswick. They have been involved in the theatre since before they were married. Brunswick Deutsch's family was the family that created Le Petit. And he had been involved with it when his mother was involved with it. Despite the fact that Rosa has more history with Le Petit than anyone else in the city, the Board treats her like dirt. They just told her that she didn't need to be on the Board anymore, that they were running the theatre. Rosa and Brunswick Deutsch have rescued the theatre more times than anyone can possibly imagine in the past 20 years. The Deutsch fortune has basically been exhausted. Yearly, she has offered a $1 million check if the Board members would simply get rid of the people who are causing these problems. Every time they elect a new executive to run things. . . . She wants to see the theatre run properly. She wants to see it run so that it can continue after she is gone. She is not seeing that happening. No one is seeing to that. I fully estimate that in one year, two years, three years tops, Le Petit will no longer exist. The Board of Directors, at this time, refuses to relinquish power. They have been dragging the theatre down for the last twenty years. Their actors are leaving left and right. I'm a prime example. My mental well-being would not allow me to continue on at Le Petit. In the twenty-six years that I have been doing theatre—regional and community, summer stock, national tours—I have never encountered the situations that I have at Le Petit. For the last four or five years, I have tried desperately to 'save Le Petit.' I think the theatre deserves to be saved. This past year, the Board had the opportunity to save the theatre properly if they would have just given the executive directorship to Sonny Borey. Every production that Sonny has ever produced and directed has been an unqualified hit. He is, without a doubt, the best musical director in the city. He is one of the best musical directors I have ever worked with. He has a wonderful amount of resources and he uses them. Le Petit Theatre put up a $10,000 budget to do Sophisticated Ladies. With his own money and his own contacts, Sonny doubled that figure . . . or no, tripled it, actually. The final budget was $30,000. When Sophisticated Ladies was over, Le Petit was $85,000 in the black for the first time in many, many years. Between Sophisticated Ladies and my next show on the main stage, The Importance of Being Earnest, the entire $85,000 had been pissed away in two productions. One of them was Keith Briggs' Laughter on the 23rd Floor—which was a moderate success. And the show that took the bulk of the money and squandered it was Lyla Hay Owen's A Christmas Carol. The show was a flop from the very beginning. Inside of a two-week span of time, Ms. Owen—first of all, Ms. Owen does her own musical adaptations of A Christmas Carol without the permission of the Board. The Board was in the process of switching over Executive Directors, having just fired one during Sophisticated Ladies and not having another one until well after Earnest.

She dismissed both of the scripts that the Board presented her with that she could use. One of them was the Menkin-Ahrens version that goes up in Madison Square every year. The other one was the Charles Webber version. She dismissed both scripts—one for having too many people, one for not having enough. The Menkin-Ahrens version that we got had a total of twenty-five people. Her version of <u>A Christmas Carol</u> originally began with sixty-four people. Within a two-week span of time, during the rehearsal period, those sixty-four people dwindled down to thirty-three. The sets were huge, bulky, completely unworkable, and not at all evocative of the period. The costumes were expensive, but inappropriate for the production. The production was ghastly, all the way across the board. Opening night was . . . the start of the show was delayed by thirty-five minutes. I have never done this in my life. I walked out in the middle. And I walked out with Uncle Wayne, who never walked out on a production in his life. Fifteen minutes into the show, he leans into me and says, 'Fuck this, Mary, let's go get a cocktail.' And for Wayne Daigrepont to do that, I mean. . . . She continued to extort money from the theatre for various and sundry things, none of which was really integral to the production. But, of course, they were all expenses that come from doing a brand new production. She did not want to stop. And the Board allowed it to happen. So by the time we got around to <u>The Importance of Being Earnest</u>, the theatre was scrambling for cash again and our production was set back on the side. And now that the Board has decided to close down Children's Corner—you see, that's why it's so important to keep Briggs as the Executive Director. He has created his own children's theatre plan. He's not happy with what Edward [Cox] is doing in the space. And the reason he is not happy is because he cannot direct musicals. He thinks he can direct musicals. He'll tell everyone he can direct musicals. But every musical that he's ever done has been a complete failure. His last production of <u>She Loves Me</u> was so critically snubbed that we thought it was going to close up within a week.

Q. So the plan is to close Children's Corner? It is definitely going to close?

A. And they're going to use that space towards the main stage. Before the space was created by John and Fanny Casey in 1969, there had been children's shows on the main stage and. . . . The space that uses Children's Corner right now was originally backstage space. The house space for Children's Corner was originally office space. When John and Fanny Casey came in, they put in a proposal to the board members to use this space. Children's theatre had been doing well at Gallery Circle when it was still open. And there was a gentleman named Luis Barroso. And John and Fanny got permission from the theatre and from Stocker Fontelieu to turn the misused office space into a theatre space and the Children's Corner space was built out of the storage space backstage. From 1970 until 1978, Luis

Barroso came in with the late Judy Latour, the late Larry Kelly, the late Freddy Palmisano, Sharon O'Brian, Ricky Graham, and Sydney Wolff, who is Freddy Palmisano's widow; and they created the shows in Children's Corner that became the award winners that made Children's Corner a nationally recognized children's theatre. Then Luis, when theatre started getting bad, children's theatre started getting a bad rap along about the late '70s because my generation was raised with so many dreadful productions, that, for all intents and purposes, my entire generation turned their backs on theatre entirely. So there was no audience anymore. That was also the beginning of some of the internal struggles at Le Petit, which eventually caused the rift. In the interim between Luis' leaving in 1978 and coming in 1985, John and Fanny Casey passed away, the space became the province of the Sciacca family on the Board of Trustees. The way that Children's Corner got changed to Teddy's Corner . . . originally, we were doing a production of <u>Make Mine Bourbon</u> which was written by Teddy Sciacca on the main stage. Well, at the beginning of the rehearsal schedule, Teddy suddenly died. Emmett Johnson, who was running the theatre at that time—another man who had no business, whatsoever, being on the stage—he's a microbiologist who has no experience in theatre. He was filled with grief and woe and, seeing a way of getting himself a little bit of extra press, forced through the issue of changing the name of Children's Corner to Teddy's Corner. Teddy's daughter,

Tammy, her widower, Frank Sciacca, during the meeting, Frank immediately popped up and said, 'Why? Teddy only ever did two shows in Children's Corner and one of them was taken to the main stage by Emmett Johnson.' She really didn't have anything to do with anything in Children's Corner. He would have nothing of it. Teddy's death was still fresh in the news at that point. It was nothing for him to run it through and change the name of the space. With the name change came a new type of apathy both from the Board and from all of us. That apathy led to some truly dreadful productions in children's theatre. Just this season alone, we began the children's season with a production of <u>Wily and the Hairy Man</u>. That was directed by a new director that I actually went to school with. It was a non-musical. The production was slow, just everything was. . . . There was none of the magic involved in this production. It was a disaster. Parents were leaving in droves. Just from that production, we lost our subscription memberships. Up until this production, the adults had been coming back because they knew Edward's [Cox] name from the original production of Children's Corner. We were beginning to get the adults back. What Mr. Briggs planned on doing, after the final performance on June 1st, the back walls will be knocked out of the stage on Children's Corner. There will be a temporary wall erected directly behind the stage. The house itself will be used for rentals. The Children's Corner stage area will be used for storage for the main stage. What he plans on doing, and this is wrong on so many different levels, it's hard to begin. He believes that he can go back to the old days, by doing small non-musical, educational-based productions on the main stage during the day. Now that's a big house. If you're doing a modern musical itself. . . . The productions are not to exceed four people, no sets, costume pieces. He's looking seriously at doing educational theatre—like safety environments, don't do drugs. He plans on busing children in from Jefferson Parish and Orleans Parish. I know, for a fact, that most of the parents from Orleans Parish are not going to allow their children to come in to the Quarter during the day or at night. What he plans on doing is nothing on the scale that we had booked with Jo-Ann Testa [a teacher], in the past. We got them interested in <u>The Secret Garden</u> because it was a novel and we had time to prepare the kids. When I called her to come in and bring the kids to <u>The Importance of Being Earnest</u>, I called her a month and a half in advance. I am very angry about this.

When Stocker finally came to me originally, he said, 'I want you to handle publicity,' the first thing in my head was, I have to call Jo-Ann and get her over here so they can see this. You know, there's still a lot of value for modern school-age audiences to enjoy. It is great literature, but it's best to see something like that on stage and then go back and read it, because you can get a better idea; you get a mental picture to go with it. I think it helps set it more in your head. And we stage all of our productions to be able to do that.

It is a by-law in the charter of Le Petit Theatre from the very beginning of the theatre on through until today: no actor who performs on stage at Le Petit Theatre is to be paid. Mr. Briggs plans on paying his actors for coming in during the day. It's not that I don't believe in paying actors; it's what I do for a living; I'm all for it. But, by going directly against that by-law, he goes directly against everything Le Petit Theatre is about. If he begins to pay these people for performing, that turns us into a semi-professional theatre. It voids the charter for the theatre. And voids a great deal of the funding that Le Petit is eligible for and currently receives. The logistics of trying to get—he plans on getting kids in there for two shows a week; and just from dealing with Jo-Ann, I know, you have a finite number of times that you are allowed to come in to do something like that. You've got to be in there by ll, and you've got to be out of there by 1. It's because of the buses. There's no way he's going to be able to do 8 shows at 45 minutes every week. There's no way he's going to be able to get that many children in and out of that space in the French Quarter during the day in the most crowded section of the Vieux Carre; it's just not going to happen. I mean, just getting the older kids up onto the bus and getting them off of the bus.

Q. Well, I don't know if you know this, but there's a Jefferson Parish rule that buses cannot drive in the Quarter between certain areas, because they had to leave us off by the

Aquarium. We had a problem with that, because that meant walking; so you have to figure that time in also. You know, that's at least a ten-minute walk, even if you walk briskly.

A. I fully believe that Mr. Briggs has not focused through entirely. I believe he is acting irrationally because, let me find a way to put this, there's no veto getting in the way of his judgment. And I don't want this to sound like I'm bashing Keith. All Keith did was apply for a job and get it. That's really all he did.
What happened with Sonny Borey was, Sonny came in to direct <u>Sophisticated Ladies</u>. Sonny told a Board member point blank during the rehearsal process for <u>Sophisticated Ladies</u>, when they were originally talking to him about taking over this place, he said, 'Do you want to know what ya'll need at Le Petit Theatre?' Every single person standing in that room. . . . He told them the truth; he told them how they were messing up; he told them the function of a Board—which is to raise money. You do not run the theatre, you raise money. You hire somebody that you have complete and total trust in to run your theatre for you, and then you leave that person alone. You raise money; we will get you in the society column; we'll get you in the newspaper. That's not a problem. This immediately caused consternation with several members of the Board. When they called him in during the rehearsal process for an interview for the position, Sonny went into the interview and, for 30 minutes, the exact same members of the Board who had been so hurt and upset by the comments attributed

to him began to lay into him. Sonny sat there, calmly and quietly as he could and then left. He just walked out of the building. What followed after that was a major explosion between one half of the Board and the other half. The one half of the Board who saw what was coming was saying, "Here is a man who is going to be able to save Le Petit and bring it back to its national prominence." The other half of the Board was people who had gotten their toes stepped on and just could not have that awful man come into their theatre. You can see it in the minutes of the meeting. Then they made the final decision to go with Keith over Sonny. Matt Chestnut said in the meeting that he did not think that Sonny would make a good steward for the theatre. This was also the same meeting that I had to find out a month and a half afterwards that I had been fired from doing publicity, but no one told me. There were comments in the notes about how Sonny would not be good working with the other Board members, that he didn't seem to have the best interest of Le Petit at heart, that he seemed to be there to serve himself.

Q. Was this a paying position? Doing publicity at Le Petit?

A. It wasn't until I got there, and I started doing publicity for the theatre during Superstar. I got the theatre more press for that one show than they had in the entire '95-'96 season. The gentleman who was running the theatre at that time, Mr. Joel Rainey, failed to alert the Board to the fact that I had done the press for the show. When Sonny came in directly after that to do They're Playing Our Song, there was a big blowup at one of the meetings. The Board wanted to know how come there was no press done for They're Playing Our Song like there was for The Secret Garden. And rather than tell the Board that one of his costumers had done the press, and I had been promised that I would be given a paid position if I did a good job doing the press, Mr. Rainey sat there and took the flak for not getting any press for the show. During Sophisticated Ladies, after Joel Rainey and all of them had been fired, Sonny and I were talking and he was mentioning all of the press that The Secret Garden had gotten and I told him that I had not done the press for The Secret Garden, and that's when I found out that he was all for it. So, thanks to Sonny, for the first time, they had a paid publicity director.

Q. How much were you paid?

A. I was to be paid $200 a show for doing the press. A measly sum, but you know, I was paid. From Sophisticated Ladies, we went into Laughter On the 23rd Floor, and because of the nature of the theatre, and because there was no press budget at all for advertising, I was forced to get as much free press as I possibly could. And that happens with every show. And as Laughter On the 23rd Floor, it happens during this past production, at the very beginning of the production process, actually, in post-production. I told the Board, "You are not going to be able to get the kind of coverage that you had for Sophisticated Ladies. It's just not going to happen. All available funds were eaten up left and right with the election and you're not a musical. So don't expect to be able to go on to the morning shows (television programs) and do something with this." I'm not going to take this to a morning show because, without an audience—

Q. It's out of context.

A. Exactly. And we fixed the problem with <u>The Importance of Being Earnest</u>; when we went on the morning shows, we went on in character and they interviewed our characters. So it made sense.

Q. That's a really good idea.

A. But, we welcomed getting the press. Mr. Briggs also suffers from, apparently, a mild form of Alzheimer's, because he cannot remember anything. Even when it was written down, he cannot remember anything. He directly circumvented my press schedule; he made problems with me for all of my press conferences which, fortunately, did not affect me then, because my press people know me, and they know the way that I work. I received reports throughout the production, that I was being blamed for everything that went wrong with the show up to and including a light board failure during one performance that forced the entire cast off-stage and, while they were trying to get the light board back up with the audience milling around the courtyard, actually was told that the cast members were yelling and bitching and complaining, "Well, I would blame that on Vatican." Mr. Briggs had gotten the cast to the point where anything that happened was my fault.
This led directly into <u>A Christmas Carol</u>. Now, I had problems, personally, with Lyla Hay Owen. Professionally, I

don't. Opening night of Christmas Carol, I was given a personal apology by Lyla for her actions during the production. But, during the production, I was told by her, to my face, she told me in the middle of the third production number, "You destroyed Keith Briggs' production, I fully believe that you are here to destroy my production." Everything that I came to her with, presswise, that was to do with her show, was immediately dismissed because, as far as she was concerned, if it came out of my mouth, it was going to hurt the show. She refused to take her cast onto the morning shows for a couple of numbers from the show; she refused to do a personal appearance on a weekend during the day at one of the local malls. It was after Thanksgiving. She refused to have anything to do with it. I got her a lot of print press, and I could not get her... and I got her onto all of the bulletin boards for the TV stations. But, I had to keep telling myself that, all the way up until the final . . . until dress rehearsal week, I can't get her to do it. And they wanted the show. They wanted the show to go in there because they had the space to fill it. And they made the space in their production specifically for me. So, after The Importance of Being Earnest, there were already problems with the Board; I had already had to go to the Board to defend myself concerning Briggs' production. The press for The Importance of Being Earnest, I had Stocker's full cooperation on everything. We had a ton of press; we had the same press we had for Sophisticated. A non-musical, and I can get that kind of press.

Q. That's great.

A. The third week of <u>Earnest</u>, I found out that I had been fired by the Board from doing press, and that the press would now be under the total domain of Keith Briggs. For the last two main-stage productions, Keith Briggs had no press whatsoever, other than theatre listings and reviews. That's it. Any press that came out here, at that point, was specifically centered on Keith Briggs. It was not centered on his productions; it was not centered on <u>The Sound of Music</u>—which was not his production—it was centered on Keith. That was his idea of doing press.
During the interim of that, Edward was put in charge of Children's Corner and I did his publicity—

Q. You're talking about Edward Cox?

A. Yes. And for his last two productions, I did the press for him for free. I figure I'm involved in the show, personally, and I may, as well, get some publicity for myself.
Another problem we've had this season is Joel Rainey's scheduling. This past season was the legacy that Joel left before he was fired by the Board for gross incompetence. Joel's scheduling of this past theatre season has been next to impossible. I mean, scheduling a show, first of all, during the middle of Jazz Fest is always a mistake. Scheduling any show during Jazz Fest is like scheduling a production during Mardi Gras. Of course, he was from out of town, so he really didn't have any clue as to how important these things are and how difficult things can be when you're a

reporter and trying to deal with Mardi Gras and festivals like Jazz Fest. It's a totally different animal from any other theatres that you're dealing with.

This next season is being planned entirely by Mr. Briggs. There is a brand new musical production of <u>Pretty Baby</u> that will be opening next season.

Q. This will be the premiere? Right?

A. Right. Yes. It would be the New Orleans premiere. It's been worked up in New York and in Texas and some other places. Supposedly, it came down here, the stories say, it's come here to get some local color and flavor and then they will take the production on to Broadway. There has been nothing but monetary problems with this product since they first began talking about it. I doubt, seriously, if this product is going to turn a profit.

Q. I kind of got that feeling.

A. Now, even—no matter how confident you are about a production, you always have a contingency plan. Because so many things can go wrong. When pressed to come up with a contingency plan for what they consider the things that <u>Pretty Baby</u> doesn't have, they decided that maybe they could do a simple musical, you know, like bring some sort of Mickey Mouse. The show with no known name? It was his idea to schedule a production with no known name. It should be able to direct itself.

Q. Keith is going to direct all the productions now? Because, I know, this year, they had some guest directors.

A. Pretty much. Keith has a couple of guest directors that are coming in from Rivertown. Edward was supposed to be able to direct a main stage production this season. His first choice was, they plan on doing <u>Coconuts</u>. And the whole show is a cartoon. And Keith will not allow it. He will not allow it. He wants Edward out of the theatre. In fact, and this is not unusual, there have been several times over the past 5 years that I have been here, new people come in and all of the old people are up about it. Everything that came before Keith is pushed out of the way, except anything that he's done during that time period. Everybody who is connected with the way things were done during that time period—out. Everything is pushed out. They either bring in their own people, or they make deals with Keith to use his key people for their support and their... everything else, exiled. I can't tell you how many people of the theatre history have been lost, forever lost. The press clippings of their productions are no longer there. There are two enormous press clipping books from the late 1950s up until the mid-'70s from both Children's Corner and main stage; both of those books are gone.

Q. I saw some, mainly of children's theatre, when I interviewed Mr. Tong. But it was his own collection.

A. Yes, they're gone.

Q. And, fortunately, some kind soul at Tulane, well it's not just one person, has kept a great vertical file and that's where

I've gotten most of my research, from Tulane, the Louisiana Collection.

A. Well, here's something you should know. For a long time, when Emmett Johnson was in charge, it looked like, if they didn't get rid of Emmett, either it was going to close—

Q. Because I've heard nothing but negative about him . . . every single person I've ever interviewed. . . .

A. Yes. The people who are on the Board now are all Emmett supporters. Every single one of them. When the theatre closes, and I can no longer say "if," it's certain. . . .

Q. You truly think it will close?

A. Yes, I truly believe that point has come. When the theatre closes, it was in the by-laws of the theatre, the property that the theatre sits on is immediately reversed to the possession of Tulane University.

Q. Won't more than one college benefit from the sale of Le Petit?

A. Actually, it would be divided among Tulane, Loyola, and LSU. I'm deeply upset by the loss of the theatre. I think, because my heart and soul, theatrically speaking, has always been with children's theatre, and I'm sort of moving away from the phrase "children's theatre." With <u>Rapunzel</u>, we began using the phrase "family musical theatre." It's because my generation was so soured on children's theatre. It still has a negative connotation; it leaves a bad taste in a lot of people's mouths.

Q. What did you call it? Family musical theatre?

A. Yes. Family musical theatre . . . which is basically what Children's Corner . . . family musical theatre. The adults and kids would come to see those shows. What saddens me the most, besides the fact that the Board is so concerned with their own social agenda, besides the fact that people are coming into the theatre these days to see the theatre, not as the grand old institution that needs to be cared for and allowed to thrive, but, rather, as a place where they can come in and have their own little power play and set themselves up as theatre guides because it is Le Petit Theatre. It's the loss of 80 years of theatrical history that involves some big names—Lady B.J. [B.J. Crosby], who is on Broadway right now with <u>Smoky Joe's Cafe</u> began at Le Petit Theatre. Melissa Marshall, who is up in New York right now. She got her start on Le Petit in <u>Applause</u> with me. That is where she began and we watched her grow. She was one of our original <u>Rapunzel</u>s. Wynton Marsalis, he was in <u>Shenandoah</u>. Sinclair Lewis performed on our stage. Up in the theatre, right next to the box office, you can see the photograph. Ethel Crumb Brett was the technical director of the theatre for 25 years, the first female technical director in this house. The Deutsches alone. There's an entire book that could be written just on the Deutsches. Let's see. Who else? There's a number of performers have come out of Le Petit. Bryan Batt. He got his start doing <u>Godspell</u> in the early '80s. Just a multitude of personalities who got their beginnings at Le Petit and all of that history almost didn't happen.

I'm sick and tired of working at places where people's personal agendas get directly in the path of the progress of the production. There is no excuse for it, in my mind, whatsoever. If you're coming in to do a show, if you've got personal problems with somebody, you wait until after rehearsal, or you wait until after the production is over, then you talk about it; you don't do it to the detriment of the production. I have found that a number of the production staff that are currently employed by Le Petit are doing just that. I find it strange that, even though everybody complains about the exact same problems in this theatre, no one is willing to stand up and say it. They are all scared to death of being blackballed, or they are scared to death of whatever "repercussions" could possibly happen. I find that aggravating because how can you improve the situation if no one's going to complain.

Q. Were you in town when there was a meeting where all the actors chose not to perform anymore at Le Petit?

A. Yes. Unfortunately, the problem there was that most of the actors who were going through that needle were not concerned with the quality of productions; they were concerned with their paychecks. The biggest bone of contention, for most of those actors, at that meeting, was that Le Petit was not paying them to perform there. Le Petit has never intended to pay them to perform. It was a testing ground. The reason why we had so many performers that got their start during the golden days of Le Petit, who are doing so beautifully right now, is because they came in as professional actors for one thing, to do a show, to just do a show. Maybe you have a supporting role in the next production; maybe you walk up to another lead.

Q. Thank you for your time.

* Here, in New Orleans, it is considered to be the oldest. However, in the rest of the country, it is considered to be **one** of the oldest.

INTERVIEWER: REBECCA HALE
INTERVIEWED BY QUESTIONNAIRE: August 6, 1997
RESPONDENT: MAURICE "MOON" LANDRIEU
Former Mayor of New Orleans

Q. How did Le Petit Theatre enrich the culture of New Orleans?

A. Le Petit has been, for many years, an important piece of the cultural mosaic of New Orleans. Live theatre is an old art form that moves and educates.

Q. What are the advantages of having a community theatre, such as Le Petit, in New Orleans?

A. A community theatre gives locals an opportunity to express themselves. They entertain the community and visitors and enrich all who participate.

Q. What did it mean to you personally (during your time in office as Mayor) to have Le Petit Theatre in New Orleans?

A. All theatre is important, but Le Petit has a tradition and its location in the Quarter added to its importance.

Q. Any other comments would be greatly appreciated.

A. Please forgive the long delay. I misplaced your request.

Q. Thank you very much!

INTERVIEWER: REBECCA HALE
INTERVIEWED: August 14, 1997
RESPONDENT: KEITH BRIGGS
Managing Director/Actor/Teacher

Q. What is your title?

A. Managing Director.

Q. What plays have you directed at Le Petit?

A. It's Only a Play
A Streetcar Named Desire
Laughter on the 23rd Floor
The Heiress
She Loves Me

Q. What plays will you direct for the upcoming season?

A. Lost In Yonkers
Master Class
Gypsy

Q. How are plays selected?

A. There's a Play-Reading Committee, mainly board members. We discuss it; I decide on the season—whether it's right for our theatre, if we can cast it. I know the actors locally.

Q. What is the status of Teddy's Corner?

A. Possibly some productions will still be in there. We may do weekends in there. It may not be feasible; we'll see. We can rent it. We can use it for rehearsals.

Q. What plays will be performed for school audiences?

A. Three productions—

Dracula for high school and middle school in late October, early November

Coconuts for high school and middle school in January, February

The Lion, the Witch, and the Wardrobe will be offered to grammar schools in April for five weeks—not part of the season subscription. A 10 A.M. performance. Full-scale production. We're paying the actors. We've not done that before. They won't be paid for nighttime. We're maintaining our status as a community theatre. The important thing is we only seat 450 people, 7,000-8,000 kids only. First come, first served. $6.00 for kids. We're attempting to get corporate funding for underprivileged kids. We hope to have some success in this area. I will send a study guide for each play. I may do a page on theatre etiquette.

Q. What positive and negative experiences have you had at Le Petit?

A. I'm a native of New Orleans. I've been associated with the theatre since I'm seven. I debuted in 1947 in Peter Pan. I remember the beautiful stage curtain. Le Petit made a great impression on me. I acted here in many plays and stage-managed a few. From '65 to '78, I was active as an actor and stage manager.

<u>The Lion in Winter</u> we did for the Southwest Theatre Conference. Lois Crandel—the first lady of New Orleans theatre—was in it.

<u>Bye, Bye, Birdie</u>—I played eight parts and had seventeen of my students in it. I was in Connecticut for six years. Your roots bring you back.

Some negatives are our air-conditioning bill can run $4,000 a month; we need a new roof—$20,000.

Q. What are the major challenges facing Le Petit today?

A. The Saenger [a theatre that has performances of professional road companies] has an extensive season and provides competition for us.

The restaurants are a big competition. It's not like New York; restaurants here don't have pre-show and post-show. At major restaurants like Brennan's, people stay a whole evening.

This is one of the safest areas, but I will be hiring a policeman for the first time. But this is safe. The worst thing here is the grunge kids.

Q. What future plans do you have for Le Petit? What is your vision for Le Petit?

A. We're in better financial shape than six months before, although membership has fallen from a high of 7,000 to 2,000.

We're trying to raise the level of volunteerism. I wish we had more high school people who could volunteer. I hope to have a high school production/workshop next summer. This will introduce many kids to theatre. I hope to increase membership and increase corporate funding. Being in Orleans Parish, we are at a disadvantage because there are so many arts organizations that get a slice of the pie.

I would like to foster a number of young directors in this area to work here.

We were contacted by the producers of <u>Pretty Baby</u> who were scouting for a place to play it before Broadway. Why not open our regular season with it? It's a chance for our audience to see something they haven't seen before. There will be some local actors in it. It's not an Equity production. Some actors will be working under an Equity Guest Artist contract.

Q. Thank you for your time.

INTERVIEWER: REBECCA HALE
INTERVIEWED: November 6, 1997
RESPONDENT: LEON CONTAVESPRIE
Le Petit Board Member/Actor

Q. Name the plays that you have acted in at Le Petit.

A. I was in Woman in Black, Laughter on the 23rd Floor, The Importance of Being Earnest, Rumors. Those were the four.

Q. Have you done any directing there?

A. No.

Q. Of these four, do you have any favorites?

A. Yes! Rumors, by far.

Q. Why is that?

A. As opposed to Woman in Black, which was an incredible live lead and a drama, I am truly convinced that comedy is the most difficult art form in the world, especially farce. It was a honing process; it was more of a growing process to learn how to hone in on your timing skills. I think out of all of them, I learned the most from Rumors. It was such a great cast, too.

Q. You said that you learned the most from Rumors?

A. Yes, just from the direction and from the fellow members in the cast.

Q. What is it like acting at Le Petit?

A. It's tradition; it's history; and I'm a relative rookie at Le Petit, and I'm also on the Board. I kind of got thrown into it at first. When I first walked into it from the stage door, it felt like . . . you know, I had just been to New York and we saw a show at the Helen Hayes Theatre, which is very small—about 750 seats. I walked in [Le Petit] and I said, "This is like being in an Off-Broadway house." The history of it, the legend and lure of the ghosts. . . . I felt like a professional. The physical plant is beautiful.

Q. How did you get to be a member of the Board of Directors at Le Petit?

A. I walked into a rehearsal for <u>Rumors</u> and Keith [Briggs] pulled me to the side and he said, "I've got to tell you something." I said, "What?" He said, "You've been nominated to be vice-president." I don't know if you are familiar with the hierarchy of the Board, but the vice-presidents are appointed board members; but they don't get a vote. They get to serve on committees and express their opinions and lobby all they want; but there is no vote. So it was unofficial until the Chairman of the Board, Jerry Dumas, called me and said, "We would like you to be a vice-president." Well, in retrospect, I had spoken to a good friend of mine, Lucy Daigle, who was the president, and she told me she had brought my name up after seeing me in <u>Woman in Black</u> and all these other shows. She said they wanted two young actors on the Board, a male and a female. They asked me and Yvette Hargis and we both accepted. The very first meeting, someone had resigned—I don't remember who it was, but someone had resigned from the Board, and Jerry bumped me up. I appreciated it and would like to take it, but I asked him about actually having a voice on this Board.

Q. So you upgraded to what?

A. A board member. Vice-Presidents are on the Board of Governors, but have no vote. There are twelve voting members.

Q. When did this all happen?

A. It was during <u>Rumors</u> . . . end of May, beginning of June.

Q. This means that you sit in on meetings?

A. Oh, yes! Now the Executive Council meetings. The Executive Council is the president, vice-president, chairman, and the treasurer. I don't sit in those meetings, but they share everything at the Board meeting, and those meetings are once a month.

Q. Who's the president this year?

A. Well, there is a Chairman of the Board and that is Jerry Domingue. And we also have a President, Lucy Daigle.

Q. Do you like being on the Board?

A. I love it. Now the actors have a voice.

Q. They really are allowing you to have a voice?

A. Well, they are listening to me. Whether they agree with me or not is because the majority of the Board is—and I don't mean this as negatively as it sounds—theatrically ignorant. Most of them have no experience. Now the few on the Board who have been on the Board for a long time really do know theatre. They go to New York; they see plays; they keep up. But there's a few who have just been appointed for business reasons, which is fine, but they don't necessarily understand the ins and outs of theatre and what's required for putting on a show. But, yes, they listen to me whether they agree with me or vote for or against me; they listen. Normally, I'm the odd man out. When there's a split vote ten to one, I'm the one. But that rarely happens.

Q. Now Yvette Hargis [actress], is she on?

A. She's a vice-president. She is not a voting member.

Q. Do they let you have input? Can you suggest plays?

A. Actually, I'm the chairman of the Play-Reading Committee. We have just narrowed it down to twelve. Keith Briggs, Yvette Hargis, myself, Nat Chestnut, and Gayle Batt. Gayle is not a board member, but anybody can be appointed to a committee. Because of her expertise in theatre, they appointed her. We have just narrowed it down to twelve [plays]. We are going to suggest those to the Board and then take six from there.

Q. Are there any things that you are trying to implement—as far as running the theatre—that you are trying to change?

A. Not so much change. This procedure, if anything. Now the box office personnel, their administrative personnel, is superb. I'm trying to change how they target their audiences, their methods of getting people into that theatre, their methods of publicity. In the '70s and late '60s, they had 6,000 members; they didn't have to publicize. You went to Le Petit because it was the only game in town. They did these great shows. I'm trying to encourage more modern attitudes about the theatre. For instance, serving coffee at intermission, which has become a Le Petit staple. However, we lose out on money. It's costing us 250 bucks a month to serve coffee. I know that sounds ridiculous. We could easily get it donated; and why we don't, I don't know. But keep it to the Sunday matinees and ditch Friday and Saturday serving coffees; and let them buy drinks. But you don't do that because it's always been done that way. You just don't change it. Something else—I want them to admit that we are broke. There are a few board members that will, but a lot of them won't admit that we have no money. Because I was the coordinator for the Halloween Gala—we raised about $8,000—in all of my press releases—that was a learning experience in itself—I announced that this was a "Save the Theatre Gala." The response we got from the media was huge. They were announcing it on the news, radio. A few of the board members were disgruntled. "How dare you say Le Petit is broke!" The last of the Southern aristocracy. You know . . . How dare you mention that! They are not coming down on me; it's just not the thing to do. I'm just trying to get them to admit that this is the problem; this is what we need to do to solve it. They want to solve it without naming it.

Q. A couple of the people I have interviewed felt that the theatre has declined and will be bankrupt in two to three years because of the problems in the Quarter, such as crime, parking, etc. They have suggested the theatre be moved. How do you feel about that?

A. Well, I could lobby both ways. The way I always felt, Bryan Batt did <u>Forever Plaid</u>; it sold out for seven weeks. <u>Sophisticated Ladies</u> sold out every night. <u>Rumors</u> was playing 350 people every night. You give them a good product, they will come down to that theatre. So that's almost an excuse to say the membership has gone down. At the same time, I don't think the theatre could ever go broke. We are in the hole about $300,000. That's the main chunk from Whitney Bank from refinancing the physical plant. The building is valued at over $5,000,000. Even if it took a half a million to pay off debts, we are still sitting on $4.5 to $5,000,000. You could buy a piece of land in Lakeview . . . Uptown, build a $2,000,000 beautiful state-of-the-art space with 350 seats as opposed to 450 seats—which is a problem now—and still keep a million in the bank, and the theatre would never have problems again . . . if it was run correctly; but in my eyes, Le Petit would be gone. It wouldn't be the same. It's Le Petit Theatre du Vieux Carre, not Le Petit Theatre du Uptown or Lakeview. The members we have, 340 new members this year, which is excellent—

however, almost to the number didn't renew. We had 300 members from last year that didn't renew. If all had renewed, we could have been up to 2,000 subscribers this year, which would have been outstanding. We are at about 1,700 now. I could be lobbied both ways. I don't want to see it go, and if you give them a good product, they will come out there to see it.

Q. Have you suggested to them about renting out to other theatre groups?

A. Yes. They all agree with that; they think that is a good idea. Another thing that has been thrown out is having a gift shop. That has been thrown out because it takes overhead. And we don't have anyone to run the box office, much less volunteers to do that. But then when they say Children's Corner, the immediate feeling is that we need to rent out the main stage. I get furious; I just get livid at these meetings because I told them, "It is a theatre, not a convention space." That's what I meant about being theatrically ignorant. A lot of them don't, many of them do; but a lot of them don't realize that you may have black nights, but you are still rehearsing, changing, touching up the set, etc. Stocker is a big advocate of "leave the main stage alone." During the summer, rent it out as much as you can. Get those conventions in there. If they can, close the grand drapes and let a group of 450 people come in there and give a talk. I have no problem with that. But the second they interfere with something going on in the show, I have a problem. That's why they think it goes hand-in-hand, but I don't. But they do think the Children's Corner needs to be rented out in some fashion. I think it's too small to sell to some kind of convention group. I think we could make some money. We could get some struggling theatre company a shot. This would help Le Petit. They get all the publicity for all these people that would come in. And the shows that would be done there would not be the same shows that would be done on the main stage of Le Petit.

Q. What about some experimental plays?

A. That's exactly what I mean. If Le Petit got the ball rolling and did some weird—well, not weird, but some—off plays you wouldn't see at Rivertown or Le Petit, or Southern Rep, then maybe another theatre company would say, "They can do it, why can't we?" And publicize. This is the beginning. If you are interested in renting the space, give us a call.

Q. How do you feel about having the school children coming to see the plays?

A. I really, really like it. There is a lot of controversy about paying the actors because, in the bylaws, which I have yet to get a copy of, no actor can be paid to perform at Le Petit. However, by contract, they are being paid for the children's shows. In theory, they are getting paid to act. It's a breach somewhere. I think it's fantastic, because for Dracula, eight performances are sold out. The kids have been loving it. I think it's fantastic.

Q. What do you think are the major challenges facing Le Petit today?

A. Filling that theatre. Getting people in the seats. We've cut down to nine performances as opposed to twelve. The theatre was, at one time, four weeks and now it's down to three. Encouraging people that it's safe, still the premiere theatre in the city, and that is being challenged over and over again. We have the cheapest prices. As a matter of fact, we will probably go up on our prices next year. $14 for a musical—that's the cheapest in the city. Some of the independent shows are charging $20 to $25. It's convincing them that it is a value, that's the challenge—getting them back in the seats and getting our subscribers back up. Yes, paying the bills. But getting donors to pay that bill, that's a short-term solution to a long-term problem.

Q. At one time, it [Le Petit] was self-sufficient. What about now with corporate sponsorship and grants?

A. They tried. They have three or four board members—I don't know who they are—who specialize in getting grants. Keith and Michael Arata are with them. It's [grant money] out there; it's only a matter of being tapped. Hopefully, eventually, we won't need that. It would still be nice if they would donate it to us. We get $1,000 from EXXON, $2,000 from Shell . . . little nickel and dime stuff that will pay for lights for one show, but nothing that's substantial.

Q. If it could be suggested that it is an educational theatre, that would help with grants.

A. Right. That's the slant they are going for now with the children's program.

Q. What goals do you think the theatre has for the future and how do you think this can be accomplished?

A. To be honest, I'm not certain they have any goals. I'm not convinced. And that is one of the things I would like to try as a board member to refocus, once they get this financial stuff out of the way. That's their goal, to pay the debt. It's not necessarily . . . they say it's to produce good theatre, but the road has been turned toward the financial. They need to focus on the theatre as the goal and getting people back in the seats as opposed to getting money in the theatre through other means. It is going to take some time. They are not going to solve this problem overnight, but, unfortunately, some of them think that it can be, or will be, if we get a grant. No one is going to give us a $300,000 grant. We are lucky if we get a $10,000 grant. On the $300,000, we are paying the interest and not the principle. Whitney is fine with it. They have no problem. We were even considering going on retreat with the board members overnight to discuss what the goals are. I think it is a good idea, but at the same time, you have a theatre that seats 450 people. Isn't the goal obvious? Let's put on some good shows and get people back in this theatre.

Q. How have you benefited from being an actor and board member at Le Petit?

A. I have learned more in the past year as an actor and a board member than I have in the last ten years. It's amazing, more as a board member than as an actor. UNO [University of New Orleans] was where I had all my training. As a board member, I have learned how the other half lives. The Board is made up primarily of society, upper class. I am strictly middle, which is interesting. There's an interesting little clash that goes on there. I don't mean a bad clash. They see this young guy, and they all respect me, and I respect them—well, they all seem to like me, let's put it that way. But it's culture clash, because I come to the meetings in shorts and a T-shirt, and they're dressed to the nines. One of them commented on the fact that he saw me dressed up, and he had always only seen me in shorts and a T-shirt. I didn't realize there was a dress code.

I have learned a lot about the press—how to handle the press. The theatre will hire an individual to do the press. But it's a matter of doing it correctly. For instance, for Dracula, three of the board members went to a symposium on the press by Angela Hill on the Overture of the Cultural Season. I had sent her a press release and she asked if anyone from Le Petit was there. And Lucy Daigle and Bill Garrett and a couple of other people raised their hands. She asked if any of them were Leon. They said, "No." She said, "Because I happen to have his cover letter." It was about a paragraph long and it said, "Dear Angela, we are hosting a Save the Theatre Benefit on Halloween night. We would appreciate you airing this because we are in the financial doldrums and we need help. If you have any questions, please call me." Lucy thought, "Oh my God, she's going to embarrass us in front of a hundred and fifty people." But Angela said, "This is exactly what you want. Short, concise, and to the point. This got my attention. It's a worthwhile cause and I will mention it on the air. If it's a two-page press release, I'm throwing it away; I'm not reading it." That has been the problem with Le Petit. They are sending out these two-page press releases on the actors, the cast, the crew. I don't want to hear all that. Just tell me who, what, where, and when. Make it short and clear.

That's it. It's learning how to bend. And board members learning how to bend. Because I have to accept attitudes. It's making me more open-minded. Because you hear horror stories about Le Petit and the fighting. And it's not like that. A few of them have some opinions that are age-old. And they have some reason for believing this. And I have to think, "Okay, she's been around here long enough and what she is saying may sound archaic, but it has to have some value."

Q. I know that there aren't as many volunteers as there once were. Is there any kind of push to try to get more volunteers?

A. We have a women's guild—The Guild, it's called. It's a group of ladies who—it acts, I'm sure primarily, as a social function, but they come in and help out at the door, and they serve coffee and things like that. No, actually, I haven't seen a huge push for volunteers. Our stage manager has a loyal crew, and they work every shift. But you should not have to rely on the same people over and over again. It's a huge imposition. Yes. I think we need some young people. I challenged each of the board members that each of them needed to go backstage and work on a show, if you haven't. Then that attitude will change—that the show just goes up. And the sets are put up by little elves. Then maybe it will be . . . "I guess we do need volunteers to help backstage."

Q. There is a big push in the schools now to get kids to do volunteer work. It's possible the schools might allow that.

A. I would like to pursue it. The only concern would be that would they want their students to come down to the Quarter. I would like to think we could overcome that. But we don't have security at night. We always walk out together, and there is never an incident. I don't feel unsafe in the Quarter. Where we are is a nice section. But I would like to even work with UNO [University of New Orleans], exchange some type of course credit. That's in the future. But they have their own theatre department, so why would they do that?

Q. Do you serve some type of a term on the Board?

A. I was a replacement. So my time ends in April. I have to be re-voted in April. Now whether I take that, I don't know. It depends upon where I'm going to be.

Q. Is it a two-year term?

A. Yes, that's correct.

Q. As opposed to other theatres, how would you rate your experience as an actor at Le Petit? Can you list the strong points they [Le Petit] have that other theatres might not have?

A. Le Petit has the benefit of having dressing rooms. They may not be kept up, but there are lights around the mirrors and everyone has their own space providing it is not a cast of thirty. If it's a normal-size cast, you have plenty of room. You have a big greenroom. There is a good monitoring system. You can hear what's going on if you want to go up in the greenroom. The physical plant is so big it makes it worthwhile. Just rehearsing on that stage is a thrill. A 250 or 150 house is a thrill. That's just the thing . . . theatres in this city—I'm not talking about Rivertown—would kill for a 150 house. Oh, you're complaining about 250 in the house last night? We only had three.

Q. How much is spent on an average production?

A. Salaries and everything. A big show like <u>Sophisticated Ladies</u> went over $40,000. Musicals should be about $25,000. A non-musical, salaries and everything, should come in between $10,000 and $15,000. I would like to think closer to $10,000.

Q. You said musicals cost more? What about <u>Sophisticated Ladies</u>?

A. <u>Sophisticated Ladies</u> was a huge, huge budget. If you really want to do a musical, well, you should spend about

$30,000. The more lavish it is, the more people will come to see it.

Q. What is the procedure for assigning a director?

A. I have asked that before. I don't know. For instance, we are considering <u>Follies</u> to open next season; and we would like to get Michael Howard, who directed at Tulane. You have certain directors in mind. You know that Stocker's going to direct one or two shows a year. That's a given. What shows depend on his schedule. Keith is a given. I'd like to get some fresher directors. Not better, just some different people.

Q. Thank you for your time.

INTERVIEWER: REBECCA HALE
INTERVIEWED: (Faxed) March 15, 1998
RESPONDENT: RICKY GRAHAM
ACTOR/DIRECTOR

Q. Please list all the productions at Le Petit Theatre in which you have acted.

A. MAIN STAGE   CHILDREN'S CORNER
    Hello, Dolly   Rumplestiltskin
    Seesaw   Tunes
    Candida   Peter, Darling!
                         Brothers Grimm Barnyard Revue
                         The Mystery of Irma Vep
                         Crackers

Q. Please list all the productions at Le Petit Theatre that you have directed.

A. MAIN STAGE   CHILDREN'S CORNER
    Three Mortal   Chicken Little
    Ladies Possessed   St. George and the Dragon Crackers
                         The Brave Little Tailor

Q. Have you worked at Le Petit in any other capacity, other than as an actor and director?

A. I wrote for the Children's Corner.

<u>Tunes</u>
<u>Peter, Darling!</u>
<u>Brothers Grimm Barnyard Revue</u>
<u>Crackers</u>
<u>Chicken Little</u>
<u>St. George and the Dragon</u>
<u>The Wizard of Oz</u>
<u>Babes in Toyland</u>

Q. What positive and negative experiences have you had at Le Petit?

A. Working in the Children's Corner with Luis Barroso in the late '70s provided some of the most exciting theatre experiences in my life. It was also the first time I was paid for performing and writing! The main stage [back in the late '70s] was as much like a Broadway theatre that one could find for miles around. It was a thrilling privilege to work there back then. However. . . .

Q. What positive and negative changes have you noticed through the years at Le Petit Theatre?

A. The Board of Le Petit over the last ten years or so has all but completely ruined the theatre. Their pettiness and stubborn refusal to keep up with the changing theatre scene in the city has alienated the talented performers and tech people of New Orleans.

Q. How important do you feel Le Petit is to the theatrical scene and the cultural life of the city of New Orleans?

A. Twenty years ago, Le Petit led the way in the local theatre community; now it can't even place in the race! The only important aspect left of Le Petit is the historical significance of the physical plant.

Q. What do you feel are the major challenges facing Le Petit Theatre today?

A. Le Petit desperately needs to face the fact that if something isn't literally done very quickly, it will close. The Board needs to be abolished, and a professional theatre business manager/artistic director has to be installed to grab the place by the scruff of the neck and set it on the right track. Major funding must be sought out to make badly-needed and long-ignored repairs to the facility, to say nothing of a good season of productions!

Q. What are your thoughts concerning the future of Le Petit Theatre?

A. I can only hope that someone with enough clout (and a strong constitution) can whip the place back into shape. So many intelligent, talented and well-intentioned people have tried over the past few years to make suggestions and help out—all of these people (myself included) have all but been told "Thanks, but no thanks. We know better." I'm afraid the general consensus of many of us now is that the place can stew in its own juice. It's not enough to help save Le Petit for the nostalgic love of the place—Le Petit has to at least meet the theatre community half way.

INTERVIEWER: REBECCA HALE
INTERVIEWED: June 4, 1998
RESPONDENT: MICHAEL ARATA
Actor/Lawyer/Chairman of the Board of Le Petit Theatre

Q. How did you get to be Chairman of the Board of Le Petit Theatre?

A. I was named Chairman of the Board on April 5, 1998. I am the youngest person to serve as chairman, and also I am the first actor to serve as chairman. I also have never been affiliated with Le Petit. I produced the play A Streetcar Named Desire at another theatre, and then the production moved to Le Petit. They were looking for someone new. I have a business background. From September to December, I was on the Board; then I was elected president in April. Since Le Petit began, actors have not gotten paid because it is a community theatre. There seems to be a lack of respect for actors; they shouldn't get paid. The Board thinks that directors and technical people should be paid, but not actors. I'd like to change that.

I think that community theatres as we know them are on their way out. Community theatres are no longer self-supporting; those days are over. Our society has changed; there is less leisure time and more responsibility. There are also so many other forms of entertainment, such as videos and sports on ESPN twenty-four hours a day. The era of volunteerism in theatre is gone. People are so busy now.

Even if we pay the actors a small amount, an honorarium, we will be telling them that we recognize that their time is valuable.

It's ingrained in the Board at Le Petit not to pay the actors. It goes back to the questions: "Do you view community theatre as a hobby or as a profession?" and "Are community theatre actors not as good as professional actors?" I think they are as good. I've acted in New York and Los Angeles, and many of the community theatre actors here are just as good.

Q. What changes were adopted at the meeting in April concerning the theatre's operations?

A. Some of the people were always on the Board because people put their friends in. There is no such thing any more as a vice-president on the Board who can't vote.
[interruption for Mr. Arata to take one of several phone calls]
Progress at Le Petit stopped from the early to mid-eighties. People on the Board were doing little; they did not make a big effort to improve the theatre's operations. I hope to change this.

Q. What plans do you have for the children's theatre? Will you allow outside groups to use the space?

A. I hope to restart the children's theatre. [It was closed last year.] We have some reconstruction plans for the space itself. I would like to use it during the day for children's plays and at night as an experimental theatre, especially for works by new local playwrights.

Luis Barroso [who started Le Petit's Children's Corner in the 1970s] will teach people how to do children's theatre the proper way. Kids have no pretensions; to them it's play. An important segment of our community has never seen plays at all. I invited the New Orleans Child Advocacy Group to hold its meeting there [at Le Petit], and there were many children in the group who were amazed to see the inside of a theatre. I want kids to know there are art forms that are accessible to do. Sonny Borey will implement my ideas for the children's theatre.

Q. What will you do to try to solve Le Petit's financial problems, and how will you attract bigger audiences to the theatre?

A. I have been pushing for a response from the business community, and the business and artistic leaders are rallying around us. They know we need their support.

All businesses need to maximize their facilities. I hope to do this by utilizing both the main stage and the children's theatre. We will rent out to other theatre groups who are interested. There aren't enough performing spaces in New Orleans for all the theatre groups who want to perform plays.

I just got off the phone with Mitch Landrieu [Louisiana Representative and former actor at Le Petit]. He called to tell me—and it's a long shot—that he is introducing a bill for the state to appropriate money for support of Le Petit.

Q. Will you seek grants for Le Petit?

A. Yes, we applied for three artistic grants through the Louisiana Division of the Arts. Actually, two are artistic and one is for staffing. If the legislature appropriates money for the theatre, it will be for improvements to the facility. We also have applied to the National Endowment of the Arts for a "Meet the Composer" grant for one of the musicians of the Marsalis family to write an original composition for a play at Le Petit. This will be a $60,000-$80,000 project.

Q. Many actors who at one time performed at Le Petit have refused to act there now. What, if anything, will you do to get them to return?

A. Ask them. Many that I've talked to are interested in performing at Le Petit again.

Q. How were the other directors, other than newly-hired Artistic/Executive Director Sonny Borey, selected to direct next season?

A. I just called different directors to ask them. I wanted to include some new directors like Tommye Myrick, a black female.

Q. How were the plays for next season chosen? Is there still a Play-Reading Committee?

A. I'm trying to get rid of the Play-Reading Committee. You barter now over plays; the best plays are not always chosen.

Some plays are outdated. We need someone with a strong vision to select the plays. [interrupted for a phone call, and he reminded me that he had a conference call scheduled shortly]

Q. What future plans do you have for the theatre? What vision do you have for Le Petit?

A. Sonny Borey [former theatre director at Jesuit High School for numerous years] was recently hired. Le Petit has run down for the last ten years; its glory is fading. I'm trying to get new people—local people, business people—interested. It's a valuable landmark for the community and theatre as a whole. Le Petit has a central location in the city. Le Petit has a prime location. I want to restore the creative bravura that this theatre needs—-like the excitement and creativity that the original people in 1916 had. Coming to the theatre is something you can't get on television. I want to restore the creative vitality of this theatre.

Q. Thank you.

INTERVIEWER: REBECCA HALE
INTERVIEWED: June 29, 1998
RESPONDENT: TERRI GERVAIS
Actor/Teacher/Director

Q. Please list all the productions at Le Petit Theatre in which you have acted.

A. MAIN STAGE   CHILDREN'S CORNER

    Hello, Dolly!   Rumplestiltskin
    1776   Beauty and the Beast
    Who Killed Santa Claus?   Emperor's New Clothes
    Peter Pan   Chicken Little
    My Fair Lady
    Pretty Baby
    Rodgers & Hart (review)

Q. Please list all the productions at Le Petit Theatre that you have directed.

A. I have never directed there.

Q. Have you worked at Le Petit in any other capacity, other than as an actor and director?

A. One time, backstage—Real Inspector Hound—props.

Q. What positive and negative experiences have you had at Le Petit?

A. Positives: It was a good training ground. Family

atmosphere. Under Stocker's regime, everyone volunteered. Social rewards. Friendships. Real team work. Opportunity to perform with an orchestra and costumes in a community setting. Always included in things such as parties and the rewards for doing the show.

Negatives: This [Positive] changed after it was run by other people. Somewhere along the way, people were driven away because of Equity. I wasn't driven away by that. Probably right now I'm not able to participate because they are not going to use Equity actors, and I'm Equity. They may not use Equity actors at all because it is a community theatre, and they are trying to save money. They have used Equity actors before, but not lately, except for Charlotte Scully. They are trying to run it like a professional theatre, but they are not paying anyone. In a volunteer situation, people want to have fun, and they weren't anymore. Lack of parking. Competition from other theatres in the suburbs. Probably the way the theatre was always sort of tied up by being run by the older Board being very set in its own parameters, for whatever reason, and limiting what sort of plays they wanted done there and not wanting to stray from certain types of plays. They had this system working against any general manager, in terms of picking plays and how things were run. Now it probably will be a positive thing in that there is a new influx of people on the Board, and there are some more people on it. There are more actors involved directly on the Board, and they are going from a move of antiquated thinking and having more control by the social people involved in the social climate of the city as opposed to the cultural climate. That Board change will probably be a positive. The old Board held theatre back a lot. They kind of kept the dust on things. With some new blood in there, probably dust things off a little bit, and move out into the 21st Century. There are some good things to retain about that, historically, but there is a lot of it that just needs to be kicked out because it's not working. That really is a big negative in the theatre having been confined to that Board. Sort of like political mucky-muck, like you get with politics, where people have their own agenda about things and they are maneuvering the whole theatre with that.

Q. What positive and negative changes have you noticed through the years at Le Petit Theatre?

A. When I did the shows twenty to twenty-five years ago, there was a feeling of camaraderie and friendship, a real social circle. Then when I did <u>The Women</u> about eight years ago, there wasn't that feeling. It was under a different management. It wasn't that they were rude or ugly to anyone, it just wasn't the same sort of feeling.
They [Le Petit Management] didn't show their appreciation of being a part of the theatre the same way Stocker would have. Earlier, there seemed to be a connection with the Board, Stocker, and the actors. Later, there didn't seem to be a connection. The way it was run before was better. With <u>Pretty Baby</u>, the producers were from New York, and they were lovely people, but they only rented the facility. They

had nothing to do with Le Petit.

In the past, Stocker had a team of people, and everyone worked well together on the shows. You were appreciated no matter what you did. They treated the actors with respect and did what they could for the actors. Not that it was a monetary compensation; it was just a social respect compensation. It was a feeling that they wanted you to come and do whatever you wanted to do, whatever you did best. They loved that you were going to contribute. People wanted to volunteer backstage; whereas now, they don't want to volunteer; they want to be paid. Actors want to get paid, too. But actors are more likely not to get paid because they do get the opportunity to be on stage, and they get the notoriety. Whereas, somebody that works backstage really doesn't get that. All they are getting out of it is that they are going to have fun at it. That's what I'm saying. There was more fun going on when people would be doing the shows. And I think there got to be a feeling—even though I wasn't really there to experience that; I had kind of taken myself out of it because of the Equity thing—where people were doing this because they got a kick out of it. They were having fun working in whatever capacity they could do. Whereas, it got to be where they expected people to be there and do what they expected them to do, but there weren't that many "Thank yous," just in the way things were run. My impression will be that that will change with Sonny Borey taking over. He is going to go back to that sort of feeling of really recognizing if somebody is going to volunteer their time, whether they are onstage or backstage or whatever, that he is going to make sure that they are welcomed and they feel appreciated.

That was the case in Peter Pan. That was the feeling from years ago, because Sonny Borey directed Peter Pan. He definitely gave that feel to it because of his personality. You had that feeling of being appreciated. What I have heard from other people, from the shows, is that they didn't necessarily make people feel that way. It wasn't a job; they weren't being paid; and yet, they were expected to act as if they were, but not get the fun out of it.

One of the other things that changed—a negative change, only noticing this through visiting and going there to see the shows—the greenroom, for example, became the pits. When Stocker was there and that whole regime, there was a lovely greenroom area and things were always clean and they had a little kitchen and that was well taken care of and the dressing rooms were always great. When other people took over, over the years it became the pits. Until Sonny came in when he did They're Playing Our Song . . . I went to see that and went into the greenroom. It was like, "What happened?" It was painted. They had furniture in it. It was cleaned up. He did that for the actors, so they would have a nice place to be. And it was still that way when we did Pretty Baby, but the theatre has definitely gone down in that respect. Things weren't being managed as well. And also the attic—where they kept the costumes, the props, and things like that—was so well organized, they would actually loan them out to people on a deposit basis. They knew where everything was. They had a nice little system there. And then that went by the wayside also, to where people don't even know what they have anymore. Things got loaned out and never returned. Nobody was managing, so they probably went through a period of 10 to 15 years where there was just no real management. It was in a state of chaos and not a particularly warm place.

I think that will change under Sonny's direction—back to the way Stocker ran things—and probably will bring the theatre back. That is my impression of what has happened in the past year. When Stocker ran things, at the end of the season, there was always an end-of-the-season party for everybody who participated in any way in the shows. There was a nice party where everybody got together, and they gave out awards to people in the terms of a subscription. They would give younger people some subscriptions; for example, if people did so many of the shows, they did something just to recognize that they had put in their time. And they always gave an award to someone—a volunteer, usually it was a backstage person—like they do with the Storer Boone awards; they did it at Le Petit. The management gave them some sort of physical award and announced their name and gave them recognition.

I think Arthur Tong may have been one person who won that one year, and there were other people. June—I can't think of her last name, and someone told me she passed away. She volunteered for years down there. Sometimes she would be in the play, but a lot of times she worked backstage; and she did stuff in the box office. She was a lovely lady. And she devoted a lot of time, because she derived enjoyment out of being there and being with these people—actors and people who worked in the theatre. So people like that, they would always give an award at the end of each year. It was a big deal for someone to receive it. To my knowledge, I think that all went out the window after Stocker left. The management was totally different. It was like, as if, I think, they were trying to view it like a professional theatre, but they weren't paying people. In a professional theatre, that doesn't go on, but people don't expect that they are going to derive this social . . . or appreciation, because they are getting paid. People can be nice, but you are expected to do what you have to do, because you are getting paid. Whereas, when you are in a volunteer situation, people want to have fun. I think that that must have hurt the theatre over the past 10 years or so, because that wasn't going on and people got tired of that. It's kind of an ordeal to go to Le Petit because of the parking, and so you want to get something out of it. That's probably been a negative for them, just in terms of the patrons, that the parking is such a problem, and also now there is competition with other theatres—other community theatres in the suburbs, across the river, across the lake, in Kenner, in Metairie. We're not the only theatre for people to attend. Now there really are legitimate touring companies that come through, so they have more to compete with.

Q. How important do you feel Le Petit is to the theatrical scene and the cultural life of the city of New Orleans?

A. Just by virtue of the building itself, that there is so much history there and it is such a pretty little theatre, quaint, and it's a beautiful space. And there is so much history, not only in terms of the building itself, but of the people that have worked there and passed through there—either short term or long term—the training that it offered. Whether people go on to do other things or not, it is a great training ground. It is very important—just where it is placed—even though it is difficult parking—where it is placed is a beautiful location for the theatre that it is and for the space that it is. It is very important. It is definitely a part of our culture. It would be a shame for it to not thrive.

Q. What do you feel are the major challenges facing Le Petit Theatre today?

A. These are the challenges as I see them:

(1) To create some sort of situation to make the parking easier for the actors as well as the patrons.
(2) To find a way to compete with the other theatres.
(3) Maybe draw in the tourist population somehow.
(4) Make it an atmosphere where people will work but not necessarily getting paid.
(5) Also to work out being able to use Equity people.

Perhaps with the Equity situation as only a monetary thing right now—and, later, that will happen, because they would leave off a lot of good people if they are eliminating anyone in the Union. My impression is that they don't want to use Equity people because they don't want to pay them. But also, because it is a community theatre, they may want to continue it along those lines, just because it is, quote unquote, a "community theatre" and, in that respect, you keep it strictly on a volunteer basis. But that also means backstage people and everybody concerned, so they would have to try to return to the way it used to be run and make it such an appealing place to be for the people donating their time and volunteering that they would really do that, which used to happen. It's a challenge to do it either way. If they choose to do that, that certainly is possible, and I'm sure it could happen. But it would also be probably beneficial to be able to include people who are in the confines of a union situation. I believe it is possible to do that, if they choose, barring any financial problem.

Q. What are your thoughts concerning the future of Le Petit Theatre?

A. I think that considering that who they have as General Manager now, that he may take a year or two to get it on its feet. I absolutely think it will come back, given that he is probably taking a lot of avenues that I wouldn't even necessarily think of—but one—in terms of writing grants and getting good advertisement, and probably just because of who he is. Sonny is a go-getter and knows the contacts. But the productions will be good. He knows how to get things done. Sonny has a following of people who know he does good work. I absolutely think he will turn Le Petit around. Given the first show he's directing [42nd Street], it will have good people in it, a lot of publicity, a real positive edge to it; and he will get a lot of people back. The theatre has lost a lot of money with many people not renewing. I bet people have gotten subscriptions when they found out he was taking over. I can even see a documentary being done on him in a year or two on one of the cable stations. Now if he wasn't the GM, I would say it probably would be closing this summer. I know they had a lot of financial problems and weren't able to pay their regular weekly bills. He's in there, and he has already started to work. Even though he has officially not taken his position yet, he started writing grants and stuff.

It is an old theatre and it does have a lot of heritage and culture and stories and history to it. There probably aren't too many theatres in the U.S. like that—that is considered a community theatre, that has survived through a lot. I don't know if Le Petit is not the oldest in the country, but probably so.

I have many fond memories, good times. I hope to get to do something else there.

Q. Thank you for your comments.

INTERVIEWER: REBECCA HALE
INTERVIEWED: July 6, 1998
RESPONDENT: EDWARD R. COX
Actor/Designer/Director

Q. What are your thoughts about the children's theatre at Le Petit?

A. We've done some magic in that space. There will never be any unity in the theatre. It's all personal power struggles. People are willing to kill other people's careers. It's terribly expensive to park; parking is not accessible. Nowadays, they don't want volunteers anymore. Volunteers get in the way, I'm told. It's the power trip. The shows never open complete. Shows lately aren't ready to open. If they had more volunteer help, shows might be ready. This is supposed to be a quality community theatre. When someone like me could say, "I want to be in a play [as a young boy]" and get in the cast. Now if you are socially, politically correct, you'll get in. No other way.
The 1970s was the Golden Age of Children's Theatre at Le Petit. Families need a place to share theatre. They needed to have weekend performances.
For Beauty and the Beast [1997], I was paid $350 to design the set. I was fighting with Keith Briggs [managing director]. Keith said the set was just a backdrop for the actors. When children's theatre productions were getting better reviews than main-stage plays, then my job was in

trouble if I opened my mouth. We [Cox and Lokey] were treated badly and told not to say anything. The minute people think you're good, they get jealous; it's as though they're working for you. There's so much competition today with films, ball games, etc. You must have a quality production to be competitive.

Q. Thank you for your candid comments.

INTERVIEWER: REBECCA HALE
INTERVIEWED: July 6, 1998
RESPONDENT: VATICAN LOKEY
Actor/Playwright

Note: This is Vatican Lokey's second interview. He was originally interviewed in 1997.

Q. You agreed to speak with me again, specifically about children's theatre at Le Petit?

A. Yes, I wanted to tell you that Edward R. [Cox] was the first recipient of Teddy's Award for Excellence in Children's Theatre. The name of the children's theatre was changed to Teddy's Corner, and then in 1996 it was changed back to Children's Corner at the discretion of the director [Cox].
My production of Rapunzel toured four states. We [Cox and Lokey] were gone from New Orleans for a season, so we ceased to exist as far as Le Petit was concerned. Le Petit wanted two Freddy [Palmisano] plays. We said we wanted to perform one established play, which was fine with them, and one new original play. Two days later, Keith Briggs was hired and squelched the idea.
When the Beverly [Dinner Theatre] burned down, people stopped doing theatre for the love of it. Applause was the first New Orleans show that I did. Elliott Keener directed it. He was not always there, so Kenny Beck, the choreographer, directed when Elliott wasn't there. The set

was the most awful you've ever seen. It was a box that rotated. Edward was cast as Dwayne. Cynthia Owen was Bonnie. The song "She's No Longer a Gypsy" was given to Cynthia, instead of Edward.

Q. What first impressions did you have of Le Petit?

A. I remember walking into Le Petit and being enchanted. Standing in the room made my hair stand up on my arms. It all tingled. The costumes were not evenly laid out. I made dividers out of cardboard for costume racks. The theatre is quaintly adequate. There's enough room for dressing backstage. The tech is grossly inadequate. The fly system needs major work. Wiring needs replacement. Luis Barroso worked at Gallery Circle, then Le Petit. The space became a children's theatre. Luis brought Arthur Tong to Le Petit. Luis controlled the children's theatre, while Stocker [Fontelieu] controlled the main stage. Later, Luis left for Atlanta.
Recently, Uncle Wayne [Daigrepont] was spoken to. All theatre photos were taken out because they would be thrown out. Trish McLain rescued them. Bill Walker, the technical director, wanted to throw out everything. I think Sonny [Borey] taking over the theatre will pull it out of the hole. There are too many power struggles now. Property values are shooting up. In the next ten to fifteen years, I don't think it will exist.

Q. What about applying for grants?

A. It's too little, too late. It's not music-based; it's not tourist-attracting. I don't see it lasting. Theatre in other parts of the country in similar situations would survive. People wouldn't let their theatre die.

Q. Thank you for your comments.

INTERVIEWER: REBECCA HALE
TELEPHONE INTERVIEW: July 14, 1998
RESPONDENT: LUCY DAIGLE
Board Member

Q. There was a meeting of the Board of Le Petit on June 14. Please comment about any changes that occurred concerning by-laws.

A. We voted to enlarge the Board from fifteen to thirty-six members.
Every year we elect or re-elect five members of the board, three from the active membership and two from the general membership.

Q. What is the difference between active and general membership?

A. We are now calling everybody general members. The active members were people who have done things for the theatre. Every member of the Board is a voting member. Honorary lifetime members are non-voting members. Rosa Deutsch is a lifetime board member. The board members elect the chairman. As of 1998, there is no president, only a chairman. Erroll Laborde initiated a form for making a person a board member. This must be approved by two members. We have a new support organization called the Friends of Le Petit, with both males and females. Another change is there are no longer student/teacher subscriptions offered to the public. We have a new box office manager named Jennifer Richardson. The inside of the theatre is being painted. There will be some repairing of the exterior of the theatre. The library upstairs has been repainted. There are new drapes. The children's theatre [closed for a short time] may be reopened, possibly with Luis Barroso directing.

We don't have our budget yet. We are paying Sonny [Borey] a much higher salary than we paid Keith [Briggs], plus Sonny's benefits are double what Keith's were.

That's about all that is happening.

A. Thank you for your comments.

INTERVIEWER: REBECCA HALE
INTERVIEWED: July 29, 1998
RESPONDENT: ROSA DEUTSCH
Actor/Board Member

Q. Please state your name.

A. I'm Rosa Deutsch, Mrs. Brunswick Deutsch. I am the daughter-in-law of the lady who started Le Petit Theatre in her house in—I believe 1916 was their first performance in her drawing room and they called themselves "The Drawing Room Players." And they, her and her group of amateur actors, were so successful with their friends, everybody enjoyed the performances so much, they said, "Oh, you should get yourself a larger space." The group went down to the French Quarter which, at that time, was a slum; rents were very cheap and they rented a large room in one of the Pontalba buildings. I'm not sure if it was the upper or lower. They constructed a simple stage—they put in some makeshift chandeliers and cheap little rush seats—and they began performing there. They were so successful, people enjoyed it so much, everyone said they ought to have their own theatre and one of the gentlemen, Harold Newman, was a financier and he said that we ought to buy our own property and build a theatre and we did! They were very successful in finding a wonderful corner, a very strategic corner, abutting Jackson Square. There was an old historic building right on that corner, but they bought three more adjoining lots which had little unimportant buildings on them. They tore down those little buildings and built a good professional, perfectly-equipped theatre building, a little more than 450 seats. They used the old corner building for dressing rooms and a reception room, where they served coffee and that sort of thing. There was a patio between the corner building and the theatre so it has made a very lovely, wonderful installation. It is very attractive for social events as well as having a perfectly well-equipped theatre. And at the beginning, I think, everybody was a volunteer and very shortly they hired a professional director, and they had a secretary who was paid and, I guess, the janitor. They had a carpenter, Jacob Wilber, and he built the sets and did practically everything around the theatre for years. The set designer who shortly came in for them was Ethel Crumb Brett, Mrs. Morris Brett. She stayed with them for about 45 years, designing the sets and the costumes—and where shall we go from there? I think they put on about ten plays a year at the beginning. And gradually, because of the ongoing expenses, they began producing, let's see, we were doing seven and then six, and last year we decided we better do only five shows a year. To utilize the theatre, we would rent it out to other groups, to give us an income without too much expense, because like so many of the art organizations today, we are strapped for money. We never have quite enough money.

Q. Do you know why, in the original charter, that if the

property is sold, it will be divided among Tulane, Loyola, and LSU? Do you know why that was done?

A. Well, they didn't want anybody to profit, any individual to profit by the sale of the theatre. Because that has now become an extremely valuable property, as you can imagine.

Q. How did you first become involved with Le Petit Theatre? How long have you been involved with Le Petit Theatre?

A. I first became involved because I, from my teens, was interested in acting, and I went to New York, and I did some TV and radio work in New York. And I came back in the '40s, and a friend said to me, "Oh, you've been acting in New York; you have to go to the Little Theatre and see if they would like to have you." And so I did go down. I auditioned, and I got the lead the first time I auditioned for them. That was the play There's Always Juliet, an English comedy . . . in the mid-'40s. I became interested in acting in the theatre. I played a number of leading roles at that time. I met Mrs. Eberhard Deutsch, who was one of the founders. She had founded the Drawing Room Players in her drawing room. And she introduced me to her son, Brunswick Deutsch, whom I, several years later, married. And so I played a number of lead parts in the late '40s, and one show we did, The Barretts of Wimpole Street, which was a famous vehicle of Katherine Cornell, and I played in that. It was later voted the most popular play they ever did up to that time.

Q. In doing research, I discovered that former Broadway actress Julie Haydon performed at Le Petit in <u>Major Barbara</u>. Do you know why Haydon chose this role?

A. All I remember is she wanted to play that part.

Q. What do you see as the strong points of Le Petit Theatre today?

A. Well, the strong point of the theatre is its plan—which is not made over from somebody's old drugstore or factory building, but built by a fine architect, Richard Koch, one of the fine architects of New Orleans, and built in perfect Spanish Colonial style to harmonize with the Vieux Carre . . . that is our very valuable and beautiful building. And then, of course, we have a loyal supporting group of members.

Q. What do you see as the weak points of Le Petit Theatre today?

A. Weak points [laughs]. Well . . . I think you always, in an arts organization, need a little more money. You never have quite enough money to do all that you want to do. We have, of course, this beautiful building, which really consists of two buildings—the theatre is on one side, the patio in the middle, and the old building where we have the coffee room. And the Children's Theatre was made in the old building which runs along Chartres Street. It's a lot of upkeep to keep up an old building, maintain the size of the building that we have. Right now, I believe we need roof repairs, and we need to replace the boards on the balcony, which runs around the outside of the building; those boards are getting rotten. There's a great deal of maintenance in an old building, which is always a big expense. And another disadvantage, in a way, is the fact that it is in the heart of the Vieux Carre, and parking is a problem. You know, people have to pay to park or come down very early in the evening at a certain time when they might be able to get a space on the street, but it's difficult. And then a lot of people nowadays are afraid of crime in the Quarter; they don't like to go home late at night. But we are on a busy corner, just diagonally across from Jackson Square. It is a problem because older people are hesitant about coming down to the French Quarter at night.

Q. Do you remember Le Petit's involvement with UNO in 1969? Why did this affiliation end?

A. I don't know . . . lack of enthusiasm, I guess, on the part of the University. . . . I really don't remember anything about that myself. Maybe a professor, at that time, suggested they didn't need that affiliation.

Q. What vision do you have for the future of Le Petit Theatre?

A. The vision I have for it is simply to continue. It's been going for eighty-two years. We have never had to cancel a production other than one night when somebody's father died. The leading lady's father died. She just felt she couldn't go on, and we canceled one evening's performance. We've been very professional in presenting our productions to our public and to our members. Now, for a long while, our members had to buy a season subscription. But sometime in the late '60s, we decided to take people in—you know, walk-ins, and that's worked out alright. And we still have a core membership of people who buy the season tickets. So that's how we operate.

Q. Why are the Managing Directors changing each year?

A. We changed because we did not find the right person for the job. We had one lady who was a wonderful actress, but she was no manager at all. And she would have checks on her desk to pay musicians or this or that, and she would just forget to pay them. People were very unhappy about that. We had another gentleman that we liked, but he decided to go back to Oklahoma to get his Masters Degree or his Doctorate in Theatre. David Cockerell—we found him quite satisfactory—but he decided he would go back and get a Doctorate. And we had—Don Marshall was the Manager for awhile. He did not direct shows, and he decided to go to another job. We changed [Managing Directors] for perfectly good reasons.

Sonny Borey is a fabulously talented man. He put on magnificent—I mean, things that looked completely professional on the stage at Jesuit High School with students. And you have to admit, they were absolutely smashing productions. And we were very happy when Sonny decided after 28 years he wanted to make a change, and he liked the idea of coming to Le Petit Theatre—a real theatre—it wasn't a high school auditorium; it was real theatre. So he's very happy with us, and we are very happy with him. But it's been only a short time that he's been our Manager . . . very dynamic person.

Q. By nature or by definition of community theatre, the actors are always voluntary. Do you ever foresee a time when that would change, and the actors would get paid?

A. The only thing that we have done recently is to say that we would pay the parking fees, because driving down to the French Quarter and trying to park every night can be expensive. With the younger people, it became a very heavy expense, so we are paying their parking fees. But, as a matter of fact, not everyone presents their parking tickets to us; so it has not been a big expense for the theatre.

Q. Anything else you would like to say?

A. I would like to say that anyone who is interested in acting and is very anxious to get on our stage because of the fact that it is practically like a professional stage, and so we never have any trouble casting. We get very talented people, of course. Twenty, thirty, forty years ago, we were the only game in town. Now, many, many groups have sprung up, so there is something of a drain on the talent pool. But still, I think when we offer a show, there is a very good turn out for the auditions.
I wanted to say something about the plays we present. . . you have to realize that we have to make our expenses; we have to be self-supporting. We do have, nowadays, in the last few years, we have had to go after corporate support. Up until eight or ten years ago, we didn't have to ask for a

penny. The theatre was self-supporting, just by its members' season tickets. But then when the gasoline shortage happened and everything went up after that time, and we realized we had to get other sources of funds . . . but that's our biggest problem—really getting enough financial support. But I think that is true of practically all the arts organizations.

Q. Mr. Arata told me the state legislature passed a bill giving some funding. Are there other grants for the theatre?

A. Yes! That's very new. We haven't gotten it yet. We have to raise $90,000 matching funds. That's a little more than a quarter of what they are promising to give us. So we feel that we can get that $90,000. We are trying to write grant applications.

Q. Do you think the theatre is in any danger of closing?

A. I don't think anyone in New Orleans would want to see the Little Theatre close. We owe a considerable note to the Whitney Bank, but they have told us that they do not want to foreclose on the Little Theatre. It would be a very unpopular thing for them to do. They have been very patient with us, and we are trying to meet our obligations. It would be a great shame to close the theatre. It would make a great nightclub; but, on the other hand, we don't need another nightclub. And I have been told we can't put a nightclub so close to the Cathedral . . . zoning would not permit that. And also the fact that we have the old building. Now the old building on the corner, which was a 1793 or

1795 building, was demolished in the '60s and rebuilt with the perfectly-matching exterior so as to be compatible in the Vieux Carre. When I say Vieux Carre and French Quarter, well that's the same thing. That building became the Children's Corner and some backstage workspace. We have had a very faithful following of members. It is something that you give your life to. It is certainly mine and my husband's main volunteer activity, as it is with many of our members. We just want it to continue. It's now eighty-something years old, and I see no reason why it shouldn't go on for another eighty or so years.

Q. Does the Guild still exist?

A. Oh, yes, definitely. That's the Ladies Guild. In fact, one gentleman said he wanted to join. The Guild does some fundraising. It has given a jazz brunch for several years. It's given some other fundraisers—dancing and things like that.

Q. For a time, there have been Sunday afternoon salons.

A. That's been fairly recent. Marda Burton, a lady who lives in the French Quarter who had been having little informal salons at her apartment, she decided that because they were becoming so popular, she asked if she could bring them to the Little Theatre. And she has done so. She gets donated refreshments and people come and pay $5.00 and she accepts any talent that wants to come. I guess that will continue. We rent to other groups—either the small theatre on the side or the main stage. We also occasionally rent to weddings. If they get married in St. Louis Cathedral, it's nice to have the reception right there. The courtyard is very pretty and we have had some replanting there. Years and years ago, the courtyard had a much larger planting bed, and we decided we needed more pavement for people to get around in during intermission, so we made the flowerbeds much smaller so we had more room for people to move. About five years ago, I decided the patio was looking a bit scruffy, and so I brought in a landscape designer and put in new plants. Of course, that sort of thing has to be maintained all the time, so I have been doing that. Recently, I found one of the gentlemen who lives in the French Quarter, and he is going to take over that job for me.

Q. Can you think of any productions in the past thirty years that have really stood out in your mind?

A. I would say <u>Evita</u>, directed by Sonny Borey, was a marvelous production. Another one that I thought was wonderful was <u>A Man for all Seasons</u>. We did a very good one by Tom Wolfe, <u>Look Homeward, Angel</u>. We did that twice, and I think the first one was the best and many people told me <u>The Barretts of Wimpole Street</u> in the late '40s was very memorable. We have done a lot of shows—seven or eight a year for eighty years. I was in <u>My Fair Lady</u>. <u>My Fair Lady</u> was very good, done by a man who no longer lives here—Max Gorgal. He directed and designed the sets.

Q. What about the children's shows?

A. Well, <u>Peter Rabbit</u> was very good a few years ago by Junya

Tanner. He was a very good director.

Q. Have there been any changes in the charter?

A. Yes, we always had a group of what we called "Active Members." And they were the people most active in the theatre. They were given certain powers, which the regular members who met only once a year did not have. But there was a lot of discussion about that recently . . . we have to check into that.

Q. Do you still have the same committee? The Play-Reading Committee?

A. Pretty much! We read plays and recommend plays to the Board. Stocker used to go to New York every year to see productions and decide what he wanted to produce. Course, it is always a problem to get the rights to any plays. Cabaret was one of our great successes. I was on the Play-Reading Committee for a long time, and I suggested it as our opening musical. Stocker said that everyone had seen Cabaret and it's been in the movies, so he didn't think we should do that. And we put out a poll to our audience and they voted "yes." It was a great show!

INTERVIEWER: REBECCA HALE
TELEPHONE INTERVIEW: July 29, 1998
RESPONDENT: LEON CONTAVESPRIE
Le Petit Board Member/Actor

Q. What is the difference between active and sustaining members?

A. Active members are the Board plus favorites of the Board. Sustaining members are all season ticket holders. All season ticket holders now have a vote as of 1998 on any by-laws. Active members could be added by the Board at any time.

Q. Who are the active members that are favorites of the Board?

A. Whoever these little snobs wanted to put on the list. The active members are supposed to be those who have served above and beyond the call of duty. There are no set rules for determining this.

Q. Are you on a committee?

A. Yes, I'm the head of the Play-Reading Committee.

Q. Now that Michael Arata has been appointed President of the Board, how will this affect Le Petit?

A. He knows how to get things done.

Q. How is the theatre doing financially?

A. The Legislature has appropriated $100,000 for every

$30,000 Le Petit raises with a cap of $300,000. This happened in June. Keith Briggs shifted the children's theatre to the main stage; and when he did, we made $15,000 on one show, as opposed to losing $800 per show. We did a two-character version of <u>The Lion, the Witch, and the Wardrobe</u> that made a profit of $7,000. This was in April.

Q. What about paying actors?

A. The charter would have to be changed to pay actors. I think the theatre needs to go professional non-profit.

Q. Thank you for your time.

INTERVIEWER: REBECCA HALE
TELEPHONE INTERVIEW: June 18, 1999
RESPONDENT: DR. AUGUST STAUB
Retired University of New Orleans Professor

Q. Dr. Staub, do you know why an alliance in 1969 between the Department of Drama and Fine Arts at Louisiana State University in New Orleans [now known as the University of New Orleans] and Le Petit Theatre dissolved after only one year?

A. Yes, I do. Le Petit was organized around the Tulane Theatre Department. The Tulane Theatre Department collapsed. L.S.U.N.O. was a new theatre department, started in 1966. Eventually, the Tulane Theatre Department thrived. Influential people on the Board at Le Petit wanted to be associated with a more established university, like Tulane, and a more established theatre chairman, like Monroe Lippman.

Q. Thank you.

INTERVIEWER: REBECCA HALE
INTERVIEWED: September 1, 1999
RESPONDENT: SONNY BOREY
Executive/Artistic Driector of Le Petit Theatre from 1998-present

Q. What is your title?

A. Executive/Artistic Director.

Q. What years have you directed plays at Le Petit Theatre?

A. I'm into my second year as Executive/Artistic Director. I believe it was 1985 when I first started directing shows here. The first show I directed was Evita.

Q. Name the plays that you have directed here.

A. Evita. After Evita, there was Peter Pan. Sweeney Todd. Then Oliver, A Chorus Line, Guys and Dolls, They're Playing Our Song, Sophisticated Ladies, 42nd Street. I just finished City of Angels, and now Grand Hotel. I believe that's all. There might be more, but, offhand, I can't recall.

Q. Describe the play selection process.

A. It depends. This past season, the Board has allowed me a lot of leeway in the shows that I would like to have. There is a Play-Reading Committee that decides the number of shows and which shows it would like to have for the season. I thought we should have shows that hadn't been done in the city before, shows that are different, that would attract a new audience. For a long time, we've let our audiences get older without trying to bring in younger people. This is something I'm trying to do right now. That's why we have the selection that I've made for this coming year. Not that we want to lose our older audience; we want to keep them, too.

Q. My next question was how much freedom do you have in the selection of plays?

A. They [the Board] pretty much let me do the plays I want to do.

Q. Do you select the other directors for each season for the plays that you are not directing?

A. Yes.

Q. Have any actors that you have worked with at Le Petit progressed to professional careers?

A. People that I've worked with both here and at Jesuit [the high school where he taught and directed plays for many years] that have gone on. Mark Calamia, who was in Chorus Line for me, here, and a number of shows at Jesuit, is in Fosse right now on Broadway.

Q. Describe the working conditions for you at the theatre. What type of staff have you had (stage manager, technical director, etc.)?

A. The staff has really increased since I've been here. We have, right now, a box office manager. We have a lady, Julia

Burka, who is in charge of marketing and development. Bill Walker is our technical director. Backstage, we have four full-time employees backstage who work with Bill. We have Derek Franklin, who's also my musical director for my shows. He works with us now; he's sort of an executive assistant. He handles a lot of the billing; he handles a lot of the artistic things that go on with the shows. We have a gentleman by the name of Jim Word who is now our historian. We're going to start having, for this coming season, an exhibit for each show that will change from show to show, that will show our past. We're trying to organize this and put it all together and eventually have a book done on the theatre.

Q. Is there a list of all the children's plays that have been done in the children's theatre?

A. Jim Word can help you with that. He's in the process of putting all that together right now.

Q. Have you noticed any differences in directing at Le Petit recently, as opposed to when you directed here in 1985?

A. Not really, because every director has their own style; things they demand, and things they want to happen. The only way I agree to direct a show, no matter where it is, is if I have control over the way the show looks. I think any director expects that. To be honest with you, no, there weren't any differences.

Q. Did you have the same number of staff people each time?

A. Well, I always bring my own people with me.

Q. What challenges do you face as Executive/Artistic Director at Le Petit?

A. There are a number of challenges. First of all, enlarging our subscription base, which has gone down for a number of years; we're trying to get that up. As well as enlarging the subscription base, I think it's very important that we have single ticket sales that are very large. Obviously, retiring the debt of the theatre. Increasing the staff. Something especially in community theatre or any type of theatrical venture, charging the prices we charge for tickets, you really need support from outside. You need corporate support. You need individual people contributing. To pay the bills is always a problem.

Q. Are these grants that you have applied for?

A. Yes, correct. The state is giving us money for renovations. Mitch Landrieu [congressman and former actor at Le Petit] had a bill passed to help us.

Q. What plans do you have for the children's theatre?

A. When I came back here, they had done away with the children's theatre. We started it again. We had three shows last year, and we have three shows this year. We would like to start writing our own shows again, like we did in the past.

Q. Are any performances being done for school children?

A. We have a program called "Educational Arts Project," where we do special shows and bring kids in three times a year. These are shows done especially for school children [not plays that are part of the regular season]. We actually have the children's season; we have our main stage season; we have director's studio now, where we co-produce with other theatre groups. Like <u>Late Night Catechism</u>, which is being performed in the director's studio, we are co-producers with them. We also have Educational Arts Project, so that's four things we have at the theatre. We'll also be co-producing a play with the Tennessee Williams Festival.

Q. How will you attract bigger audiences to the theatre?

A. I think, by the quality of the productions. If people see that you are doing quality shows and doing it consistently, and you're not doing it "hit or miss," people will come. If the product is there, people will come.

Q. What are your plans for the future of the theatre? What vision do you have for Le Petit?

A. Right now, I'm in the process of trying to make the building itself work. We're trying to renovate. This past year, we've instituted a lot, doing director's studio, doing the Educational Arts Project, the different types of shows that we're doing. Things have got to progress; we have to make this work. And then we'll go from here.

Q. Where would you want to "go from here"?

A. The future is going to tell us that. We need to see how we're doing now.

Q. Have the season subscriptions increased this year?

A. I'll be able to tell you that in September. I know that we're getting a lot of new subscriptions.

Q. Would you care to make any other comments?

A. So much has gone on in this theatre in eighty-three years, and I don't think there's any organization that lasts eighty-three years and doesn't have its ups and downs; everyone does. I think the future looks very bright for this theatre, whether I'm here or not. My main challenge is I want to leave such a foundation for this theatre that whether I'm here or not, it will succeed.

Q. How do you think this theatre has added to the cultural life of New Orleans?

A. Oh, tremendously. Just the building itself, the physical facility itself. Where else can you find something like this? In any city you go to, it's few and far between. Especially the location we're in. Everybody bemoans the fact that we're in the Quarter and all the parking problems. I think it's wonderful we're here. It's absolutely fabulous.

INTERVIEWER: REBECCA HALE
INTERVIEWED: September 16, 1999
RESPONDENT: JIM WORD
Historian/Business Manager/Actor/Designer

Q. You are the official Historian of Le Petit?

A. Yes. I am employed as the official historian of Le Petit. It's a part-time paid position. I began my career here in 1966 as a volunteer. I became part of the paid staff from 1968 to 1972. I started out as a Senior Technician here. In 1972, I left New Orleans to pursue a professional career as a scenery/lighting/costume designer and an actor in Atlanta, New York, Florida, and up and down the Eastern Seaboard. This actually relates to your topic. After doing that for a while, I ended up as artistic director for the High School for the Performing Arts in Atlanta; and after I retired from that, I always wanted to come back to New Orleans, so I came back here. I had visited the theatre [Le Petit] during the time that I was away. I had seen it go through some very good periods, some very bad periods . . . a lot of roller coaster stuff. The past 15 years or so, the theatre has been on a decline. I noticed the archival collection, which at one point a lot of attention was paid to, that was in really disastrous condition for a lot of reasons. I'm very careful not to blame previous administrations of this theatre for what happened, because, in reality, they did the very best that they could; and sometimes it was more important to pay the light bill and to pay the taxes on the building than to make sure the archives were in the right shape. In any case, I wrote a proposal to the current Board of Governors and the current director to come in and pull all this stuff back together and get it in an actual archive state so that it could be preserved either at this building or, should this building ever close or the theatre ever close, it would be given to the Historic New Orleans Collection. That's how I got here . . . how I started this project.

Q. Is there a list of all the Children's Theatre productions ever done?

A. Yes. I have not been able to pull it up on the computer yet because of the operation of <u>Grand Hotel</u>. If you can give me a week to fourteen days, I'll do all of that. We have the show running; the theatre's all torn up. The early years will be fairly easy to do because I was the first resident designer for the children's theatre when it first started. You might want to put in your notes that the children's theatre program started in 1970 under the direction of Luis Barroso. Prior to that, there had been occasional children's offerings through the Junior League, the same situations they have in a lot of cities. The Junior League sponsors children's theatre at various organizations. But there had never been a resident children's program here. The Board of Governors at that point decided that they wanted a permanent in-house children's theatre season with at least three shows a year. At that point, Gallery Circle Theatre on Madison Street, which is no longer in existence, had their own children's theatre and Luis was the director of that program. The problem they had over there was they had one performance space. The children's shows would have to be done on the same set that the evening shows were being done on; it was a mess. The Theatre [Le Petit] hired him in 1970 to come here and that was the beginning of what was called the "Plan des Enfants," which means the Children's Forum. That period from 1970 up to, I would say, 1978, was known in New Orleans as the golden age of children's theatre. We were—Luis, myself, a lot of people that you know around town today—Becky Allen, Peggy Scott LaBorde, Pam Vergas, John Garret, Kenny Wesson—all of those performers . . . Ricky Graham . . . all of them came out of that children's theatre program. So it was not only great entertainment for kids, it was a terrific audience development tool for all of the theatres in town—not just this one—but it also produced some of the first line talent that you see in the city today.

Q. What does your position as historian entail?

A. At this point, the proposal is developed in several phases. The first phase was to locate, classify, and catalog all of the photographs of the productions of the theatre since its inception, some of which were kept, as I said in the declining years, some of which were kept in albums, some in locked cabinets in the library, but only about two thousand of them were there. At this point, we have six thousand photographs and we are working our way to eight thousand, and those were just in boxes and file folders that were thrown into the attic years and years ago . . . some of them very badly damaged, some of them in very good shape. The whole point of the first phase is to find everything—identify everything—catalog it, classify it, and classify it as to musical, comedy, drama, etc. And the major part of that is the development of a database to put on the computer. Oddly enough, this is the 84th season; none of this was actually written down anywhere. Even the photograph albums that were kept in the '20s, '30s, and '40s have just pages of photographs and a program. There is no actual identification of the photographs as to what actor this is, what scene that is. It's a big, big job in putting that data in a database so that where there is a computer that you can actually pull up what is here and what's supposed to be here because, over the years, sadly, a lot of stuff has just walked out the door. In the past, this theatre had probably the best collection of period costumes, period furniture, and props of almost any theatre I have ever seen or worked with; and I have worked with a lot of them. Through the years, it has all disappeared. Now, occasionally, when the theatre was in really bad financial trouble, they would hold yard sales. People would come in and buy stuff. I understand, pretty much, to a degree, why that had to happen, but it pretty much decimated the theatre's furniture and costumes. But, back to your original question . . . part of Phase I is this photo exhibit which is something that needs to happen but also is a way to let people become aware that this process is going on. And all through this season, every play, there will be a new photographic exhibit in the lobby of photographs from particular genres of shows. This one is musical; the next one will be comedy from 1917 all the way up to the present. It is a way to let the public know what a real treasure this is. It's a fun way to get people involved. I have a wonderful committee that I put together of about twenty-five people of former board members, actors, new people, old people that have been involved in this theatre over the years; and they do a lot of the work as far as getting stuff together.

Then Phase II is doing the same thing with the existing documents about the theatre because there are Board minutes; we have the original rent receipts from when the theatre moved to the Pontalba building in 1916, and things like that; but they are just lying around. Mold and mildew are getting to them, and they get rotten. Like I said, they are not identified, catalogued, or classified either, so the documents will be the next phase. Probably the less glamorous project, but to a degree, the most important one. And there are other things that are coming out of this; there is a possibility of videotapes being made, a documentary video being made. There is a producer in Texas who is interested in it. We are in preliminary discussions with him right now about a possible historic documentary that he feels he could market to A&E, Discovery, and other channels like that. And then, at the end of that . . . the primary goal, of course, is to make sure that some sort of legal document is set up, that this collection is maintained exactly as we put it together no matter what happens to the theatre. Should anything horrendous happen to the theatre, probably it would be transferred to the Historic New Orleans Collection. But we hope that will never happen.

Q. When I interviewed Sonny Borey, there was mention of a book?

A. Yes, one of the goals down the line is a book. There was a little tiny booklet written in 1928. And that is really the only thing published, other than things that have resided in Tulane Library—Masters Theses and one Doctoral dissertation that were done on the place. There has never actually been a history written and that is a goal eventually, too. What we want is for this work to be divided in some manner so that it just doesn't lie around.

Q. What vision do you have for the theatre? How do you see the future of Le Petit?

A. Actually, I'm sure that is a question, I'm sure, you asked Sonny, and he is the most qualified to answer it. But I do have my own vision of what I would like to see happen. I would like it to continue to be a vital and vibrant producing organization that does quality theatre for an audience that, I'm sure, exists in New Orleans, even though it gets harder and harder to get people to come down here. Although I think we are winning that battle little by little. But I would also like to see it become almost an umbrella arts organization for other types of endeavors—into operating our own subscription season and our own Children's Theatre season. I would like to see it become a home for other arts organizations that wouldn't necessarily be a part of Le Petit but who would produce work here almost in a co-production type of situation. There is a little bit of that going on now with the Tennessee Williams Festival producer here with us. I would like to see it become more active in that area because, I think, there was a time when there were 7,000 members here and every show had to run for a week in order to satisfy that membership. I'm not sure that membership theatre, per se, not just here, but nationally . . . I'm just not sure if it is all that viable anymore. I think it's an important component of it, but I don't think you can operate a theatre as a private subscription theatre anymore. There are just too many considerations—people don't want to commit to being in the same place, the same night for nine months of the year. They need flexibility in scheduling; there are just too many things preventing that from happening. I think any arts organization that wants to succeed is going to have to, like I said, produce its own works, but also become an umbrella organization so that other arts groups can move in and out in some sort of loose confederacy. I think that will help to solidify the position of the theatre. During the '20s and '30s, this theatre really had a national reputation as a leader in the Little Theatre movement, and that reputation is still there. It's just that nobody knows about it anymore; through dissertations and things like that, people eventually find out.

In order for this building to remain the storehouse and treasure that it is theatrically, it's going to have to change with the times. And, as you know, particularly in New Orleans, one of the things that we enjoy about being here, the charm of living here, is that things don't change much down here. It is possible to live in a memory even today. But in order to survive, the theatre is going to have to change its focus in one way or another. That probably means a different vision for the Board of Governors. I hesitate to say this, but let's say, less "arthritic." Let's keep the antiquity in the building, in the patio, and in the history of the place, but we have to become more forward looking; or, otherwise, it's going to become like the Cabildo. It will be a museum that people come and walk in. That should not happen. I believe, as does Mr. Borey, the director, there are a lot of excuses offered for why we just don't want to come to Le Petit anymore—we don't like parking in the Quarter, there's all that trash down there, there's all that noise, and blah, blah, blah, blah. . . . But if you offer a product that is good enough, people will find a way to deal with the parking. They will find a way to come down here. That show Late Night Catechism proved it. I look at the guest register from that show every weekend. And, you know, where did they all come from? They come from Arabi, from Chalmette, from Marrero, from Kenner. All of the suburban people who said, "We just don't want to deal with the mainstage program at Le Petit anymore," will come down here for something like that. So if you give them quality, they will come. Also, like I said before, I think that's a national problem. Being involved in theatre as many places as I've been, we are in a bad period for art. People just can't seem to find time or money to commit to it like they used to. Fortunately, movies and films are helping us a lot. I keep my mouth shut about movie ticket prices because if they get higher, it may be worth it to come see something live rather than go to the Palace [movie theatre] with popcorn and a Diet Coke.

Q. Is Le Petit involved in sponsoring the Tennessee Williams Festival? They weren't originally.

A. No, they weren't, originally, but how it has worked out through the years. What happens is that we co-produce, in a sense. I don't really understand the intricacies of that arrangement. You could probably find out more from Peggy Scott LaBorde because she is so involved with the Williams Festival. But the Williams Festival develops the production. We co-produce it and it becomes part of our season. One of the reasons is that the constitution and bylaws of this organization historically require that this is a community theatre and actors cannot be compensated. In the early '70s, there was some discussion, and nothing ever came of that, there was some discussion of making it a professional or semi-professional organization, never an Equity house, but paying the actors, and that sort of dried up. Because of the restrictions of the constitution and the bylaws, actors are not supposed to be compensated, so anytime actors are compensated, which they generally are for the Williams productions, it has to be a co-production that is brought in by an outside company. We just can't produce it ourselves. I don't really understand the intricacies. I'm not the General Manager . . . Sonny or Peggy Scott LaBorde would be better to explain that to you. I don't really even want to know. The people who run the Williams Festival—you know how territorial people are in New Orleans—they don't want to. . . . I remember several years ago there was some discussion about combining the two organizations—and this is just gossip; also heard, at one point when things were really, really bad here, we went through director after director—no one stayed . . . it was just a mess. There was some discussion at that point of the Williams Festival taking over the theatre, but the active membership went, "Absolutely not!" I'm glad that didn't happen. See, I see it in the reverse. I see for Le Petit to be the umbrella organization and the Williams Theatre to be a component of that . . . a separate entity. I don't know if you are familiar with the Arts Alliance in Atlanta. The Memorial Arts Center in Atlanta was created as a memory to all of Atlanta's art people who died in a plane crash at Orleans, France. There is one organization called the Arts Alliance and under it are the Alliance Theatre, the Atlanta Symphony Orchestra, the Museum of Art, the Atlanta Children's Theatre . . . all these separate entities. The Arts Alliance acts as an umbrella and handles all the funding, passes out the money. It is very effective because they get millions and millions of dollars in grants because they are this large organization. And if Le

Petit could be the over-arching organization and fund the Williams Festival and fund other things that could come in here . . . it could work very interestingly. But, of course, the Williams Festival doesn't want to give up their montage.

Q. To get back to your position as historian, you set your own hours as to when you work here or . . . how does that work?

A. Basically yes, because I am retired, and I like being retired. Usually I am here on Tuesday, Wednesday, or Thursdays, but that's flexible. If I have something I need to do or a meeting I need to attend, I set my own hours. But I have to be here for 22 hours a week. I don't have to punch a time card. It is a situation where the product tells them I'm doing my job. That photo exhibit tells them I'm doing my job.

Q. I know you have been working a lot during the summer.

A. I started in January. Brought the proposal to the theatre in November. It was approved at the end of December and I began on January 6th, I believe.

Q. Do you see this as an ongoing project? Once the main work is done, there still would be updating?

A. Yes, because, you see, one of the things that is happening, we've done a wonderful job of bringing all this musical history together and right up to the present. However, there are shows going on right now that . . . every show needs to be documented in one way or another, and filed . . . so it will be an ongoing thing. I don't know if it will necessarily be me. I committed to this as an open-ended project and the theatre committed to me also to a certain number of things being accomplished. Once those things are accomplished, I don't know what will happen, but there will need to be some ongoing curator to keep up with it. I don't know that it will be me . . . maybe me . . . might be you.

Q. Thank you for your time.

INTERVIEWER: REBECCA HALE
INTERVIEWED: October 23, 1999
RESPONDENT: LUIS BARROSO
Actor/Director/Teacher

Q. Your last name is spelled Bar—

A. —Barroso. Luis. Luis, middle initial Q.

Q. My first question was to name the productions that you directed and those that you acted in at Le Petit.

A. During 1970-1978?

Q. Yes. Any of them that you have done. My time period starts in 1968.

A. I directed all of the Children's Corner productions from 1970-1978. On the main stage, I directed Tunes II, which was a musical revue that we actually started in the Children's Corner. I rented the Children's Corner one summer. I didn't realize that you were going to ask me about that. Can we stop the tape while I find my notes? I acted in Gideon.

Q. Was that main stage?

A. Yes. Main stage. I acted in Fiddler on the Roof. I acted in The Real Inspector Hound. I also was in Tunes II. I'm trying to think of some others. I can't remember.

Q. That's fine. I am really concentrating on the children's

plays. I just wanted a list. You also acted in some of the children's plays?

A. Oh, yes, I sure did. I acted in The Brothers Grimm. I acted in Pinocchio. I did several of the children's shows. In the '90s, I acted in The Emperor's New Clothes. That was 1990. I was the phantom in The Phantom of the French Opera in the '95-'96 season. I acted in The Little Mermaid. That was later. I acted in Cinderella. I was the prince. And The Brothers Grimm. I was Wilhelm. I was the father in Hansel and Gretel. And I often went in for actors that got sick. So those—

Q. You probably don't remember my sister, but she was in, I think, The Emperor's New Clothes.

A. Was it the one in 1990?

Q. No. They didn't do one around 1972 or 1973?

A. Yes. We repeated The Emperor's New Clothes. That's not on here.

Q. Around 1972 or 1973?

A. No. No. It was later than that.

Q. '74 maybe?

A. At least. If not later.

Q. Here it is . . . The Emperor's New Clothes, summer rep.

A. Yes. But that wasn't a summer rep. That was an actual production. I don't know what this summer rep thing is, but

I'll find out. We have it in the book. All these books are filled with all that information.

Q. Her name is Nancy Fichter. She was also in <u>My Fair Lady</u> and <u>Hello, Dolly!</u>

A. On the main stage?

Q. Yes. She is a professional singer in Dallas. In fact, that was what got me started going to Le Petit, was to see her plays.

A. There are so many kids that went through . . . I have been doing this forever, thirty years now, so it's been a complete succession of actors and actresses, singers and dancers.

Q. Can you tell me what positive and negative experiences that you have had at Le Petit? Both as a director and an actor.

A. Positive experiences: Having the opportunity to develop this work, a lot of it . . . not a lot. But all of it was original works that I commissioned through local writers, musicians, composers. And during this particular period, 1970-'78, I was given free reign to run the children's theatre. I had been at Gallery Circle for two years. I started my career at Gallery Circle in 1968. I was there in '68, '69, and '70. And 1969, 1970, those two seasons returned another set of sparkling careers. In 1970, a couple of board members at Little Theatre and the Executive Director at that time, Stocker Fontelieu, called me over because they had the Corner Theatre available, and they wanted to do something with it. They had tried experimental theatre, and for some reason, the Board didn't go for it. So when they had seen—

they were aware of the success we had had at Gallery Circle with children's theatre—they called me over and asked if I would start a children's theatre at Le Petit, and that's now Children's Corner. . . . Actually, they tried at that time to make it Le Petit Théâtre du Vieux Carré French. It was really called Les Quandre Enfant. That lasted maybe all of six months. People didn't respond to it, so we just changed it to the Children's Corner. And even though the name has been changed to Teddy's Playhouse, a lot of people still just call it the Children's Corner. That was in 1970, so the positive thing was the fact that the space was made available to me and I was able to go in and I was given the opportunity to create wonderful shows with—all done by local writers. I was able to create a group there that was. . . . They were very creative years—very, very creative. On the negative side, I guess, to a certain degree, even though we were very successful almost from the beginning, I'd say by the third show, we were pretty much sustaining ourselves. The audiences just grew and grew. You know, marketing . . . I was very fortunate to have Arthur Tong, who taught me a lot. And we did a lot of creative marketing . . . targeted the Girl Scouts and all that . . . so by the third show, <u>The Wonderful World of the Brothers Grimm</u>, we were already selling out and being very successful. And that stayed throughout the eight years that I was there. We were at capacity and beyond capacity for some of the shows. We had to hold some of the shows over, in fact. But, on the negative side of that—and this is not negative, this is something that can be very clearly understood—there was a main stage at Le Petit and the children's theatre . . . I want to say . . . was a child . . . was the bold kid on the block. Therefore—I don't know how to put this politely . . . I don't want to say stepchild . . . we were a child. It was the kind of thing where, of course, the main stage was it and we were second, I guess, is a good way to put it. But that didn't impede us from doing things that we wanted to do. And we, both the main stage and the children's theatre, for the most part, co-existed very peacefully. It's hard to have a lot of things running as a theatre. Any time that there was any kind of scheduling, of course, the main stage superceded the children's theatre. But we sat down and talked about it and tried to work things out so that we could all have successful rehearsals and running—particularly, the running of the shows were very carefully . . . We had to schedule that we would come in between main-stage shows so that we could have a full three or four weekends. We used to do, at that time, four. They are only doing three now. We grew to four full weekends, sixteen performances. 1:00 pm and 3:00 pm on Saturdays. 2:00 pm and 4:00 pm on Sundays. So that was the only major negative thing—being second.

Q. Now the Board lets you choose. . . .

A. Yes. They admitted that they were completely unschooled in children's theatre. So they just trusted me to do what I could do. I had been doing it successfully for two years, and they knew that I knew what I was doing. Actually, my training was not necessarily in children's theatre. I was a directing major at Tulane University, so I got my training in directing. But directing children's theatre . . . it's like . . . it's the material that's different. You still use the same principle no matter what, so. . . . It just happened that that is where fate led me, to children's theatre.

Q. Did they give you a budget to work with?

A. Yes.

Q. Did you go in and say, "I need 'X' amount of dollars," or did they just say, "Luis, this is the amount of money you have to work with?"

A. It worked both ways. I worked out a budget and then they either approved it or asked if I could work with a little bit less. Money was never a major issue. When I was approached about the children's theatre, Le Petit really wanted it to be a service to the community. They were not looking to make a profit or anything. We eventually did make money. But the initial approach was to make it a service to the community. At that time, the theatre was very successful. I mean, they had over six thousand members from the main stage. So when they approached me about the children's theatre, I was approached in a way that they wanted it to be a service for the community. They wanted it to be a place where we could start audiences for the future. Also, a lot of parents would bring their kids to the shows; whereas, they would not go themselves to the theatre. And some of them would join in the membership of the main stage once they saw the children's theatre. So we did bring new audiences into the theatre with their kids who would eventually join the main stage. So it was a dual purpose of service to the community and audience development for the main stage, to a certain degree. So that's how the Children's Corner was mainly seen. There wasn't a whole lot of money, but sometimes not having a lot of money makes you a little more creative. And luckily, because of the main stage, I was called "The Scavenger." Once they tore down sets on the main stage, I was there collecting things I could use. And there were many, many sets on the Children's Corner that were made from leftovers from the main stage. I would take them and rework them. I did a lot of my own designing for a while there, and then eventually, I was able to get people to design for me and become staff over there. It was a gradual development in terms of the staff. For a long time, I was the only staff member for Children's Corner with the help of a lot of volunteers who were interested in children's theatre.

Q. I was going to ask you about the volunteers.

A. Arthur. Arthur was with me at Gallery Circle. . . . He was a volunteer at Gallery; and when I left, he came with me and he is there still. He came to Little Theatre in 1970. Oh, there was a score of volunteers of people who wanted to see us make a go of it.

Q. Now did you have parents? Like parents of kids who were in the plays?

A. No. Well, I didn't have kids in the plays.

Q. That's right. It was adults.

A. It was teens and adults. My children's theatre was not with kids unless a kid was called for . . . we used a kid in <u>Hansel and Gretel</u>. If it was called for a child, then I would; but I don't do that. That was not my idea of children's theatre.

Q. Did you do the costumes yourselves?

A. No.

Q. No? Was it a volunteer?

A. Yes. For a long time, it was CeCe Casey who did the costumes. She was a board member who was also—I don't know what you would call the children's theatre liaison to the Board. And she designed and made a lot of the costumes for us. We had several tech designers. I'm trying to remember when it was I actually got a technical director—when we were able to afford, from the children's theatre to here, a second person—and that was David Potter. I don't remember exactly when he came.

Q. He also worked on the main stage?

A. He also worked on the main stage. And eventually we were able to offer him a salary to just be Children's Theatre Technical Director. All the other staffing was on a per-show basis—your musical director, the writers, the choreographers, etc.—they were on a per-show basis, which is the way most theatres worked.

Q. The third year, I believe the theatre won an award, the

Winifred Ward Award?

[Here Mr. Barroso is showing Becky Hale a photo of the award.]

Q. This is great. Now how do you win this award? Did you have to submit?

A. Yes. What happened was that there had been a Southwest Theatre Conference held here in town, and a couple of people. . . . We performed a children's show—I can't remember which one—for them, and a couple of people suggested us to the awards. And they wrote us and said if we would send in samples, pictures and stuff like that. In 1978, when I retired, the New Orleans Music and Drama Foundation gave an award to the Children's Theatre. I don't think they exist anymore.

Q. When you left in 1978 to go to Atlanta?

A. No, no, no. In 1978, I left to go to Minacapelli's Dinner Theatre. I was at Minacapelli's for two years. I resigned at Little Theatre in May; and then that June, I started at Minacapelli's. A friend of mine, Bill Holiday, asked me to come and direct The Odd Couple. He was working over there at that time, a local comedian. And stayed for two years. He and I produced shows there for a couple of years. I had been guest directing in Atlanta at the Center of the Puppetry Arts when he offered me a full-time job. I was tired of doing dinner theatre and traveling to Slidell. So in 1980 I went to Atlanta to the Center for Puppetry Arts, which is the only center in the U.S. dedicated to the art of puppetry. That grew out of a group called the Vagabond Mime. They do a show of mime every once in a while, even though I left in '89. I have done a little bit of writing myself, or adapting, is more like it. Last year they (Center for Puppetry Arts) did my adaptation of <u>Alice in Wonderland</u>.

Q. It is the Center for Puppetry Art?

A. Art. Yes.

Q. When you left Le Petit in 1978, can you comment on why you left? Did you?

A. It was the first time there was Board interference, something very petty. I had. . . . In order to expand my audiences, I had bought a set of little chairs. I bought the set of little chairs because I had a little bit of money left over from one of my budgets. So I bought the chairs out of a production budget. And a board member said that that was a capital investment. These little plastic chairs. They are still using them. Those little plastic chairs. And they just gave me a lot of grief about it. And I guess that I was just at a point where I was just indignant that I was being given grief over something. You see, this particular person was not aware; and somehow or another, that one person was able to infiltrate and turn all the board members against me. She was a very mean-spirited woman, but that's another story, you know. I've forgiven her. She really did me a favor. When you're an artist, you have to move on. . . . I don't know how much longer I would have stayed after 1978 anyway. It was just probably time to go. She just gave me the incentive. But it was over that. It was over their chairs. How many chairs did I buy? Maybe thirty or forty little chairs? I can't remember. And they didn't cost over $3.00 or $4.00 each. But I had enough money left over on one of my budgets to be able to buy the little chairs, but they were a capital investment. I was slapped on the hand over that. So I had done. . . . Freddy Palmisano wrote a lot of the music and shows for me. We put together a musical revue called <u>Tunes</u>, which I rented the Children's Theatre at night to do the show because there were also some rentals in the theatre. And <u>Tunes</u> was so successful that they asked that we do it on the main stage; and therefore, it became <u>Tunes II</u> on the main stage. Then we did another show called <u>Peter Darling</u>, and that was also. . . . I rented the Children's Theatre again at night . . . very successful. We brought it back again at Christmas because there was another break in there between children's shows. That all went fine. Then we wrote . . . well, we hadn't finished writing . . . but we wanted to make sure we had the theatre for another show called <u>Night Time Naughties</u>. Well, they thought we were doing <u>Rocky Horror Show</u> or something. They felt <u>Night Time Naughties</u> was a naughty title for Le Petit. . . . They didn't trust us that it was going to be, you know, a fun show. It just had a picturesque title. So they denied me the rental in the summer of 1978. So between the chairs and that denial of trust about bringing in a tasteful show. . . . You know, <u>Peter Darling</u> was a little trashy, but it was not dirty or anything like that. It was just picturesque.

I think that you're back to why the children's theatre was started in the first place. They were doing crazy shows; and before the children's theatre was started and the Board got out of joint, they were a very conservative people at that time; and I'm not too sure that they still aren't. But we'll see . . . they are doing some picturesque shows this year—Falsettos, and all that. So we'll see what happens. So that was the second straw when they denied me to produce Night Time Naughties. But, you know what? Again, things always work out for the best. It played at the Beverly Dinner Theatre. They changed the title; the title was a little suggestive for them, too. What did they call it? Night Time Naughties . . . because . . . Night on the Town? It went through several titles. I don't think it was called Night Time Naughties again. But the show did go on to the Beverly Dinner Playhouse. Without having a job or anything coming up, I just said, "Enough! I'm out of here!" As soon as that happened and Bill Holiday called me and said, "Hey, I'm doing Odd Couple at Minacapelli's; can you direct it?" I said, "Well, I don't have a job. Sure." And again, we made a success at Minacapelli's. Two years over there, we built it back up. Do you remember that?

Q. Oh, yes. I went to a number of productions. I think I saw The Odd Couple. I enjoyed going there.

A. The food was delicious.
 [At this point, Mr. Barroso is showing Becky Hale programs from that time.]

<u>Sunshine Boys</u>, <u>Bell, Book, and Candle</u>, <u>Alice in Wonderland</u>. . . .

Q. That is wonderful that you kept these. Because that is one of the problems Le Petit is having. Everything seems to be thrown around and. . . .

A. This is the eight years I was over at Le Petit. Here is <u>Fiddler on the Roof</u>.

Q. I have this article.

A. This is astounding. This is when Little Theatre was at its height in terms of membership and all that. I did a lot of work outside Le Petit. This is at the People's Playhouse. We did <u>Three Sisters</u>. I played Lyla's husband.
Was this <u>Becket</u>? Yes, it is <u>Becket</u>. I did <u>The Funeral</u> for Summer Lyric. Did a lot of work at Summer Lyric. Did <u>The Sound of Music</u>. Also during that time in 1973, there was a new company, Royal Comedy Company. And we opened this show on Bourbon Street for them. It didn't last long. That was the only show they did. But I tried to work with other non-profit groups. I did. . . . Here is me as the witch in <u>Hansel and Gretel</u>. I did some work at Tulane. I did some things for Nancy Staub. Now Nancy had some children's theatre over at Le Petit before I did. But they were sporadic puppet shows here and there.
[Mr. Barroso is showing Becky Hale several programs.] Lord. . . . Opera. . . . Something with the New Orleans Symphony. See, Nancy and I worked very closely together. And during this time, she was running The Puppet

Playhouse on Magazine Street—5900 Magazine. And she did a lot of outreach stuff with the orchestra and went to schools. Did the <u>Three-Penny Opera</u> at People's Playhouse. Oh! <u>Gideon</u>! How could I forget <u>Gideon</u>? Did that at Little Theatre. I was the only one that got a good review. [Quoting from review.]
"There was a large cast that worked subvertly . . . particular impact being made by Luis Q. Barroso's performance as a reluctant fighter." I was the only one that got mentioned. Oh, this was such a terrible show. I don't know why they ever did it.

Q. Did you notice any differences in acting and directing lately? Because you have been back at Le Petit as opposed to when you were there in the '70s. Far as facility being different, or anything at all.

A. Just . . . between now and the '70s. . . . There was more communication in the '70s. They were . . . like I said, when you are running a space like that where you have as many activities as are going on, you really had communication. And it seemed to me that there were more staff meetings, more just getting together to work things out than there are now. There is a lack of communication that has been some of the downfall of the theatre . . . lately, anyway.

Q. What about the volunteer staff?

A. The lack of volunteers? They had a lot of volunteers, and now you don't see them. But that also comes from, you know, we are twenty years later, and people expect to get paid for things that they do. There wasn't as much of that then. At that time . . . back then when I worked at Little Theatre, it was like a privilege to be asked to work there. That has gone out the window mainly because there are so many other theatrical places here in town now, so many other groups, that Little Theatre is not the only game in town—or not the major game in town. At that time, it was Little Theatre and Gallery Circle Theatre and that was it. Then you had the Beverly Dinner Theatre, but that was a different story, because they were completely professional. But between Le Petit and Gallery . . . Le Petit having the building and all that; and Gallery had a raggedy . . . 525 Madison Street, with some brilliant work and plays, don't misunderstand me. . . . They were the only game in town. Now you have Rivertown Repertory, the Dog & Pony, JPAS. The talent has certainly spread out. The talent now is going mostly where they can get paid. And Little Theatre still supposedly doesn't pay exactly what the Equity contracts are. . . . You know how that is. I have no idea how that is working out . . . on who is paying for that . . . according to the Charter, they aren't supposed to pay people, so I don't know how they work that out. I am an Equity member and I work Equity when I do work. They haven't done anything that I wanted to try out for. They have an audition today for a show. They haven't done anything that interests me.

Q. How has Le Petit contributed to the cultural life in New Orleans?

A. A lot. I mean they are in their 82nd year. They must have something going on in order to last that long. Particularly that the children's theatre is still going on . . . barely wearing loose threads, but it is still happening. It did have one year. This one year that it didn't exist . . . the year that Keith Briggs decided not to have children's theatre. I'm not sure . . . what was your question again?

Q. How has Le Petit contributed to the cultural life in New Orleans?

A. Well, like I said, for a while there, Le Petit was the only game in town.
I can't say from its very beginning in the '20s, or whatever, but obviously, they have built a beautiful theatre. They started out in the Pontalba . . . a group of interested people, you know, whatever, and eventually they built that beautiful theatre, which in itself is a cultural landmark. And, as I said, I can't imagine that they have not made some sort of very positive. . . . The thing about it is that they are so intent on being a community theatre, but I'm not sure that community theatre is a thing of the past. It's very hard when you're a very small town and most of the larger towns' community theatres have gone mostly to regional theatre. They have the Alliance Theatre and the Augustian . . . ever since the '60s, the focus has gone mostly to regional theatre. We did have a regional theatre here in New Orleans for a couple of years—New Orleans Repertory Theatre. But, unfortunately, it didn't last. But again, they brought in

people from out of town who didn't understand . . . New Orleans is a very peculiar town in terms of theatre and what the theatre public would want. And once the money ran out for that and they weren't able to capture the imagination of the New Orleans audience, it did . . . Havoc [June] . . . came in and tried to make a go of it . . . even she couldn't. I think they set their goals a little too high. Regional theatre uses a lot of local people. You have to start with your local actors and all that. Remember the New Orleans Repertory Theatre used to bring in people from all over the place—I mean they used a few. . . . Lyla did a couple of shows. . . . There was just a lot of mistakes that they made. They brought in all the top brass from out of town. I have noticed here in town, whenever someone local gets to the helm of an arts organization, that's when it really does well. The Arts Council during the '70s was a mess. They kept bringing these people from out of town... blah, blah, blah. And when Shirley Trusty Cory took over, that is when it really took off. A local person caring about local needs. You just can't beat it . . . someone who understood the local theme. But the Arts Council for a long time hired all these executive directors from other cities and just made New Orleans a stop between gigs until they found something better. The same thing happened to the Contemporary Arts Center. Look at that man . . . the last person to run it before Jay . . . he ran it for a couple of years. His big thing was to bring Edward Albee in because they were friends. Then Edward Albee comes in and does this terrible production of one of his old plays. Anyhow, the man . . . it was just a stopping place for him between gigs. When I came back to New Orleans in 1989, I had great hope because I was up for the job of Theatre Director with the Contemporary Arts Center. I had been interviewed and sent in applications and all that and had shown them that I had an affinity for New Orleans. I had lived here before and had run a successful company, the Children's Corner. But then they hired this girl, Julie Hebert, somebody from California, or somewhere, who came here and started doing her own crazy plays that nobody understood. And ran the theatre into the ground. There hasn't been another theatre director since she left. So I truly believe if they hire local people for these positions . . . like I'm just in awe of what Shirley Trusty [Cory] has done with the Arts Council. None of the other executive directors have been able to do that. They didn't care. Shirley does. I got off the question again.

Q. How has Le Petit contributed to the cultural life in New Orleans?

A. Oh, yes. Le Petit has had quite an impact since Stocker . . . Stocker was there a long time. It has been a succession of executive directors. And again, it takes someone who puts the theatre and the organization before their own ego. And that's what we had there at that time. Of all the people who were there, during the '70s anyway, all put the organization and the success of the organization before ourselves. We wanted Le Petit to be a success and, ergo, we would all be successes too, because we were attached to it. For some reason, we took the pride in the building . . . keeping it up, and that hasn't happened with people who came in afterwards. There was not that pride in the place. There was more ego than let's keep this organization. . . . If you look at any artistic organization—arts organization—it's always taken a person—one person—like the big instance I can think of is the Center for Puppetry Arts where Vincent Anthony had this vision for the place—the organization—and has seen it through to the point where it's. . . . He is Mr. Puppetry in Atlanta. He put the Center and what the Center is doing beyond his own . . . the drive is for the organization as opposed to himself. This has happened in various arts organizations around the country where it has taken the vision of one person to see it through. And with the succession of executive directors in the theatres around town, it just hasn't happened. There has been a couple or three from out of town there (Le Petit) who have not understood what Le Petit is all about . . . what New Orleans is all about. You have to understand the psyche of the city and its inhabitants and what the public . . . theatre, as a consumer. You have a product. You have the public buy it. You have to understand your public. I'm not saying that you can't also be artistic because as an artist, you have to satisfy yourself; but it's got to be a medium in some way of satisfying your artistic self and being able to please the public, too. Sometimes, it's kind of hard and you have to make some adjustment to your artistic vision. I think Gallery at one time had down pretty well the stride. They did these wonderful musicals that the public loved; but then in between, whenever they did not need the money raised by those musicals, they could do Edward Albee. . . . He did a wonderful Tiny Alice in between. . . . We made enough money on. . . . I can't remember which musical. Then we could do an Edward Albee or a BF Rock—which there was an audience for—but not as much as for the musicals. So there is a way of doing it. You've got to, to a certain degree, sacrifice your artistic vision in order to give the public what they want; and then little by little, you give them something that you want, that you hope they will like, too. But you can't beat them over the head. New Orleans people you can't beat over the head that much. I was very lucky that I was doing children's theatre. But even in children's theatre, if you notice all these titles were popular titles. I found that if I did a title . . . if I were to do a title the audience didn't know, they wouldn't come. But then these titles . . . we took great liberty, because most of these titles could be done in five minutes. We decided to make them into major musicals. We gave them what they wanted. . . . I'm a musical comedy fan, so I enjoyed doing all those musicals. I was surrounded by wonderful people. And Judy Latour, my choreographer, we put together a nice little team.

Q. Some of these were repeated?

A. Yes. We repeated, expanded, reworked them. A lot of the shows, we were very lucky . . . every four years the audiences changed. We kept a pretty decent mailing list at that time. And we would write the initials of the person that would come. We found that every three or four years, our audiences changed, so we were able to repeat the shows so each time we repeated the show, we would work on it a little bit more and refine it to the point where there were a couple or three of these shows that are just really great. Let's see, <u>Rapunzel</u> is an excellent show. <u>The Emperor's New Clothes</u> is a really good show. There are several of them that were repeated and we worked on them a little bit more. Then there were some done during the '80s of these shows that no one came back to see.

Q. What do you mean? There were some shows in the '80s that no one worked?

A. No. No extensions. No refinement. We worked . . . even when I did <u>Puss 'n Boots</u> just recently, last year, we did a lot of reworking on it. These shows were written in the '70s; and now you've got to reach kids of the '90s; and there is a difference. I always kept real in touch with what children were into during those eight years, even during the years at the Center. First thing I did over was children's puppet shows. And as an artist, you have to keep in touch with your audience. Then you are competing with television. You are competing with movies. You are competing with toys that are out. You try to keep up with all of that; and also, the technology of the theatre has changed a lot over the years. You have to take advantage of the technology advances.

Q. What are your thoughts concerning the future of Le Petit?

A. I think that no matter what, it is going to continue. It is too entrenched an organization . . . by hook or crook, it is going to continue. I think that it needs to. . . . They need to come to the present. They are too entrenched in the past in terms of how they deal with things. If it is going to continue to be a community theatre, they need to look back at what a community theatre is and realize whether it can go back to being a true community theatre, which is. . . . A community theatre is a place of training. There is no training whatsoever there. You get people who are of the community. . . . It seems to me, for a while, they would look to the established actor, or whatever, as opposed to giving a chance to community people, or people that are just starting out, and again giving training to those people . . . something we used to do . . . part of it . . . particularly in children's theatre. There were some people that were regulars in the children's theatre, but there was always room for new people to come in and learn. The idea of community theatre . . . they need to explore that and see what is a community theatre. And where the theatre fits into that, or whether it needs to become something else. I personally would like to see Little Theatre become more of a New Orleans Repertory Theatre, the professional theatre. But I don't know how much their charter would have to change. Or they would have to sell the theatre to another group or what it would need to become that. But it needs to move forward into the millennium with modern times. I think that they are too much entrenched in the old ways.

One of the things that it really, really needs is a working Board . . . not just a Board of people that come there every four to six weeks and such. One of the Boards I have always particularly liked is the Board over at Baton Rouge Little Theatre where it's a working Board. Each board member has a job to do and they do it. Another thing they need is a Board that raises money so that the artists can do their work . . . and be more astute in the hiring, which they certainly don't have a good track record of in the past few years. They have had some executive directors who have not brought the theatre forward, and know their audiences. . . . Again, it's a consumer product.

Q. What do you think of the fact that they have a person who's an actor as Chairman of the Board? Do you think that's a benefit?

A. No. I think the Board membership should be people who can go out and raise money. I think actors should stay on stage and act. I'm an actor; and I know when I'm an actor how selfish I can be. When I'm an actor, I put myself ahead of anything else. So how can an actor put an organization above himself?

Q. Good point!

INTERVIEWER: REBECCA HALE
TELEPHONE INTERVIEW: October 26, 1999
RESPONDENT: LUCY DAIGLE
Board Member

Q. What happens if Le Petit is sold?

A. As of April of 1998, the Board would decide which group would oversee the theatre. We thought schools would be in conflict with each other, so we changed the by-laws. Le Petit must be maintained as a theatre. In the event of the need to sell Le Petit, it would be sold to an entity approved by the Board of Directors and subject to approval of two-thirds of the membership. There wouldn't be an exchange of money.

Q. How has the audience response to the plays been this year?

A. The Play-Reading Committee didn't get to choose much. Subscribers said they didn't care much for the season. You have to give the subscribers what they want or what they think they want. If we don't have the audience, we don't have the plays.
We have a fundraiser on November 13 that is $125 per person and $250 for patrons. There will be an auction and four bands.
We hope to get some grant money. We did get $300,000 from the state for the preservation of the building itself; it

can't go into operating expenses. We also received $50,000 from the Gertrude Ford Foundation. We need to renovate bathrooms to be able to accommodate the handicapped. Rosa Deutsch has been the biggest contributor to the theatre, especially the last two years. She is an honorary life board member.

Q. How has the Tennessee Williams Festival helped Le Petit?

A. The festival rents space at Le Petit. They have given us publicity. They put us on the map. People come from all over the country to attend.

Q. Does Le Petit still sponsor a Sunday Salon?

A. No, we haven't had Sunday Salons lately because we are using the Children's Corner. There is not enough space. The Salon was fun at first, but then it was not profitable.

Q. Thank you very much for your responses.

INTERVIEWER: REBECCA HALE
INTERVIEWED BY E-MAIL: November 4, 1999
RESPONDENT: VELEKA GRAY
Actress/Teacher (Leading Lady on Soap Operas)

Q. How did your experiences in acting at Le Petit prepare you for a professional career?

A. In my case, Stocker Fontelieu and Le Petit took me to the next ring in my career. Since I was five years old, I had done extensive modeling, print work, and enough local commercials at WWL and WDSU [television stations] to be well known in the city. But even when the regional and national commercials I was cast in enabled me to join the actors' unions so that I was recognized as a professional actress, it was my training at Le Petit that I credit with having transformed me from a mere artisan into an artist. The people with whom I worked at the theatre instilled a respect in my soul for the art of acting and induced me to find the best in myself in performance. This was enormously valuable tutelage for the work I would soon be doing on national TV.

INTERVIEWER: REBECCA HALE
Telephone Interview: November 7, 1999
RESPONDENT: LEON CONTAVESPRIE
Le Petit Board Member/Actor

Q. Please comment on the smaller stage at Le Petit and how it is being used.

A. The Director's Studio of Le Petit Théâtre du Vieux Carré provides an alternate space for other theatre companies. It is called Teddy's Corner when children's theatre is being produced.
For Late-Night Catechism, Sonny [Borey] couldn't produce the show, because in the by-laws someone working at the theatre can't make a profit. He got a friend to produce it. Le Petit receives $2,000 per week in rental fees. If the Board would have known how successful this play would be, Le Petit would be making more from it.

Q. Why were the by-laws changed concerning the profit by universities of the sale of Le Petit?

A. Numerous rumors existed two years ago about the closing of Le Petit. Officials from Loyola and Tulane got word about this, and their fangs were out. We can't turn it over to universities. They would sell it, close it, and use the money for their programs. The law was changed in April of 1998. If Le Petit is sold, a private entity would have to run it as a theatre.

Q. How is the theatre operating financially?

A. We are property rich but cash poor. Operating expenses are $25,000 per month. We have $300 in the bank. We get $2,000 per week for <u>Late-Night Catechism</u>. The marketing director [Julia Burka] will be axed. Derek Franklin may get the axe for mismanagement. We may consolidate the business manager and marketing position. Two interns from the Arts council are working with us, learning to help with fundraising. Sonny [Borey] insisted on doing shows of his choice. Next year it's back to basics. Maybe one innovative show, the rest traditional. Next season we want to do <u>Barnum</u>, <u>Noises Off</u>, <u>Not About Nightingales</u> for the Tennessee Williams Festival, <u>No, No, Nanette</u>. The people in charge of the Tennessee Williams Festival have a problem understanding they are renting the theatre. We will tell them next year: these are our dates. We want a partnership. This year <u>Cat on a Hot Tin Roof</u> is a co-production with the festival. We can't rotate our season around their festival. They can agree to use our Tennessee Williams production under our guidelines.

Q. What about the children's theatre?

A. Adults who were kids in 1970 are now returning with their kids. Children's theatre has gone back basics. The costs are between $8,000 and $10,000, and we are making only $2,000. I would like college kids to perform in them for little kids. I would like to see interactive theatre with simple costumes and make-up. Kids don't need elaborate costumes and sets. I would love to start an education program. I would like to see more scaled-down productions with simple costumes and sets. Like the two-person <u>The Lion, the Witch, and the Wardrobe</u>.

We have a meeting tomorrow night. Call me the next day, and I'll let you know if anything happened that you should know.

INTERVIEWER: REBECCA HALE
TELEPHONE INTERVIEW: November 9, 1999
RESPONDENT: LEON CONTAVESPRIE
Le Petit Board Member/Actor

Q. You had a Board meeting last night at Le Petit.

A. Yes. Cheryl Sims, a representative of the Ford Foundation in Mississippi, loved the production of <u>Hay Fever</u> and donated $50,000 to the theatre to be used for anything. We had an architect discuss repairing the stairwell. Nobody was fired at the meeting, as I had thought might happen. Nothing changed with Franklin or Julia Burka. The Board hired two people from the Arts Council to help with fundraising. The Board paid an application fee to the Arts Council for these interns; the interns are not being paid. These two people were at the meeting. Stuart Gahn, a board member, became very heated and resigned. That's all that happened.

Q. Thank you for this information.

INTERVIEWER: REBECCA HALE
TELEPHONE INTERVIEW: December 6, 1999
RESPONDENT: SARAH KARY
Board Member/Box Office Director - The Footlight Club

Q. In researching community theatres, I discovered that the Footlight Club was established in 1877. Le Petit Theatre in New Orleans has always billed itself as the oldest continuously-running community theatre in the United States. Please comment.

A. Yes, the Footlight Club began in Jamaica Plain, Massachusetts, in 1877. The American Association of Community Theatres says we're the oldest continuously-running amateur community theatre in the United States.

Q. Please elaborate.

A. The Footlight Club began performing in 1877 in a building that was built in 1830, called Eliot Hall. The Theatre, located near Boston, was begun by a group of socialites. We are still performing in the original building, although in the 1980s the building underwent a facelift. The organization owns the building.

Q. Has the theatre performed every year since its opening?

A. Yes.

Q. Is there an open box office, or does the theatre operate on a subscription basis?

A. We have an open box office, but we offer season subscriptions for four of the five shows in the season. The fifth play is a fundraiser. Season memberships cost $45. Individual prices are $15 per show. We try to pick shows that we know will attract our audiences. The plays run for three weekends on Friday and Saturday nights. We have active and associate memberships. The active members, about 50 people, do something for the theatre; they form the base of our volunteers. The associate members are those who buy tickets only. In the early history of the theatre, you had to be a member to go to plays, but a few years later, they established the open box office. Also, until the past twenty years, you had to be a member to audition for any of the plays.

Q. How is the Footlight Club doing financially?

A. The last five years have been the strongest financially, but it fluctuates. At one time, finances were so tight that we were carefully unscrewing nails to reuse them. We tend to stay in the black now.

Q. Is there a children's theatre?

A. Not an active children's theatre. We do try to do one show per year that includes children.

Q. Are plays performed during the summer?

A. Usually in the summer, we do one-acts; this gives an

opportunity to those who haven't had a chance to act. Last year [1998] we had a play by a new unpublished playwright. This past summer because of renovations and cleaning, we had no one-acts. We also rent the theatre to other groups at reasonable rates.

Q. Have any famous people performed at the theatre?

A. Joe McIntire from the band, New Kids on the Block. He and his family have performed here. He has been generous with us. When we performed Falsettos, the playwright, William Finn, came and enjoyed it. Also, one of the original Broadway actors, who happened to be in the area, attended a performance.

Q. Is there a Play-Reading Committee?

A. Yes, it was established three or four years ago. Before that time, the Board picked the season. Each season there were two musicals, two dramas, and one comedy.

Q. How are the directors chosen?

A. We interview directors. There are different directors for each production. As of the last five years, the directors and musical directors are equally paid. The actors are not paid. This is not an Equity theatre.

Q. How many people does the theatre hold?

A. The theatre holds between 270 and 300 people. We have movable chairs. We usually sell about 250 memberships. We have a variety of ages in our audiences, young and old.

On our Board, the youngest is twenty-three, and the oldest is fifty.

Q. What plays will be performed this season?

A. <u>Torch Song Trilogy</u> opens our season. Then we have <u>Jesus Christ Superstar</u> for our annual fundraiser, <u>Into the Wood</u>, <u>To Kill a Mockingbird</u>, and we close with <u>Auntie Mame</u>.

Q. Thank you for your time.

A. I enjoyed chatting with you.

INTERVIEWER: REBECCA HALE
TELEPHONE INTERVIEW: January 26, 2000
RESPONDENT: LEON CONTAVESPRIE
Le Petit Board Member/Actor

Q. Have there been any changes at Le Petit since I last spoke to you?

A. Yes. Jim Word, formerly our historian, is now our business manager. He is in charge of all finances. He is a full-time business manager, and he answers to the Board, not to the Executive/Artistic Director (Sonny Borey). Since he is retired, he agreed to a salary of $22,000. We are saving money because Julia Burka resigned. Julia was development director, in charge of guiding the theatre, and she became a fundraiser. She couldn't do either. Jim will do all the accounting and write all checks. He will handle grants. The Board itself will work on fundraising. A volunteer committee will do the work that Jim was doing as historian. The committee will work on a display of all dramas, a pictorial history, for next season, much like Jim did for the musicals this year.

Q. How is the theatre doing financially?

A. Much better. We are okay financially because of the success of Late Night Catechism. The play brings in $50,000 per month, with a net profit of $35,000-$40,000. We've [Le

Petit] taken over the rights to the show. We get all the money, and we have control. Also, the $300,000 grant from the state is coming in. Some of the money will be used to install a new bathroom for the handicapped.

Q. Has the Board decided on the plays for next season?

A. We will be doing <u>Noises Off</u>, <u>Not About Nightingales</u> (if we can get the rights to it), and <u>The Mystery of Edwin Drood</u>. We don't know about the others yet. Two other plays that we wanted to do we had to drop because both directors that we wanted have other commitments.

Q. Thank you for your comments.

INTERVIEWER: REBECCA HALE
INTERVIEWED: September 29, 2000
RESPONDENT: VATICAN LOKEY
Actor/Costumer

<u>Note:</u> *Vatican Lokey originally was interviewed in 1997 and then again in 1998.*

Q. When I first interviewed you in 1997 and then in 1998, you said that you would never again perform at Le Petit. However, you have performed there again. What changed your mind?

A. Two names. Sonny Borey and Derek Franklin. Both treated me like a million bucks. They give actors and those who work under them professional respect—more than anyone else in town. I was in <u>Rapunzel</u> at Le Petit. I did that and then I went into <u>City of Angels</u>, which was a different singing role for me,—difficult music to sing. Derek had us rehearse for seven weeks. Then I went into <u>Grand Hotel</u>. I am proudest of <u>Grand Hotel</u> and <u>Falsettos</u>, more than anything else I've ever done.

Sonny knows how theatre works, how it affects people, how it affects audiences. He can do anything he sets his mind to. Derek and Sonny work in entirely different ways, but get the job done. <u>Kiss of the Spider Woman</u> and <u>Falsettos</u> were both critically successful. I don't particularly like the play, Kiss of the Spider Woman, but Le Petit's production was as good as it could be. Barnum [performing, as of this interview] is an excellent production. It has been playing to sold-out audiences, and the run has been extended. I'm playing "Jasper Johns" in The Mystery of Edwin Drood, later this season.

Sonny and Derek have fought hard to turn the theatre around, especially concerning the Board.

Q. How have they done this?

A. When the Board realized that we do need Sonny, some board members listened and some didn't. Leon Contavesprie [board member] helped to get some of what is being done today. Sonny and Derek looked for actors in the community. The board members are now talking more about the theatre. They are actively recruiting new talent to perform at the theatre. Sonny and Derek have done a lot to dispel the idea that Le Petit Theatre is unapproachable [from an actor's standpoint]. For years when I got here, you are a Le Petit person, or a Bayou Dinner Theatre [no longer in existence] person, or a NORD [New Orleans Recreation Department] person. Since Sonny and Derek have taken over, actors from other theatres have flocked to audition at Le Petit. This one show—Barnum—could put the theatre back in the black. Late Night Catechism [performing in the Teddy's Corner space] has been running for over a year, and Le Petit is making a lot of money from that show.

Q. Will you be performing in any children's plays in the future at Le Petit?

A. The Thanksgiving show in November is the debut at Le Petit of <u>The Bepuzzled Pilgrim</u>, written by Wayne Daigrepont. I'm playing the part of "Xavier." We've performed this play before with the Porta-Puppet Players. Wayne wrote it in 1993, and we're writing a new song for the show.
Wayne [Daigrepont] is becoming the children's theatre director. Edward Cox had a breakdown during <u>Rapunzel</u>. It was a medical condition. He walked out on <u>Rapunzel</u>. There were threats. He's fine now, but his reputation isn't. No one in the theatre there was even remotely concerned. Michael Arata was less than kind, though very professional. After <u>Rapunzel</u> closed, the directing went to Wayne Daigrepont. Shows in Teddy's Corner have a shorter run because of <u>Late Night Catechism</u>.
<u>Pilgrim</u> is the quintessential Porta-Puppet Show. We're changing the show to fit the space. We're hiring a second puppeteer. There will be a fall children's show and a spring children's show in Teddy's Corner.

Q. What are your thoughts of the future of Le Petit?

A. The only way Le Petit will survive is with Sonny Borey. No one else in the city has the experience, the bulldog determination, and the money to keep the theatre running. Sonny has sunk so much of his family's fortune into the theatre. Bills have been paid off. He is rebuilding the idea that Le Petit is the premiere theatre in town. The play <u>Late Night Catechism</u> is responsible for a lot of this. It has been running for over a year. While one sister [the only character in the play] is on stage, two sisters are doing it at conventions, parties, etc.

I love being back at Le Petit. The biggest problem is Jim Word [now the business manager who is also in charge of publicity]. Jimmy had gone to Atlanta right after Luis [Barroso]. Jimmy saw <u>Beauty and the Beast</u> [at Teddy's Corner], and he changed fourteen shades of green. I bring this up because I have seen this happen before with the Cuban [Luis Barroso]. There is no excuse for why <u>Barnum</u> was not publicized more. Sonny Borey is the best thing about Le Petit since Stocker Fontelieu. Sonny has a healthy respect for Le Petit.

<u>Falsettos</u> [1999 season] was the most emotionally draining show I've done. Derek Franklin is more responsible for last season than Sonny. Derek knew they'd lost money, but it was worth it to get an audience to see what can be done at Le Petit. Derek was a complete joy during the entire production of <u>Falsettos</u>. It was a marvelous experience. Everyone desperately wanted to do the show.

The Board at Le Petit is 85% of the way it needs to be for actors. There are still some members of the old regime bringing up lesser of two evils. The biggest problem with Michael Arata is he is an ACTOR. Actually, Michael could do good work if given the right director. Michael is a good chairman as long as he realized he's there for physical reasons; he looks good. It's 75% positive with Michael being chairman.

I'm trying to convince Derek and Sonny to do a concert version of a show on the main stage or the children's theatre. It could be marketed as a concert series. It keeps the audience educated and interested. Le Petit is a hotbed for revolution. Sonny is smart enough to know he has to watch his back.

Q. Thank you for your time.

INTERVIEWER: REBECCA HALE
TELEPHONE INTERVIEW: November 11, 2000
RESPONDENT: LEON CONTAVESPRIE
Le Petit Board Member/Actor

Q. Have there been any changes at Le Petit since we last spoke?

A. The term limits for the Board. If someone is appointed after one member resigns, the year doesn't count toward the term. It used to count. A person could serve eight years, then sit out a year, and then can serve again.
Also, there was a motion at the meeting to take out the by-law saying we are an amateur theatre. The motion was tabled indefinitely.

Q. Are any actors paid at Le Petit?

A. We pay no one. However, Bert Pigg was paid Equity for <u>City of Angels</u> but not for the latest play.

Q. Who signs the checks?

A. If an Equity member wants to be on stage, he/she can perform, but won't be paid by us [the Board].

Q. How many season subscriptions were sold for 2000-2001?

A. 680 subscriptions. The largest attendance we had for <u>Noises Off</u> [November 2000] was 125 people.
We got a grant from the state for $300,000. A new lighting system cost $100,000. Renovating a bathroom to make it

handicap-accessible and renovating the outside balcony cost $100,000.

Q. Explain the play selection process. Does the Board consider what is happening in the city—current events?

A. We start with a master list of play titles. We don't take into account what's happening in the city. We do keep in mind what other theatres are doing. The more timely, the less likely people will vote on it. I wanted to do <u>Twilight of the Golds</u>, which I thought was very timely, but the Board said audiences wouldn't come to see it. Things that are timely and should be done aren't done. We always have traditional musicals on the list. Sonny is into extravagant musicals— [<u>Kiss of the Spider Woman</u>], rather than <u>Fiddler on the Roof</u>, etc. The feeling of the staff is that the old-line patrons represent only one-tenth of what walks in. When we tried a new, innovative season, it flopped. <u>Barnum</u> [September 2000] had good attendance with two hold-over performances, averaging 125 people for the extra performances, not sold-out.

Q. I've noticed that reviews of the plays often appear a week after opening night. Doesn't this hurt business?

A. I've seen the press for our shows. We send it in, but it's up to the <u>Times-Picayune</u> what gets in. It's a matter of what the <u>Times-Picayune</u> feels like putting in.

Q. How is Teddy's Corner doing?

A. Teddy's Corner is a money pit. We did three children's shows last year. One cost $5,000 and didn't bring in $2,500. I would prefer a two-person version of The Lion, the Witch, and the Wardrobe. Last year doing Sammy, the Sorcerer cost $6,000 and brought in only $2,500. Sonny is taking control of the children's theatre. We are currently discussing what will be done.

Q. There has been some discussion of eliminating the Play-Reading Committee.

A. As long as I'm on the Board, there will be a Play-Reading Committee. I should tell you that we received a grant of $5,000 from Harrah's Casino for Little Shop of Horrors [January 2001] for production costs. The grant is for programs that cater to the ethnically diverse. Le Petit has been criticized for not being racially mixed enough with a city that is heavily black. Yet blacks don't support black productions like Ma Rainey's Black Bottom [1999]. Little Shop of Horrors has an ethnically-diverse cast.

I like to give Sonny free rein on musicals. Barnum was budgeted at $60,000 but cost $75,000. Late-Night Catechism is attracting 30% tourist business. Barnum attracted 10% tourist business. We put computer displays in hotels to advertise our plays. We used to have a banner on the balcony, announcing the play. When we did this for Hay Fever [1998], one hundred tourists came to the production. I don't know why we stopped doing this. I must check on this.

Regarding paying actors, Sonny flew in Patrick Mendelson for Grand Hotel. Sonny used his own money.

Q. Thank you for your comments.

INTERVIEWER: REBECCA HALE
TELEPHONE INTERVIEW: January 14, 2001
RESPONDENT: LUIS BARROSO
Actor/Director/Teacher

Note: In researching the children's theatre at Le Petit, I read two reviews by S. Joslyn Fosberg, now deceased. One review was The Emperor's New Clothes in 1974, and the other review was Rapunzel in 1978. Fosberg wrote the same criticism of Le Petit and Luis Barroso's play in 1978 that she had written in 1974. She felt that Barroso had not changed as a director from 1974 to 1978. I contacted Barroso for a second interview, via telephone, and asked him to comment on the reviews.

Q. Did Ms. Fosberg's criticisms affect your directing in any way?

A. No.

Q. Did you change anything in the way you directed after her reviews?

A. No. Let me tell you about Suzanne Fosberg. She wrote a couple of plays for Le Petit, like Cinderella. She used simple sets, like grabbing a couple of boxes as set pieces. She thought my shows were more adult-oriented than child-oriented. In spite of that, we did her Cinderella, and she let me do what I wanted to do with it.

Q. In her 1974 review, Fosberg wrote: "Nothing ever surprises me at the Children's Corner. The scripts are all written according to pat formula." Would you comment on this?

A. They were formulaic, based on the classics. I always asked my writers to stick to the original story as much as possible. That's what they were formulaic. When a kid came to my show, they saw the story. I enjoyed doing them, and the audience enjoyed them.

Suzanne was one of the most brilliant people I have ever met, but she was crazy. She painted; she wrote; she was a true renaissance woman.

Once those children walked into the theatre, they saw magic. In <u>The Emperor's New Clothes</u>, they saw farthingales and high wigs. In <u>Raggedy Ann and Andy</u>, I set it in the 1930s, so they saw costumes from that time period.

Q. Fosberg said in the review that she thought children's theatre should be educational. How do you feel about that?

A. To me, theatre, first and foremost, should be entertainment. People don't want to be hit over the head. I think the kids were educated; they saw lights, scenery, costumes.

Q. Fosberg also said that children's theatre should be performed by children. Please comment.

A. Using kids is okay as long as that's the specific goal of the program. I always went for the right age of the characters. I think it's great for schools to use children in plays. Ty Tracy [long-time director at New Orleans Recreation Department] did it at NORD at that time. I used children in <u>Hansel and</u>

Gretel, when it was appropriate. They [directors at Le Petit] tried doing stuff with little kids in the '80s, and it killed them.

Q. She also stated: "We must think very little of children's capacities. Don't we believe that children are capable of coping with fear, and wonder, with love, and disappointment? If we give kids nothing but sugar-candy reviews, how will they ever develop a taste for Shakespeare. . . ." Please comment.

A. She's underestimating kids herself. If by sugar-coating, she means that the plays weren't scary, she's mistaken. When watching Sleeping Beauty, the kids trembled when the witch came on.
I hold no ill will towards Suzanne. I was doing theatre professionally, and she was writing for five dollars an article for the Vieux Carre Courier, which went out of business after a few years. She was a frustrated writer, actor, director, painter. She had her own agenda. She was a brilliant mind, but success managed to escape her. When I did Lafitte, the Pirate, the man who played Lafitte was a Viet Nam veteran, and the Vieux Carre Courier harped on that, instead of his role in the play. Just because Ray was a Viet Nam veteran. . . . That was the gist of the Vieux Carre Courier.
The children's laughter and applause was important. The children left the theatre knowing the story. I insisted that the story be there. I was blessed that I could do the classics. The parents wanted shows that they were familiar with.

Q. Thank you so much for your comments.

INTERVIEWER: REBECCA HALE
TELEPHONE INTERVIEW: January 16, 2001
RESPONDENT: LEON CONTAVESPRIE
Le Petit Board Member/Actor

Q. Leon, I had asked you about attendance figures and revenue.

A. Yes, I have some information for you concerning the last few years. That's all I could find. I'll list them for you.

1997 - <u>Lost in Yonkers</u>:

    1,647 total attendance
    1,243 season tickets sold
    284 general admission tickets at door

1998-99 - <u>42nd Street</u>

    1,253 season tickets sold
    4,240 total house
    $61,485 just for walk-ins
    $65,653 with the bar

[Note: Alcoholic and non-alcoholic beverages are now sold at intermission with alcoholic beverages costing between $2 and $4.]

<u>Hay Fever</u>:

    2,098 total attendance
    $16,259 outside sales
    $17,674 with the bar

$36,442 with season subscriptions

<u>Hay Fever</u> is the most successful non-musical ever in terms of single tickets and in terms of cash. It came on the heels of <u>42nd Street</u> with Ken Risch who was a popular director. It got great reviews and was during Sonny Borey's first season.

<u>The Innocents</u>:
    1,416 total house
    $ 6,561 ticket sales
    $ 7,319 with the bar

<u>Ma Rainey's Black Bottom</u>:
    2,015 total house
    $16,362 ticket sales
    $17,729 with the bar

Tickets for non-musicals are usually $18; but since this play was during the Tennessee Williams Festival, we charged $20.

<u>City of Angels</u>:
    3,361 total house
    $43,719 ticket sales
    $46,597 with the bar

For the whole 1998-99 season:
    13,130 in attendance
    $141,386 ticket sales
    $10,596 the bar
    $151,982 total

There were 2,099 ticket exchanges, exchanging one night for another. We now charge $2 to exchange tickets.

For Teddy's Playhouse – 1998-99:

Rapunzel   2,277 tickets sold ($7.50 per ticket)
                                 $17,077.50 total (no bar)
                                 115 complimentary tickets distributed

Cast members get two complimentary tickets per actor.

Rumpelstiltskin - Spring 2000:

         736 people in attendance for three weekends
         1,375 in attendance for all performances
         $5,497.50 ticket sales
         $705.73 in donations
         $6,203.23 total
         $7,564.92 in expenses – we lost money.

Main Stage:

Cat on a Hot Tin Roof [with the Tennessee Williams Festival]:

         $34,238 total box office
         50% of entire box office goes to the Festival
         $17,119 to Le Petit, plus $5,000 rental from the Festival for all functions held at Le Petit.
         $22,119 total to Le Petit

The Tennessee Williams Festival paid for all production costs.
         688 season ticket members saw it.
         2,024 non-members saw it.

Tiger Tails – March 2001:
Le Petit is paying everything except for two nights that the Tennessee Williams Festival splits. If Equity actors are used, they will be paid by the Festival, not by Le Petit.

Falsettos – January 2000: $20,693.18 production costs
$22,817 box office, including season members
$13,025 walk-ins
$ 9,792 season members
576 season members
755 non-members
$ 3,000 from the Krewe of Armeinius

[Note: The Krewe of Armeinius is a gay Mardi Gras krewe that buys out the final dress rehearsal of each musical. This has been occurring for the past three years.]

$902.50 Actors' Night [Actors pay what they want to see play.]
$26,719.50 Grand Total
$19,193.98 expenses
$ 7,600 royalties
$ 7,525.52 profit

1999-2000

Grand Hotel: $46,269.60 box office
$44,162.67 expenses

Lettice and Lovage: $14,792.88 all tickets
$10,169.26 expenses

It only brought in $2,000 in outside sales. It was the biggest bomb.

Teddy's Corner:

    <u>Sammy the Sorcerer:</u> $2,512.50 all tickets
                                                $2,160.00 expenses

    <u>Robin Hood</u>: $1,702.50 all tickets
                                                $2,646.87 expenses

Our business manager suggested that we have to re-vamp the children's theatre.

Main Stage:

    <u>Kiss of the Spider Woman</u> – June 2000:
                                                $34,154.80 box office
                                                $44,542.54 production costs

In the children's theatre at night, <u>Late-Night Catechism</u> has been running since 1999.

August 1999-August 2000:
                                 $457,752.56 box office
                                 $222,841.73 expenses,
                                 including salary and royalties

We split the box office with Theatrics, Inc., the producer, listed as Bert Pigg. No one who volunteers or works for Le Petit can make money off of productions; that's why Theatrics, Inc., is listed as producer. Theatrics, Inc., gets 50% of the box office and pays the royalties. Le Petit gets 50% of the box office and does not pay the royalties. We now have three "Sisters" for <u>Late-Night Catechism</u>. Amanda Hebert is the main sister and performs most often. The other two actresses perform once a month each. Teddy's Playhouse holds 135 adults (it holds 150 kids for children's productions), and we've been averaging 75 per house for <u>Catechism</u>.

Q. Thank you for all this information. Is there anything else that I should know?

A. Some members of the Board proposed taking out of the by-laws the words <u>amateur theatre</u>. I told them I want to know what Equity would say about this. I see no rush to meet with Equity about this.

Oh, I have figures for one other play.

<u>Noises Off</u> – 2000: $ 8,615 total box office
                                     $12,074.55 production costs
                                     We lost $4,013.81.
                                     We do pay parking for actors.

Q. Thank you for your time.

INTERVIEWER: REBECCA HALE
INTERVIEWED BY E-MAIL: February 27, 2001
RESPONDENT: DAVID CUTHBERT
Times-Picayune Critic/Writer/Lyricist

Q. Why was the name Battistella used in the title of your play Cinderella Battistella?

A. The title, "Cinderella Battistella," came from the show's composer, Freddy Palmisano, who just liked the rhyming aspect of it. And, because it was a familiar New Orleans name, it made everybody laugh at the juxtaposition. As Freddy said, "If you can make an audience laugh at the title of your play, you're halfway home already."

INTERVIEWER: REBECCA HALE
INTERVIEWED: April 20, 2001
RESPONDENT: GARY RUCKER
Actor/Playwright/Teacher

Q. I understand that you and Dane Rhodes are performing Limerick Junction in the children's theatre at Le Petit.

A. Yes, that's right.

Q. What about the play that was supposed to be perfomed in April?

A. Limerick Junction is replacing Lafitte the Pirate because the Board felt there was not enough time to mount a production of Lafitte the Pirate. Le Petit is producing Limerick Junction. They asked Dane at the last minute.

Q. Who are the members of the cast?

A. Myself, Dane and one child, Danny Neese.

Q. How many performances will you be doing?

A. Eight performances over three weekends, with performances at 12:00 p.m. It's interactive theatre and is an attempt to get kids to enjoy poetry. It should be fun.

Q. Thank you.

INTERVIEWER: REBECCA HALE
INTERVIEWED BY E-MAIL: May 28, 2001
RESPONDENT: DOUGLAS LEAL
Actor

Q. How did your experiences of acting at Le Petit affect your career as an actor? I know that you performed in <u>Brighton Beach Memoirs</u> and <u>Amadeus</u>.

A. You mentioned my main stage work [<u>Brighton Beach Memoirs</u> and <u>Amadeus</u>, directed by Audley Keck; and <u>Biloxi Blues</u>, directed by Elizabeth Barron] but in the studio space [a.k.a. Children's Corner], I also did <u>It's Only a Play</u>, directed by Keith Briggs, and <u>Mass Appeal</u>, which I directed myself.

Le Petit was the premier stage in New Orleans when I was there. It certainly had the best physical plant of any theater in the city, including the university stages. Its facilities were equivalent to many of the smaller professional regional theaters I'm familiar with. The technical staff was very professional and did excellent work. You felt more like a professional actor there than in some other theaters, in that you never had to worry about building sets, finding props, doing your own costumes, etc. You were really taken care of, and it's an experience I have had only rarely, even in working with Equity companies in Chicago and Los Angeles.

I credit LPT with the foundation for my career. Not having an academic background in theater, I honed my acting skills in my work at Le Petit. Opening night of Brighton Beach, I got such a rush that I decided to pursue acting as a career right then and there. (You can read more about it in an interview I did with Dodds in the Picayune, 8/4/89.) The camaraderie and family spirit of all the shows I did there made it great fun. I made some great friendships, too. Audley became a real mentor to me, and my roommate in Los Angeles is Wayne Camp, whom I met doing Biloxi Blues.

In some ways, LPT was neither fish nor fowl—a community theater with professional facilities and professional quality—and this tension accounted for some of the negatives I experienced. The "membership club" atmosphere still lingered and was a little off-putting. I remember being approached after a Brighton Beach matinee by one older lady, obviously a Garden District doyenne, who asked me with a sweet but slightly condescending smile, "So, how did you enjoy performing on *our* stage?" What, I thought at the time, made it *her* stage.

LPT didn't think like a professional theater, either. Both Brighton Beach and Amadeus were selling out even after their extensions, but LPT didn't even consider extending further. Brighton Beach, in fact, was the final production of the year and could probably have run all summer long.

It was also difficult sometimes to be the only creative artists in the production not being paid. The TDs, designers, directors, etc., were all paid, union musicians were used for the musicals, and here were the actors, sometimes having to pay for parking just to rehearse, getting nothing. I thought a community theater should either provide for non-professionals of all disciplines to participate [designers, directors, musicians] or should give up the "community" pretense and compensate everyone. Excluding the actors, while I understood the reason, denigrated our contributions somewhat. The attitude seemed to be that "the applause, and the opportunity to work on our stage, should be enough."

I finally made the decision that my time and talent were important and stopped working for free; soon thereafter I moved to Chicago. Ironically enough, I'm back working virtually for free in Los Angeles. I'm part of a membership theater company, which means I pay dues of $45 a month; do a company job and a technical assignment; and when I act, I get the princely sum of $7 a show under the Equity 99-seat plan. But it's all in hopes of getting paid work in film or TV. That possibly was out-of-reach in New Orleans. Unfortunately, my LPT credits were of little use to me elsewhere. I've auditioned for professional theaters all over the country, and no one has ever recognized LPT, except for one director in Chicago, who said he knew the artistic director in the '70s. I mentioned that I knew Stocker very well, but that was not the name he recalled, so I believe he was mistaken. It's impossible to be sure, of course, as some directors and casting directors might have recognized the credits but not said anything to me.

Even if someone would recognize the credit, I don't know if they would know what prestige the stage had in the New Orleans theatrical community. LPT is officially "community" theater, and that designation makes any actor's work there count for far less than work at a professional theater, no matter the quality. In an audition just last week, I had a stage director ask me which theaters on my résumé were Equity. Apparently I would get more "points" in his mind for those productions.

I value the opportunities I was given at LPT. I believe I did some of the best work of my career there; for various reasons, I have not had the chances elsewhere that I had at LPT. But Eugenes and Mozarts come from all over the country to Chicago, New York, and Los Angeles every day, and they're my competition. Now, I know and you know that my work at LPT probably surpassed their efforts even if they worked in Equity houses, but no one else knows this. This is not a slight against LPT, however. There are very few regional theaters with name recognition among stage directors, and far fewer that TV and film CDs recognize. Here in Los Angeles, I've had a few CDs see that I'm from Chicago and ask if I worked at Steppenwolf—as though that were the only theater in the city and as though I would keep such a credit off my résumé!

All in all, I have very fond memories of my work at LPT, and I am proud of all the shows I did there. There's an actress in my company who worked twice at LPT a few years after I left town, and we were talking just the other day about what a unique place it was, and how it provided such a rare opportunity. I'm glad you're drawing some attention to it through your dissertation. I'd love to hear your conclusions.

INTERVIEWER: REBECCA HALE
TELEPHONE INTERVIEW: October 9, 2001
RESPONDENT: ERROL LABORDE
Chairman of the Board of Le Petit as of 7/1/2001.

Q. I understand that the charter of Le Petit was recently changed. Please comment.

A. The word amateur has been deleted from the charter. This doesn't mean we're a professional house. There have been situations where key persons had to be paid, like actors in Equity. We are not a professional theatre. Sonny [Borey] will negotiate with the actors. An example of this was in Barnum where one of the actors was paid. If someone was key to a show, we'd pay them.

Q. What are your plans for the theatre?

A. I'm responsible for business accountability and trying to rebuild the Board. We need people who are interested and competent on the Board. We need better grant writing. Harrah's has given us a $5,000 grant. We need to develop administratively. We need a grant writer on staff, not just someone who comes in once.

Q. How did you become involved with Le Petit Theatre?

A. I became involved with the theatre through the Tennessee Williams Festival. Le Petit is to the Tennessee Williams

Festival like Jazz Fest is to the Fairgrounds. The facilities at Le Petit are used for the Tennessee Williams Festival. The Tennessee Williams Festival brings people to the theatre.

Q. Do you have any other plans for the theatre?

A. I'm redefining jobs. My job is basically to worry about behind-the-scenes things. Financially, we are not desperate. We're living on the edge, but we're not over the edge yet. I don't worry about casting or scenery. My job is behind the scenes.

Q. Good luck to you as the new chairman. Thank you for your time.

INTERVIEWER: REBECCA HALE
TELEPHONE INTERVIEW: March 3, 2002
RESPONDENT: STEPHEN THURBER
Former Technical Director/Set Designer at Le Petit

Q. You are mentioned in Victor Klein's book <u>New Orleans Ghosts II</u> and in the documentary "Haunted History: New Orleans" concerning your encounters with ghosts at Le Petit. Please elaborate.

A. My two colleagues were with me. I was feeling ill at ease. Lights were coming up incorrectly, and we were the only humans in the building. The circuiting was wrong. Our plan was to check on the wiring. We went upstairs to the library. As I approached the door, I had an eerie feeling. I want to add that I was not on drugs, nor was I on alcohol, as some people would like to suggest. As we were coming up to the door, I said, "Don't open the door." I started turning my back. My friends made fun of me. As my friends opened the door, this vision (we later named him Jim) knocked me down. It was the most horrific, scary thing. His face was so close to mine. My friends said I flew back six or seven feet. As I flew back, this thing, this vision hit me. I needed six stitches in my lip and I had no insurance, so I had to go to Charity Hospital. In talking to the doctor, he said it was impossible that I just bit my lip. I also asked the doctor if I could have hit myself. He said with the severity of the hit, I would have had red marks, which I didn't, if I had hit myself.

Q. Exactly what did this vision look like?

A. From the waist up, he looked like a person. From the waist down, it just drifted off. The anger and ferociousness of the thing was just horrible.

Q. You also mentioned the ghost Caroline?

A. Yes, I saw her two weeks ago at Le Petit. The current technical director Bill Walker asked for my help since I used to work at Le Petit. I now work at the Jefferson Performing Arts Society. Anytime I couldn't find something at Le Petit, I asked for Caroline's help, and then I found the object I needed. Caroline takes the shape of a woman in a wedding gown. I've been told by some people at Le Petit, "Stephen, every time you walk in here, Caroline's here." I know this is weird to see something that's not there that is there. I'm from New Orleans, born and raised here. I've toured all over Europe with productions. I didn't believe in ghosts until I had these experiences.

Q. Thank you very much for your comments.

A. If your professors or anyone else want to talk to me about this, feel free to give them my phone number. I'd be glad to tell them about it.

Appendix B

CHILDREN'S THEATRE PRODUCTIONS AT LE PETIT

1970-71

The Emperor's New Clothes adapted by Sharon O'Brien and
    Fred Palmisano
Aladdin and the Magic Lamp adapted by Luis Barroso and Fred
    Palmisano
The Wonderful World of the Brothers Grimm adapted by Fred
    Palmisano
The Little Mermaid adapted by Lyla Hay Owen and Fred
    Palmisano
Mary Poppins adapted by Ivan Kivitt

1971-72:

Pinocchio adapted by John Simons
The Red Shoes adapted by Lyla Hay Owen
Cinderella adapted by Suzanne Fosberg
The Brothers Grimm Follies adapted by Luis Barroso and Fred
	Palmisano
Babes in Toyland adapted by John Simons and Ricky Graham

1972-73

Beauty and the Beast adapted by Ricky Graham and Fred
	Palmisano
The Merry Adventures of Robin Hood adapted by Sharon
	O'Brien and Fred Palmisano
Hansel and Gretel adapted by John Simons and Fred Palmisano
Sleeping Beauty adapted by John Simons and Fred Palmisano

1973-74

Rumplestiltskin adapted by Sharon O'Brien and Fred Palmisano
Aladdin and the Magic Lamp adapted by Luis Barroso and Fred
	Palmisano
Rapunzel adapted by Sharon O'Brien and Fred Palmisano

Summer Repertory:
The Emperor's New Clothes adapted by Sharon O'Brien and
	Fred Palmisano

Rapunzel adapted by Sharon O'Brien and Fred Palmisano
Take Me to the Treasure by Claire Jones

1974-75

Mother Goose adapted by Sharon O'Brien and Fred Palmisano
The Snow Queen adapted by Lyla Hay Owen
Lafitte! by Sharon O'Brien and Fred Palmisano

1975-76

Pinocchio adapted by John Simons
The Adventures of Raggedy Ann and Andy by Lyla Hay Owen

1976-77

Beauty and the Beast adapted by Ricky Graham and Fred Palmisano
The Merry Adventures of Robin Hood adapted by Sharon O'Brien and Fred Palmisano
The Further Adventures of Raggedy Ann and Andy by Lyla Hay Owen
Puss in Boots adapted by Sharon O'Brien and Fred Palmisano

1977-78

The Brothers Grimm Barnyard Revue by Fred Palmisano, Ricky Graham, Lyla Hay Owen, and Luis Q. Barroso

Raggedy Ann and Andy's Musicland Capers by Lyla Hay Owen
Peter Darling by Ricky Graham and Fred Palmisano
Rapunzel adapted by Sharon O'Brien and Fred Palmisano
Rumplestiltskin adapted by Sharon O'Brien and Fred Palmisano

1978-79

Earthlings by Dave Barton and Matt Bond
The Pied Piper adapted by Sydney Wolf and Fred Palmisano
Wiley and the Hairy Man adapted by Jack Stokes
The Brave Little Tailor adapted by Aurand Harris

1979-80

Robin Hood, Too! by Sharon O'Brien and Fred Palmisano

1980-81

The Littlest Angel by Charles Tazewell

1982-83

Babes in Toyland adapted by John Simons and Ricky Graham
Rapunzel adapted by Sharon O'Brien and Fred Palmisano
The Brothers Grimm adapted by Fred Palmisano

1983-84

Alice's Adventures in Wonderland adapted by Brainerd Duffield

1984-85

Mother Goose adapted by Sharon O'Brien and Fred Palmisano

1986-87

Rapunzel adapted by Sharon O'Brien and Fred Palmisano
Androcles and the Lion adapted by Aurand Harris
The Wizard of Oz adapted by Ricky Graham and Fred
   Palmisano

1987-88

The Masque of Beauty and the Beast by Michael Elliott Brill

1987-88

Chicken Little adapted by Ricky Graham and Fred Palmisano
Rumplestiltskin adapted by Sharon O'Brien and Fred Palmisano

1988-89

Puss in Boots adapted by Sharon O'Brien and Fred Palmisano

Winnie the Pooh adapted by Kristen Sergel

1989-90

Pinocchio adapted by John Simons
Cinderella Battistella by Fred Palmisano, Bob Bruce, and David
    Cuthbert
The Golden Touch by Teddy Sciacca
Mother Goose adapted by Sharon O'Brien and Fred Palmisano

1990-91

The Emperor's New Clothes adapted by Sharon O'Brien, Fred
    Palmisano and Sydney Wolf
Snow White and the Seven Dwarfs adapted by Jessie Braham
    White
Jack and the Beanstalk adapted by Bob Rafferty
The Trial of the Big Bad Wolf by Bob Bruce and David
    Cuthbert

1991-1992

Hansel and Gretel by adapted by John Simons and Fred
    Palmisano
Goldilocks and the Christmas Bears by Eleanor Harder
Aesop's Fables adapted by Kim Esop Wylie
Peter Rabbit adapted by Denys Gawronski

1992-93

Lafitte! by Sharon O'Brien and Fred Palmisano
The Little Mermaid adapted by Lyla Hay Owen and Fred Palmisano
The Pied Piper adapted by Sydney Wolf and Fred Palmisano

1993-94

The Golden Touch by Teddy Sciacca
The Snow Queen adapted by Lyla Hay Owen
The Merry Adventures of Robin Hood adapted by Sharon O'Brien and Fred Palmisano
Sleeping Beauty adapted by John Simons and Fred Palmisano

1994-95

How To Stay Young Forever by Teddy Sciacca
The Red Shoes adapted by Lyla Hay Owen
Sleeping Beauty adapted by John Simons and Fred Palmisano
Peter Rabbit adapted by Denys Gawronski

1995-96

Treasure Island adapted by Charles DeWald
The Phantom of the French Opera by Lyla Hay Owen
The Jungle Book adapted by Craig Sodaro
Aladdin and the Magic Lamp adapted by Luis Q. Barroso and

Fred Palmisano

1996-97

Wiley and the Hairy Man adapted by Jack Stokes
Pinocchio Commedia by Fred Palmisano and John Simons
Beauty and the Beast adapted by Ricky Graham, Fred
    Palmisano, and Edward R. Cox

1998-99

Puss in Boots adapted by Sharon O'Brien and Fred Palmisano
The Brothers Grimm Barnyard Revue adapted by Ricky
    Graham, Lyla Hay Owen, Fred Palmisano, and Luis
    Barroso
Rapunzel adapted by Sharon O'Brien and Fred Palmisano

Educational Arts Program:
The Lion, the Witch, and the Wardrobe adapted by Aurand
    Harris
The Gift of the Magi adapted by Anne Coulter Martens

1999-2000

Sammy the Sorcerer's Unsightly Halloween by Wayne
    Daigrepont
Rumplestiltskin adapted by Sharon O'Brien and Fred Palmisano
The Merry Adventures of Robin Hood adapted by Sharon

O'Brien and Fred Palmisano

2000-2001

The Bepuzzled Pilgrim by Wayne Daigrepont
Limerick Junction by Dane Rhodes and Gary Rucker
An Afternoon with Aesop by Wayne Daigrepont

2001-2002

You're a Good Man, Charlie Brown by Clark Gesner
Schoolhouse Rock, Live! Book by Scott Ferguson, George
    Keting, and Kyle Hall; Songs by Lucy Aherns and Bob
    Dorsey
Cinderella by Richard Rogers and Oscar Hammerstein II

2002-2003

Honk! book and lyrics by Anthony Drewe; music by George
    Stiles; based on The Ugly Duckling by Hans Christian
    Anderson
Free To Be . . . You and Me by Marlo Thomas
Bye Bye Birdie by Charles Strouse, Lee Adams, and Michael
    Stewart (This was Teddy's Corner production performed on
    the main stage.)

2003-2004

Snoopy by Charles M. Schulz
Once Upon a Mattress based on the story The Princess and the Pea by Mary Rogers

2004-2005

Chicken Little by Ricky Graham and Fred Palmisano
Cinderella Battistella by Bob Bruce, David Cuthbert and Fred Palmisano
Saint George and the Dragon by Ricky Graham and Fred Palmisano

2005-2006

Season cancelled due to Hurricane Katrina (August 29, 2005)

Appendix C

MAIN-STAGE PLAYS AT LE PETIT

The Drawing Room Players (performed in members' homes)

1917-1918

The Beau of Bath by Constance D'Arcy Mackay
Ashes of Roses by Constance D'Arcy Mackay
Maker of Dreams by Oliphant Dawn
The Prince of Court Painters by Constance D'Arcy Mackay
How He Lied to Her Husband by George Bernard Shaw

The Drawing Room Players of Le Petit Théâtre du Vieux Carré (Lower Pontalba Building)

1919-1920

Pierrot Home from the Wars by Thomas Wood Stevens

Suppressed Desires by Susan Glaspell and George Cram Cook
Maid of France by Harold Brighouse
The Romancers by Edmond Rostand
The Land of Hearts Desire by William Butler Yeats
Le Passant by Francois Coppee
Big Kate by Charles Frederick Nirdlinger
Everybody's Husband by Gilbert Cannon
Two Crooks and a Lady by Eugene Pillot
No Smoking by Jacinta Benavente
Spring by T.B. Murray
The Four-Flushers by Cleves Kinkead
Moonshine by Arthur Hopkins
Just As Well by J. Hartley Manners
Bagatelle by Samuel Louis Gilmore

1920-1921

Interior by Maurice Maeterlinck
A Good Woman by George Middleton
Helena's Husband by Phillip Moeller
Allison's Lad by Beulah Marie Dix
Ruby Red by Clarence Stratton
The Turtle Dove by Margaret Scott Oliver
Joint Owners in Spain by Alice Brown
Sabotage by Messrs. Hellem, Valcros, and Pel d'Estor
The Unseen by Alice Gerstenberg

409

The Florist Shop by Winifred Hawkridge
L'Arlesienne by Alphonse Daudet
Woman Proposes by Paul Armstrong
Portrait of a Policeman by Sara Bennett
Riders to the Sea by John Millington Synge
The Pot-Boiler by Alice Gerstenberg
The Game of Chess by Kenneth Sawyer Goodman
Boccacio's Untold Tale by Harry Kemp
The Farewell Supper by Arthur Schnitzler
The Dear Departed by Stanley Houghton
A Night at an Inn by Lord Dunsany
What, Again! By Natalie Vivien Scott and Samuel Louis Gilmore
The Importance of Being Earnest by Oscar Wilde

1921-1922

The Sweetmeat Game by Ruth Comfort Mitchell
A Well-Remembered Voice by James M. Barrie
The Bear by Anton Chekhov
Beyond the Horizon by Eugene O'Neill
The Philosopher of Butterbiggen's by Harold Chapin
Ten Seconds by Robert Courtney
Another Way Out by Lawrence Langner
He and She by Rachel Crothers
A Sunny Morning by Serafin and Joaquin Quintero
The Mollusc by Hubert Henry Davies
The Rights of the Soul by Giusseppe Giarosa

The Dark Lady of the Sonnets by George Bernard Shaw
The Monkey's Paw by W.W. Jacobs and Louis N. Parker
Lady Windermere's Fan by Oscar Wilde

1922-1923 - (inauguration of the new theatre at 616 St. Peter St.)

The Falcon and the Lady by Margaret Penney
The Little Stone House by George Calderon
The Man in the Stalls by Alfred Sutro
Candida by George Bernard Shaw
The Trysting Place by Booth Tarkington
The Man Who Married a Dumb Wife by Anatole France
Le Fanion by M. Paul Ginisty
The Constant Lover by St. John Hankin
The Wife with a Smile by Denys Amiel and Andre Obey
Children of Earth by Alice Brown
For Distinguished Service by Florence Clay Knox
O'Flaherty, V.C. by George Bernard Shaw
The Gods of the Mountains by Lord Dunsany
The First and the Last by John Galsworthy
The Twelve-Pound Look by James M. Barrie
Torches by Kenneth Raisbeck

1923-1924

Pomander Walk by Louis N. Parker

Drums of Oude by Austin Strong
The Shirkers by C.M.S. McClelland
Fourteen by Alice Gerstenberg
The Master by Herman Bahr
Julian by Louis Gilmore
Overruled by George Bernard Shaw
The Green Cockatoo by Arthur Schnitzler
R.U.R. by Karel Capek
The Torchbearers by George Kelly
He Who Gets Slapped by Leonid Andreyev

1924-1925

The White-Headed Boy by Lennox Robinson
The Yellow Jacket by George Hazelton
Fame and the Poet by Lord Dunsany
The Cradle Song by G. Martina Sierra
The Ship by St. John Ervine
You and I by Philip Barry
Pygmalion by George Bernard Shaw
The New York Idea by Langdon Mitchell

1925-1926

The Honeymoon by John Tobin
The Pigeon by John Galsworthy
Belinda by A.A. Milne
Lackeys of the Moon by Mary Cass Canfield

Big Kate by Charles Frederick Nirdlinger
Mardi Gras by John Beach
The Joy of Living by Herman Sudermann
The Sabine Women by Leonid Andreyeff
Dear Brutus by James M. Barrie

1926-1927

The Swan by Ferenc Molnár
Sun-Up by Lula Vollmer
Doctor Knock by Jules Romains
If by Lord Dunsany
A La Creole by Flo Field
Declasse by Zoe Akins
The Romantic Young Lady by G. Martinez Sierra

1927-1928

The Mask and the Face By C.B. Fernald
John Ferguson by St. John Ervine
The Rose and the Ring by Harris Dean
Anna Christie by Eugene O'Neill
The Adventurer by Hugh Ross
Children of the Moon by Martin Flavin
Mr. Pim Passes By by A.A. Milne

1928-1929

Anthony and Anna by St. John Ervine
The Good Hope by Herman Heijermans
The Magic Sword by Harris Deans
Craig's Wife by George Kelly
The Women Have Their Way by Serafin and Joaquin Quintero
Seven Women by Sir James M. Barrie
The House with the Twisty Windows by Mary Pakington
How He Lied to Her Husband by George Bernard Shaw
Saint Joan by George Bernard Shaw
Outward Bound by Sutton Vane
The Queen's Husband by Robert E. Sherwood

1929-1930

Spread Eagle by George S. Brooks and Walter B. Lister
The Devil's Disciple by George Bernard Shaw
Twelfth Night by William Shakespeare
The House by H.F. Rubinstein
The Silver Cord by Sidney Howard
Reefs by Virginia Shaw Putnam
Saturday's Children by Maxwell Anderson

Summer 1930

The Front Page by Ben Hecht and Charles MacArthur

1930-1931

The Painted Ship by Eleanor Carroll Chilton and Herbert Agar
Hotel Universe by Philip Barry
Prunella by Lawrence Housman and Granville Barker
Icebound by Owen Davis
The Apple Cart by George Bernard Shaw
The Poor Nut by J.C. Nugent and Elliott Neugent
Hedda Gabler by Henrik Ibsen
The Truth by Clyde Fitch

Summer 1931

The Last Mile by John Wexley

1931-1932

The Vinegar Tree by Paul Osborn
Death Takes a Holiday by Alberto Casella
They Knew What They Wanted by Sidney Howard
Laughing Boy by Otis Chatfield-Taylor
On Approval by Frederick Lonsdale
Caesar and Cleopatra by George Bernard Shaw
Michael and Mary by A.A. Milne

Summer 1932

What Price Glory by Laurence Stallings and Maxwell Anderson
The Bad Man by Porter Emerson Browne

1932-1933

Once in a Lifetime by Moss Hart and George S. Kaufman
The Cherry Orchard by Anton Chekhov
The Man Who Pays the Piper by G.B. Stern
Hay Fever by Noel Coward
Fata Morgana by Ernest Vajda
The Marquise by Noel Coward
The First Mrs. Fraser by St. John Ervine

Summer 1933

Art and Mrs. Bottle by Benn W. Levy
Trial by Jury by Leo Delibes
H.M.S. Pinafore by W.S. Gilbert and Arthur Sullivan
Coppelia a ballet-pantomime, adapted by Lelia Haller
The Streets of New York by Dion Boucicault
To My Husband by William H. Fulham

1933-1934

Let Us Be Gay by Rachel Crothers
What Every Woman Knows by James M. Barrie
The Mikado by W.S. Gilbert and Arthur Sullivan
Both Your Houses by Maxwell Anderson
Biography by S.N. Behrman
Dangerous Corner by J.B. Priestly

A Lady with Five Husbands by William H. Fulham

Summer 1934

The Road to Rome by Robert E. Sherwood
Whistling in the Dark by Laurence Gross and Edward Carpenter
Caprice Espagnol an original ballet to the music of Rimsky-Korsakov's Caprice Espagnol, adapted by Lelia Haller
Le Portrait de Manon by J. Massenet

1934-1935

Three Cornered Moon by Gertrude Tonkonogy
Il Tabarro by Giacomo Puccini
The Secret of Suzanne by Ermanno Wold-Farrari
Night Over Taos by Maxwell Anderson
Good-bye Again by Allan Scott and George Haight
Yellow Jacket by Sidney Howard and Paul DeKruif
The Divine Drudge by Vicki Baum and John Golden
By Candlelight by Siegfried Geyer, adapted by P.G. Wodehouse

Summer 1935

The Cuckoo's Nest by H. Stuart Cottman and LaVergne Shaw
The Late Christopher Bean by Sidney Howard
Judgement Day by Elmer Rice

1935-1936

The Chocolate Soldier adapted by Bernauer and Jacobson, from
George Bernard Shaw's Arms and the Man
Elizabeth the Queen by Maxwell Anderson
Accent on Youth by Samson Raphaelson
Counsellor-At-Large by Elmer Rice
Kind Lady by Edward Chodorov
Liliom By Ferenc Molnár
Clear All Wires by Bella and Samual Spewack

Summer 1936

The Hairy Ape by Eugene 0'Neill
The Royal Family by George S. Kaufman and Edna Ferber
June Moon by Ring Lardner and George S. Kaufman

1936-1937

Twentieth Century by Ben Hecht and Charles MacArthur
Mary of Scotland by Maxwell Anderson
Holiday by Philip Barry
Spring by Colin Campbell Clements
Bury the Dead by Irwin Shaw
Personal Appearance by Lawrence Riley
The Firebrand by Edwin Justus Mayer
Call It a Day by Dodie Smith

Summer 1937

Cox and Box by Sir Arthur Sullivan and F.C. Burnand
The Last Night of Don Juan by Edmond Rostand
He by Alfred Savoir, adapted by Chester Erskin
The Night of January 16th by Ayn Rand

1937-1938

First Lady by George S. Kaufman and Katherine Dayton
Pride and Prejudice dramatized by Helen Jerome from the novel by Jane Austen
A Bill of Divorcement by Clemence Dane
The Play's the Thing by Ferenc Molnár
Peer Gynt by Henrik Ibsen
The Taming of the Shrew by William Shakespeare
Idiot's Delight by Robert E. Sherwood

Summer 1938

Escape by John Galsworthy
The Hutchinsons, Bless Them by Edward J. Levy

1938-1939

Penny Wise by Jean Ferguson Black
Charles the King by Maurice Colbourne
Topaze by Marol Pagnol

Libel by Edward Woll
Our Town by Thornton Wilder
Street Scene by Elmer Rice

Summer 1939

A Doll's House by Henrik Ibsen
The Torchbearers by George Kelly

1939-1940

Patience by W.S. Gilbert and Arthur Sullivan
The Dark Tower by Alexander Woollcott and George S. Kaufman
Cyrano de Bergerac by Edmond Rostand
Excursion by Victor Wolfson
Shadow and Substance by Paul Vincent Carroll
Kiss the Boys Goodbye by Clare Booth Luce
Au Destin by William H. Fulham
The Torchbearers by George Kelly

1940-1941

Margin for Error by Clare Booth Luce
Storm in a Teacup by Bruno Frank, adapted by James Bridie
The World We Make By Sidney Kingsley
Gaslight by Patrick Hamilton
Une Robe De Soie by Henriette Charasson

Love Is the Best Doctor by Moliere
The Doctor in Spite of Himself by Moliere, adapted by Gerhardt Lindemulder
The Gentle People by Irwin Shaw
Tonight at 8:30 by Noel Coward
Ways and Means by Noel Coward
Fumed Oak by Noel Coward
Family Album by Noel Coward

1941-1942

The Man Who Came to Dinner by George S. Kaufman and Moss Hart
Invitation to a Murder by Rufus King
She Stoops to Conquer by Oliver Goldsmith
Youth at the Helm by Paul Volpius, adapted by John Coman
Fashion by Anna Cora Mowatt
George Washington Slept Here by Moss Hart and George S. Kaufman
The Pursuit of Happiness by Lawrence Langner and Armina Marshall Langner

1942-1943

The Contrast by Royal Tyler
The Heart of the City by Lesley Storm
Jason by Samson Raphaelson
Out of the Frying Pan by Francis Swann

The Eve of St. Mark by Maxwell Anderson
The Damask Cheek by John Van Druten and Lloyd Morris

1943-1944

Major Barbara by George Bernard Shaw
Her Master's Voice by Clare Kummer
The Witching Hour by Augustus Thomas
There Shall Be No Night by Robert E. Sherwood
Dark Eyes by Eugenie Leontovich and Elena Miramova
Ladies in Retirement by Edward Percy and Reginald Denham
Janie by Josephine Bentham and Herschel Williams
There's Always Juliet by John Van Druten

1944-1945

The Skin of Our Teeth by Thornton Wilder
Skylark by Samson Raphaelson
Uncle Harry by Thomas Job
The Great Big Doorstep by Frances Goodrich and Albert Hackett, from the novel by E.P. O'Donnell
For Keeps by F. Hugh Herbert
Misalliance by George Bernard Shaw
A Bell for Adano by Paul Osborn, based on the novel by John Hersey
Much Ado About Nothing by William Shakespeare

1945-1946

Over Twenty-One by Ruth Gordon
Blithe Spirit by Noel Coward
Hope for the Best by William McCleery
The Deep Mrs. Sykes by George Kelly
The Visitor by Kenneth White
Ghosts by Henrik Ibsen
When Ladies Meet by Rachel Crothers
Fling at Fifty by John Beach

1946-1947

Boy Meets Girl by Bella and Samuel Spewack
Of Mice and Men by John Steinbeck
Ah, Wilderness by Eugene O'Neill
Thunder Rock by Robert Ardrey
Biography by S.N. Behrman
Small Miracle by Norman Krasna
Dream Girl by Elmer Rice
Petticoat Fever by Mark Reed

Summer 1947

Laura by Vera Caspary and George Sklar

1947-1948

Golden Boy by Clifford Odets

The Philadelphia Story by Philip Barry
Outward Bound by Sutton Vane
Arms and the Man by George Bernard Shaw
The Late George Apley by George S. Kaufman and John P. Marquand
Kiss and Tell by F. Hugh Herbert
Medea by Euripides
The Time of Your Life by William Saroyan

1948-1949

An Inspector Calls by J.B. Priestley
The Merchant of Yonkers by Thornton Wilder
Memorial by Allen White also kow as Clay Shaw
The Petrified Forest by Robert E. Sherwood
The Glass Menagerie by Tennessee Williams
The Barretts of Wimpole Street by Rudolf Besier
Command Decision by William Wister Haines
On Borrowed Time by Paul Osborn
Yes, My Darling Daughter by Mark Reed

1949-1950

The Lady from the Sea by Henrik Ibsen
The Play's the Thing by Ferenc Molnár
Light Up the Sky by Moss Hart
Right You Are (If You Think You Are) by Luigi Pirandello
Two Blind Mice by Samuel Spewack

Berkeley Square by John L. Balderston
Therese by Thomas Job, from Emile Zola's Therese Raquin
Made in Heaven by Hagar Wilde

1950-1951

The Guardsman by Ferenc Molnár
Summer and Smoke by Tennessee Williams
My Sister Eileen by Joseph A. Fields and Jerome Chodorov
Rain by John Colton and Clemence Randolph
The Silver Whistle by Robert McEnroe
Dangerous Corner by J.B. Priestley
Strictly Dishonorable by Preston Sturges
The Enchanted by Jean Giraudoux, adapted by Maurice Valency

1951-1952

Detective Story by Sidney Kingsley
September Tide by Daphne Du Maurier
Junior Miss by Jerome Chodorov and Joseph Fields
Abe Lincoln in Illinois by Robert E. Sherwood
Payment Deferred by Jeffrey Dell
Second Threshold by Philip Barry
You Can't Take It With You by Moss Hart and George S. Kaufman
The Happy Time by Samuel Taylor

1952-1953

State of the Union by Howard Lindsay and Russel Crouse
Come Back, Little Sheba by William Inge
The Madwoman of Chaillot by Jean Giraudoux
Tony Draws a Horse by Lesley Storm
Guest in the House by Hagar Wilde and Dale Eunson
Stalag 17 by Donald Bevan and Edmund Tracinski
The Women by Clare Boothe Luce
The Country Girl by Clifford Odets

Summer 1953

The Male Animal by James Thurber and Elliott Nugent

1953-1954

Gigi by Anita Loos, from the novel by Collette
Death of a Salesman by Arthur Miller
Affairs of State by Louis Verneuil
Point of No Return by Paul Osborn
Angel Street by Patrick Hamilton
Southern Exposure by Owen Crump
The Ladies of the Corridor by Dorthy Parker and Arnaud D'Usseau

1954-1955

The Lady's Not for Burning by Christopher Fry

My Three Angels by Sam and Bella Spewack, based on the play
    La Cuisine des Anges by Albert Jusson
Sabrina Fair by Samuel Taylor
The Fourposter by Jan de Hartog
The Caine Mutiny Court Martial by Herman Wouk
The Birds by Aristophanes
King of Hearts by Jean Kerr and Eleanor Brooke

1955-1956

The Remarkable Mr. Pennypacker by Liam O'Brien
Dial "M" for Murder by Frederick Knott
Darkness at Noon by Sidney Kingsley
The Rainmaker by N. Richard Nash
The Solid Gold Cadillac by Howard Teichmann and George S. Kaufman
Anastasia by Marcelle Maurette, adaptation by Guy Bolton
Our Town by Thornton Wilder

1956-1957

The Ponder Heart by Joseph Fields and Jerome Chodorov, adapted from the story by Eudora Welty
Time Limit by Henry Denker and Ralph Berkey
The Corn Is Green by Emlyn Williams
The Great Sabastians by Howard Lindsay and Russell Crouse
The Chalk Garden by Enid Bagnold
Harvey by Mary Chase

Edward, My Son by Robert Morley and Noel Langley

1957-1958

Tiger at the Gates by by Gean Giraudoux, adapted by Christopher Fry from the play Le Guerre de Troi N'Aura pas Lieu
The Desk Set by William Merchant
Speaking of Murder by Audrey and William Roos
Inherit the Wind by Jerome Lawrence and Robert E. Lee
White Sheep of the Family by L. duGarde Peach and Ian Hay
Middle of the Night by Paddy Chayefsky
On Approval by Frederick Lonsdale

1958-1959

Ring Round the Moon by Jean Anouilh
Separate Tables by Terence Rattigan
Bell, Book and Candle by John Van Druten
The Hidden River by Augustus Goetz
The Teahouse of the August Moon by John Patrick
The Man by Mel Dinelli
Marriage '59 by by Virg Engeran

1959-1960

Who Was That Lady I Saw You With? By Norman Krasna
Morning's At Seven by Paul Osborn

Cyrano de Bergerac by Edmond Rostand
The Fifth Season by Sylvia Regan
Tonight at 8:30 by Noel Coward
Hands Across the Sea by Noel Coward
The Astonished Heart by Noel Coward
Red Peppers by Noel Coward
The Autumn Garden by Lillian Hellman
Once More, With Feeling by Harry Kurnitz

1960-1961

Once in a Lifetime by Moss Hart and George S. Kaufman
A Touch of the Poet by Eugene O'Neill
Anything Goes music and lyrics by Cole Porter, book by P.G. Wodehouse and Guy Bolton, revised by Howard Lindsay and Russell Crouse
Rebel Without a Cause by James Fuller
Life With Father by Howard Lindsay and Russell Crouse
Breath of Spring by Peter Coke
Monique by Dorothy and Michael Blankfort

Summer 1961

They Knew What They Wanted by Sidney Howard

1961-1962

Strange Bedfellows by Florence Ryerson and Colin Clements

Five Finger Exercise by Peter Shaffer
Send Me No Flowers by Norman Barasch and Carroll Moore
The Boy Friend by Sandy Wilson
Night Must Fall by Emlyn Williams
The Great Big Doorstep by Frances Goodrich and Albert Hackett, from the novel by E.P. O'Donnell
A Thurber Carnival by by James Thurber

1962-1963

Everybody Loves Opal by John Patrick
The Best Man by Gore Vidal
Come Blow Your Horn by Neil Simon
Barefoot in Athens by Maxwell Anderson
The Pleasure of His Company by Samuel Taylor and Cornelia Otis Skinner
The Deadly Game by James Yaffee, adapted from the novel by Fríederic Dürrenmatt
The Imaginary Invalid by Moliere

1963-1964

The Visit by Fríederic Dürrenmatt, adapted by Maurice Valency
Sunday in New York by Norman Krasna
A Majority of One by Leonard Spigelgass
The Devil's Advocate by Dore Schary, from the novel by Morris West
The Happiest Millionaire by Kyle Crichton

Guys and Dolls by Frank Loesser, Abe Burrows, Jo Swerling, and Damon Runyan
The Mousetrap by Agatha Christie

1964-1965

Golden Fleecing by by Lorenzo Semple, Jr.
Macbeth by William Shakespeare
A Thousand Clowns by Herb Gardner
First Love by Samuel Taylor
Not in the Book by Arthur Watkyn
Mary, Mary by Jean Kerr

Summer 1965

The Pajama Game by Richard Bissell, George Abbott, Richard Adler, and Jerry Ross

1965-1966

Never Too Late by Summer Arthur Long
A Man for All Seasons by Robert Bolt
A Case of Libel by Henry Denker
Catch Me If You Can by Jack Weinstock and Willie Gilbert
The Miracle Worker by William Gibson
You Can't Take It With You by Moss Hart and George S. Kaufman

1966-1967

West Side Story by Arthur Laurents, Leonard Bernstein,
Stephen Sondheim, based on a conception by Jerome Robbins
Pygmalion by George Bernard Shaw
Any Wednesday by Muriel Resnik
The Barretts of Wimpole Street by Rudolph Besier
The Seven Year Itch by George Axelrod
Victims of Duty by Eugene Ionesco
The Diary of Anne Frank by Frances Goodrich and Albert Hackett
Barefoot in the Park by Neil Simon

1967-1968

Bye Bye Birdie by Michael Stewart, Lee Adams, and Charles Strouse
The Aspern Papers by Roger Cornish, based on a novella by Henry James
The Odd Couple by Neil Simon
Who's Afraid of Virginia Woolf? By Edward Albee
A Bug in Her Ear by Georges Feydeau
The Playroom by Mary Drayton
Enter Laughing by Joseph Stein

1968-1969

Kiss Me, Kate by Cole Porter, based on Shakespeare's Taming

of the Shrew
The Lion in Winter by James Goldman
Light Up the Sky by Moss Hart
Wait Until Dark by Fredrick Knott
The Star-Spangled Girl by Neil Simon
The Night of the Iguana by Tennessee Williams
White Liars by Peter Shaffer
Black Comedy by Peter Shaffer

1969-1970

Li'l Abner by Norman Panama and Melvin Frank
Everything in the Garden adopted by Edward Albee, from the play by Giles Cooper
The Subject Was Roses by Frank D. Gilroy
The Killing of Sister George by Frank Marcus
The Amorous Flea by Moliere
The Prime of Miss Jean Brodie by Jay Allen, from the novel by Muriel Spark
Visit to a Small Planet by Gore Vidal

1970-1971

Oklahoma! by Oscar Hammerstein II and Richard Rogers
Don't Drink the Water by Woody Allen
Gideon by Paddy Chayefsky
Look Homeward, Angel by Ketti Frings, from the novel by Thomas Wolfe

Cactus Flower by Jo Swerling
Witness for the Prosecution by Agatha Christie
Born Yesterday by Garson Kanin

1971-1972

Fiddler on the Roof by Joseph Stein, Sheldon Harnick, and Jerry Bock
The Importance of Being Earnest by Oscar Wilde
The Price by Arthur Miller
Forty Carats by Barillet and Gredy
A Funny Thing Happened on the Way to the Forum by Stephen Sondheim, Larry Gelbart, and Burt Shevelove
Hadrian VII by Peter Luke
Plaza Suite by Neil Simon

1972-1973

Hello, Dolly! By Jerry Herman and Michael Stewart
The Last of the Red Hot Lovers by Neil Simon
Ten Little Indians by Agatha Christie
My Daughter, Your Son by Henry and Phoebe Ephron
I Do! I Do! by Tom Jones and Harvey Schmidt
Becket by Jean Anouilh
Play It Again, Sam by Woody Allen

1973-1974

My Fair Lady by Alan Jay Lerner and Frederick Loewe
Night Watch by Lucille Fletcher
Private Lives by Noel Coward
Another Part of the Forest by Lillian Hellman
The Little Foxes by Lillian Hellman
Sherlock Holmes and the Affair of the Amorous Regent by John Fenn
Absence of a Cello by Ira Wallach

1974-1975

1776 by Peter Stone and Sherman Edwards
Promenade, All by David V. Robison
Who Killed Santa Claus? by Terence Feely
All the Way Home by Tad Mosel
Next! By Terrence McNally
The Real Inspector Hound by Tom Stoppard
The Last of Mrs. Lincoln by James Prideaux
6 Rms Riv Vu by Bob Randall

1975-1976

Funny Girl by Jule Styne, Bob Merrill, and Isobel Lennart
The Prisoner of Second Avenue by Neil Simon
The Time of the Cuckoo by Arthur Laurents
All the King's Men by Robert Penn Warren

Picnic by William Inge
Tunes II by Fred Palmisano, Sharon O'Brien, and Luis Barroso
The Sunshine Boys by Neil Simon

1976-1977

Shenandoah by James Lee Barrett, Peter Udell, Gary Geld, and Philip Rose
The Gingerbread Lady by Neil Simon
Ladies in Retirement by Reginal Denham and Edward Percy
A Streetcar Named Desire by Tennessee Williams
Two By Two by Richard Rodgers and Martin Charnin
Scapino! by Frank Dunlap and Jim Dale
My Fat Friend by Charles Laurence

1977-1978

Seesaw adapted by Michael Bennett from William Gibson's Two for the Seesaw
Habeas Corpus by Alan Bennett
The Curious Savage by John Patrick
The Country Girl by Clifford Odets
Rodgers & Hart: A Musical Celebration by Richard Rodgers and Lorenz Hart
God's Favorite by Neil Simon
Unexpected Guests by Jordan Crittenden

1978-1979

The Unsinkable Molly Brown by Meredith Wilson
A Community of Two by Jerome Chodorov
Vanities by Jack Heifner
Butterflies Are Free by Leonard Gershe
The Decline and Fall of the Entire World As Seen Through the Eyes of Cole Porter by Ben Bagley
The Shadow Box by Michael Cristofer
California Suite by Neil Simon

1979-1980

Mack & Mabel by Michael Stewart and Jerry Herman
The Chalk Garden by Enid Bagnol
Same Time, Next Year by Bernard Slade
Dames at Sea by George Haimsohn, Robin Miller and Jim Wise
The Ritz by Terrence McNally
Something's Afoot by James McDonald, David Vos, and Robert Gerlach
Blithe Spirit by Noel Coward

1980-1981

Cabaret by John Kander, Fred Ebb, and Joe Masteroff; based on Berlin Diaries by Christopher Isherwood
Chapter Two by Neil Simon
On Golden Pond by Ernest Thompson

Dracula by Hamilton Deave and John Balderston, based on the novel by Bram Stoker
The Roar of the Greasepaint, The Smell of the Crowd by Leslie Bricusse and Anthony Newley
Tribute by Bernard Slade
The Boys from Syracuse by Richard Rodgers and Lorenz Hart, based on Shakespeare's Comedy of Errors

1981-1982

Pippin by Roger O. Hurson and Stephen Swartz
Lunch Hour by John Mortimer
Cleavage by David and Buddy Sheffield
Chicago by Fred Ebb, Bob Fosse, and John Kander
The Rainmaker by N. Richard Nash
The Man Who Came to Dinner by Moss Hart and George S. Kaufman
Side By Side By Sondheim by Stephen Sondheim, Leonard Bernstein, Mary Rodgers, Richard Rodgers, and Jule Styne

1982-1983

Gypsy by Arthur Laurents, Jule Styne, and Stephen Sondheim
The Philadelphia Story by Philip Barry
Auntie Mame by Jerome Lawrence
Deathtrap by Ira Levin
The Robber Bridegroom by Alfred Uhry and Robert Waldman
70 Girls 70 by John Kander and Fred Ebb

Summer 1983

Grease by Jim Jacobs and Warren Casey

1983-1984

South Pacific by Richard Rodgers, Oscar Hammerstein, and Joshua Logan
Godspell by Stephen Schwartz, based on the Gospel According to St. Matthew
The West Side Waltz by Ernest Thompson
Room Service by John Murray, Allen Borets, and George Abbot
How to Stay Young Forever by Teddy Sciacca
I Love My Wife by Michael Stewart and Cy Coleman

1984-1985

Sweet Charity by Neil Simon and Cy Coleman
The Dining Room by A.R. Gurney
The Winslow Boy by Terence Ratligan
The Fantasticks by Tom Jones and Harvey Schmidt
The Elephant Man by Bernard Pomerance
The 1940s Radio Hour by Walton Jones

Summer 1985

Make Mine Bourbon by Theodora Sciacca

1985-1986

Evita by Andrew Lloyd Webber and Tim Rice
The Desperate Hours by Joseph Hayes
The Gin Game by D.L. Coburn
Pigeons by Tom Atkins
Tintypes by Mary Kite, Mel Marvin, and Gary Pearle
Nora (A Doll's House) by Henrik Ibsen

1986-1987

Peter Pan by James M. Barrie
The Foreigner by Larry Shue
The Dresser by Ronald Harwood
Cat on a Hot Tin Roof by Tennessee William
Le Veau Qui Tete (The Suckling Calf) by Dalt Wonk
Brighton Beach Memoirs by Neil Simon

1987-1988

The King and I by Richard Rodgers and Oscar Hammerstein
Children of a Lesser God by Mark Medoff
Amadeus by Peter Shaffer
The Rose Tattoo by Tennessee Williams
Sweeny Todd by Stephen Sondheim
Gaslight (Angel Street) by Patrick Hamilton

1988-1989

<u>Oliver</u> by Lionel Bart, based on <u>Oliver Twist</u> by Charles Dickens
<u>Biloxi Blues</u> by Neil Simon
<u>Educating Rita</u> by Willy Russell
<u>A Streetcar Named Desire</u> by Tennessee Williams
<u>Show Boat</u> by Jerome Kern and Oscar Hammerstein II, based on the novel by Edna Ferber
<u>A Chorus Line</u> by James Kirkwood, Nicholas Dante, Edward Kleban, Marvin Hamlisch, and Michael Bennett

1989-1990

<u>Annie Get Your Gun</u> by Irving Berlin
<u>I'm Not Rappaport</u> by Herb Gardner
<u>The Threepenny Opera</u> by Kurt Weill and Bertolt Brecht
<u>Orpheus Descending</u> by Tennesee Williams
<u>Man of La Mancha</u> by Dale Wasserman, Joe Darian, and Mitch Lee
<u>The Women</u> by Clare Booth Luce

1990-1991

<u>Guys and Dolls</u> by Frank Loesser, Abe Burrows, Jo Swerling, and Damon Runyan
<u>The Crucible</u> by Arthur Miller
<u>Candida</u> by George Bernard Shaw

The Glass Menagerie by Tennessee Williams
The Mikado by W.S. Gilbert and Arthur Sullivan
Broadway Bound by Neil Simon

1991-1992

My Fair Lady by Alan Jay Lerner and Frederick Loewe
The Lion in Winter by James Goldman
Fences by August Wilson
Sweet Bird of Youth by Tennessee Williams
Fiddler on the Roof by Joseph Stein, Sheldon Harnick, and Jerry Bock
Applause by Betty Comden, Adolph Green, Charles Strouse, and Lee Adams

1992-1993

How to Succeed in Business Without Really Trying by Frank Loesser, Abe Burrows, Jack Weinstock, and Willie Gilbert
M. Butterfly by David Henry Hwang
The Nerd by Larry Shue
Summer and Smoke by Tennessee Williams
Look Homeward, Angel by Ketti Frings from the novel by Thomas Wolfe
The Music Man by Meredith Wilson

442

1993-1994

West Side Story by Arthur Laurents, Leonard Bernstein, Stephen Sondheim, based on a conception by Jerome Robbins
The Baby Dance by Jane Anderson
Music, Music, Music a musical tribute to various composers
Jake's Women by Neil Simon
The Pirates of Penzance by W.S. Gilbert and Arthur Sullivan
The Taming of the Shrew by William Shakespeare

1994-1995

Hello, Dolly! by Jerry Herman and Michael Stewart
Trophies by William S. Seward
Some Enchanted Evening by Richard Rodgers and Oscar Hammerstein II
A Life in the Theatre byDavid Mamet
La Cage aux Folles by Harvey Fierstein
The Sisters Rosenweig by Wendy Wasserstein

1995-1996

Carmen Jones by Oscar Hammerstein II
The Heiress by Ruth and Augustus Goetz
Steel Magnolias by Robert Harling
The Woman in Black by Stephen Malatratt
The Secret Garden by Marsha Norman and Lucy Simon, based on the novel by Frances Hodgson Burnett

They're Playing Our Song by Neil Simon, Marvin Hamlisch, and Carole Bayer Sager

1996-97

Sophisticated Ladies conceived by Donald McKayle, based on the music of Duke Ellington
Laughter on the 23rd Floor by Neil Simon
A Christmas Carol by Charles Dickens
The Importance of Being Earnest by Oscar Wilde
She Loves Me by Joe Masteroff, Jerry Bock, and Sheldon Harnick
The Sound of Music by Richard Rodgers and Oscar Hammerstein
Rumors by Neil Simon

1997-1998

Pretty Baby by Anne Rose and Hugh McElyea
The Passion of Dracula by Bram Stoker
Lost in Yonkers by Neil Simon
Master Class by Terrence McNally
A Streetcar Named Desire by Tennessee Williams
Gypsy by Arthur Laurents, Jule Styne, and Stephen Sondheim

1998-1999

42nd Street by Mark Bramble, Michael Stewart, Harry Warren,

and Al Dubin
Hay Fever by Noel Coward
The Innocents by William Archibald
Ma Rainey's Black Bottom by August Wilson
City of Angels by Cy Colman, David Zippel, and Larry Gelbart

1999-2000

Grand Hotel by Luther Davis, Robert Wright, George Forrest, and Maury Yeston
Lettice and Lovage by Peter Shaffer
Cat on a Hot Tin Roof by Tennessee Williams
Falsettos by William Finn
The Kiss of the Spider Woman by John Kander, Fred Ebb, and Terrence McNally

2000-2001

A Christmas Carol by Charles Dickens, adapted by Buzz Podewell
Barnum by Cy Coleman, Michael Stewart, and Mark Bramble
Noises Off by Michael Frayn
Little Shop of Horrors by Howard Ashman and Alan Menken
Tiger Tails by Tennessee Williams
The Mystery of Edwin Drood by Rupert Holmes, suggested by Charles Dickens' unfinished novel

445

2001-2002

George M! by George M. Cohan
Art by Yasmina Reza
Leader of the Pack by Ellie Greenwich
Sweet Bird of Youth by Tennessee Williams
Chicago music by John Kander; lyrics by Fred Ebb; book by Fred Ebb and Bob Fosse

2002-2003

Anything Goes by Cole Porter
The Ritz by Terrence McNally
Five Guys named Moe songs by Louis Jordan; written by Clark Peters
The Rose Tattoo by Tennessee Williams
Hello, Dolly! book by Michael Stewart; music and lyrics by Jerry Herman; based on the original play by Thornton Wilder

2003-2004

Forever Plaid by Stewart Ross; musical arrangements by James Raitt
The Mystery of Irma Vep by Charles Ludlam; original music composed by Peter Golub
Grease by Jim Jacobs and Warren Casey
When Ya Smilin' by Ricky Graham

Dames at Sea by Jim Wise, Robin Miller, and George Haimsohn

2004-2005

A Day In Hollywood/A Night In The Ukraine music by Frank Lazarus and lyrics and book by Dick Vosburgh
Tru by Jay Presson Allen
Eating Raoul book by Paul Bartel, music by Jed Feurer and lyrics by Boyd Graham
Oh, Coward! by Roderick Cook
Pageant book and lyrics by Bill Russell and Frank Kelly; music by Albert Evans

The following were not part of the main season:

At the Club Toot Sweet on Bourbon Street by Ricky Graham and David Cuthbert
The Bible: The Complete Work of God (Abridged) by the Reduced Shakespeare Company

2005-2006

* Hurricane Katrina caused the cancellation of most of the 2005-2006 season.

And the Ball and All by Ricky Graham

Appendix D

LE PETIT CHILDREN'S THEATRE PRODUCTIONS PERFORMED AT OTHER LOCATIONS

The Calliope Players was the name of the Le Petit acting troupe that performed at venues other than Le Petit Theatre.

1969: Marco Polo - Performed at Trinity Church
1971: Pinocchio - Performed at the Travel Lodge Motel
1971: Rumplestiltskin - Performed at the Oakwood Mall
1973: Rumplestiltskin - Performed at the Clearview Mall
1984: Pinocchio - Performed at the Italian Village of the Louisiana World Exposition

About the Author

Dr. Rebecca Hale resides in Metairie, Louisiana with her husband Richard, a musician. She teaches drama to high school students in Jefferson Parish. She also teaches adult acting classes and workshops. She is the owner of Hale Talent, a talent agency.

www.ingramcontent.com/pod-product-compliance
Lightning Source LLC
Chambersburg PA
CBHW020632230426
43665CB00008B/136